AF378644

LONDON AT NIGHT

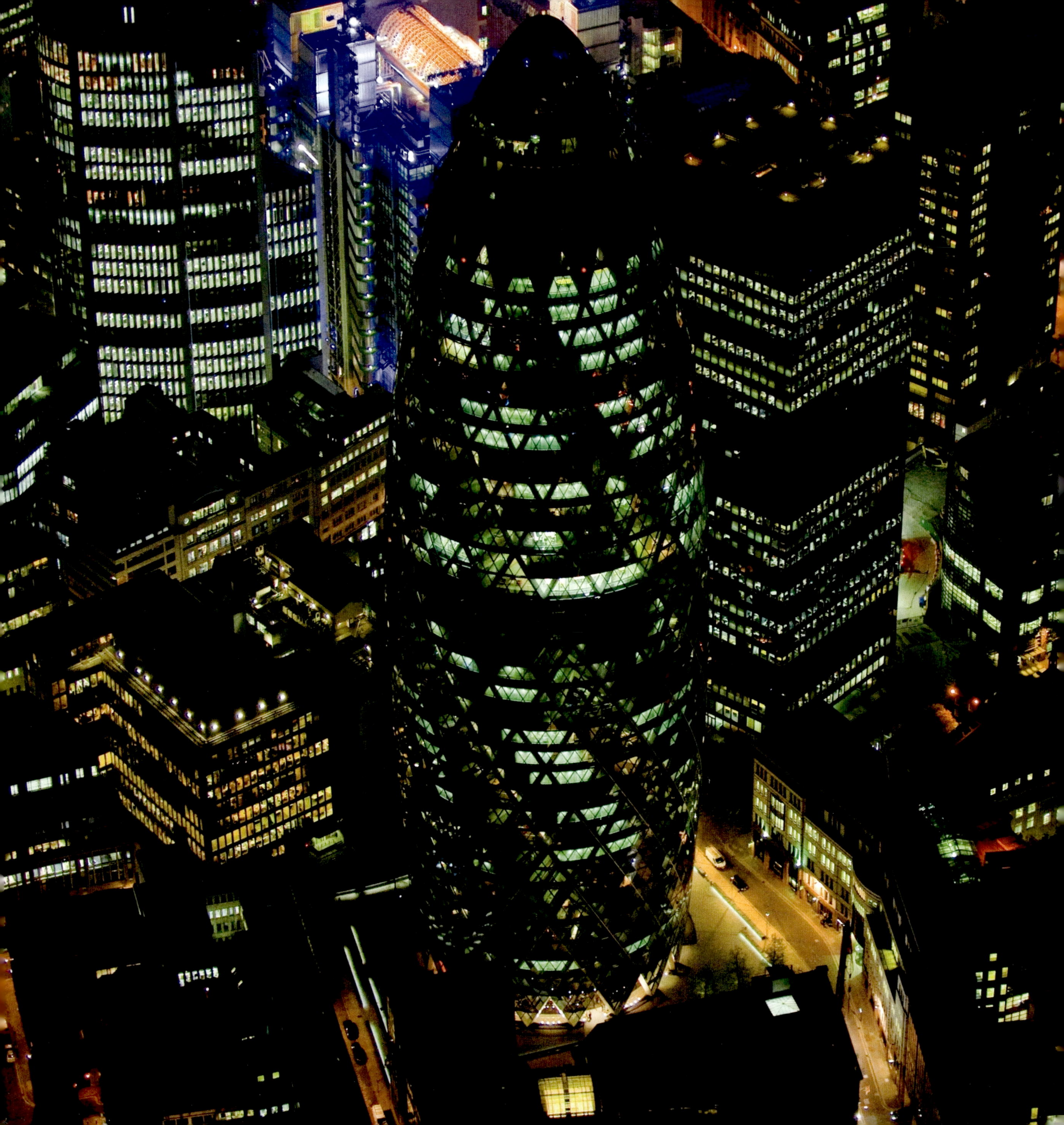

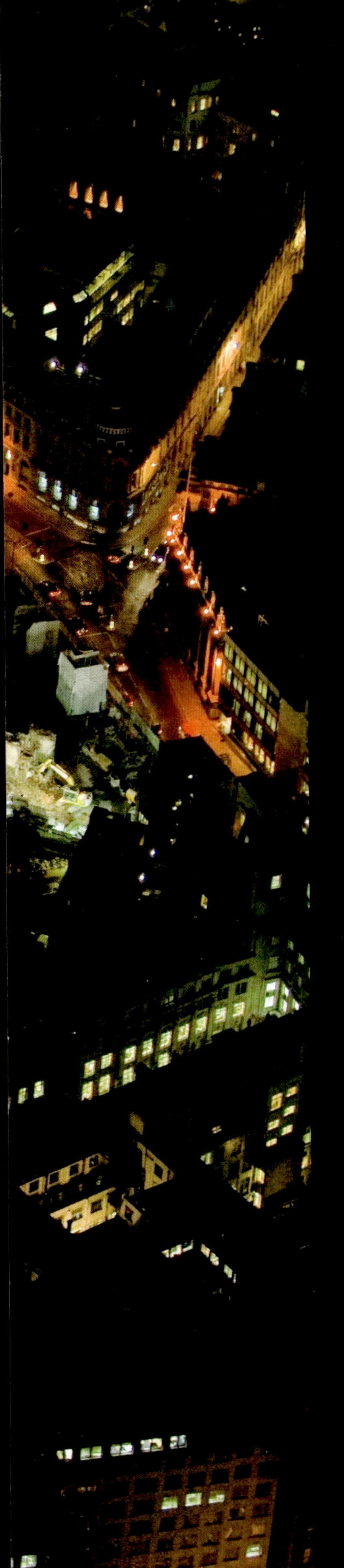

LONDON AT NIGHT

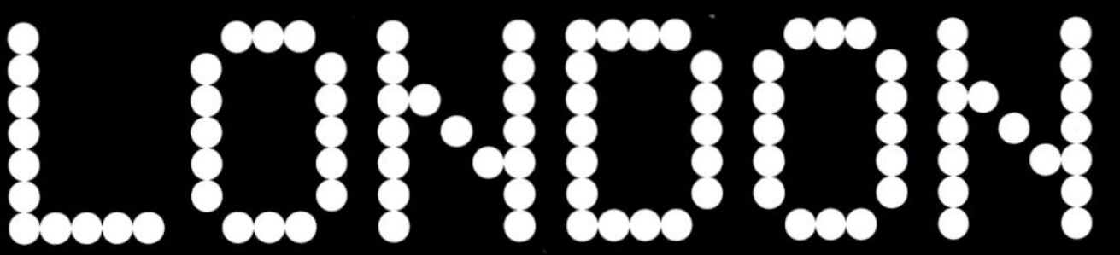

JASON HAWKES
INTRODUCTION BY KENNETH POWELL

MERRELL
LONDON · NEW YORK

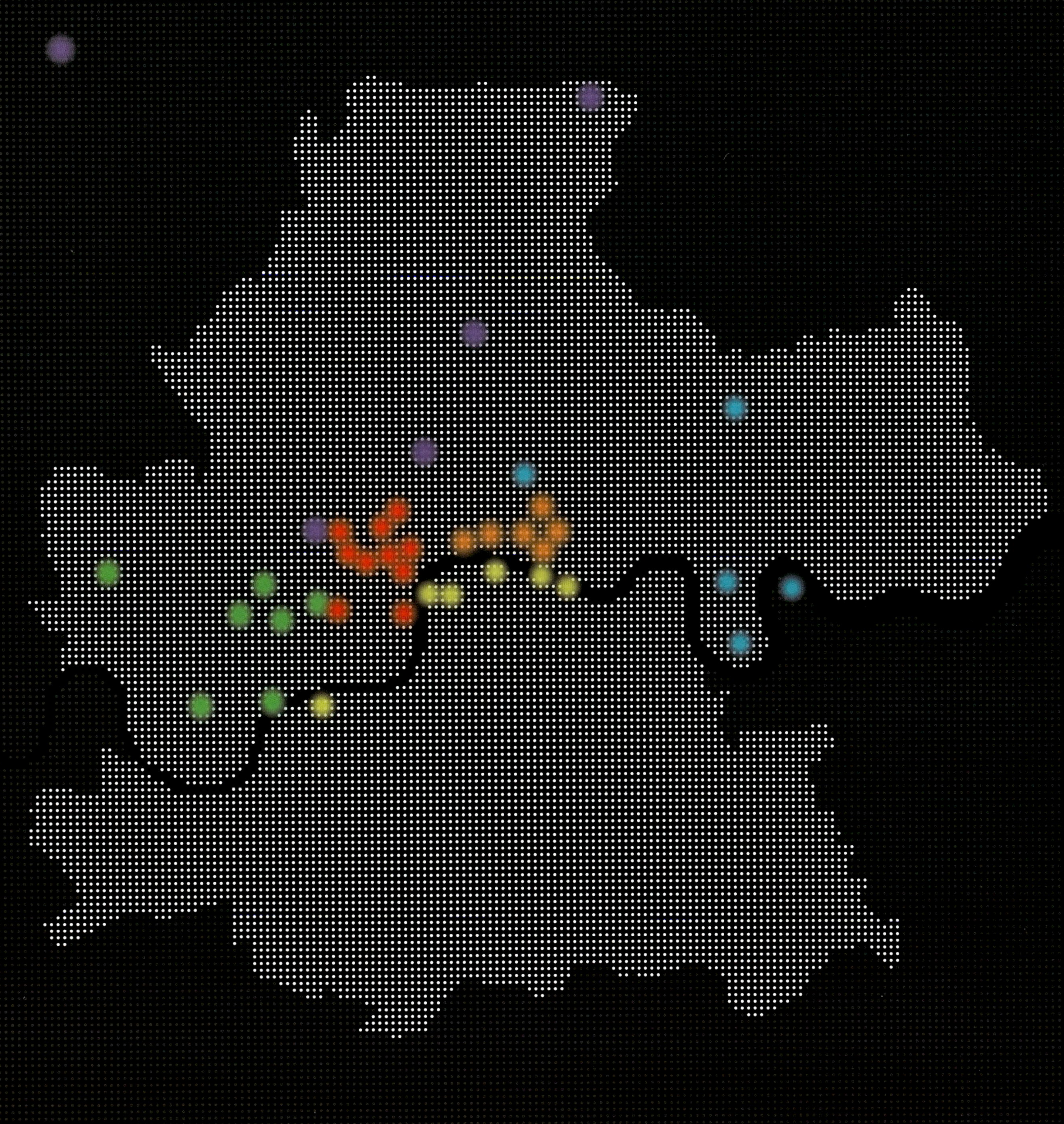

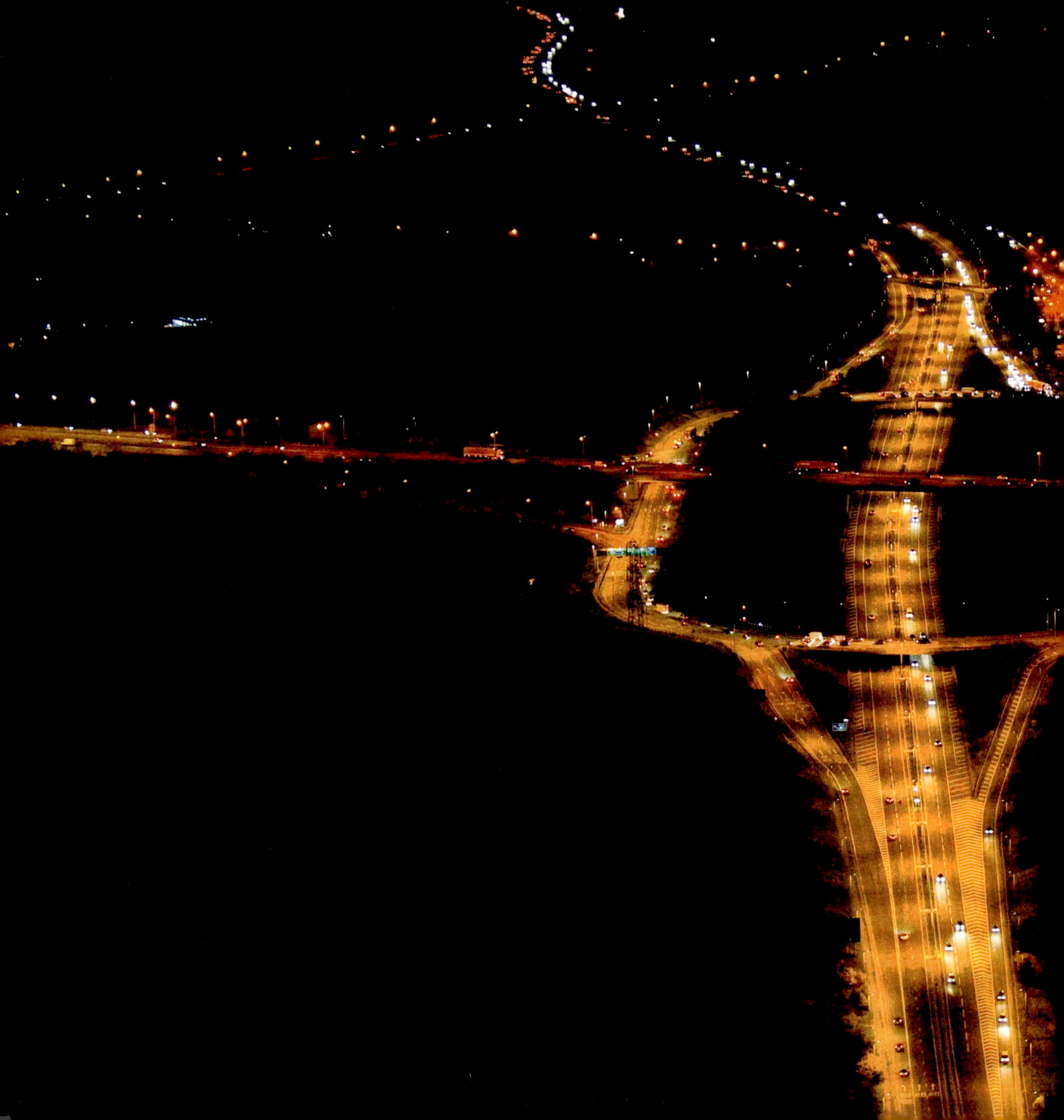

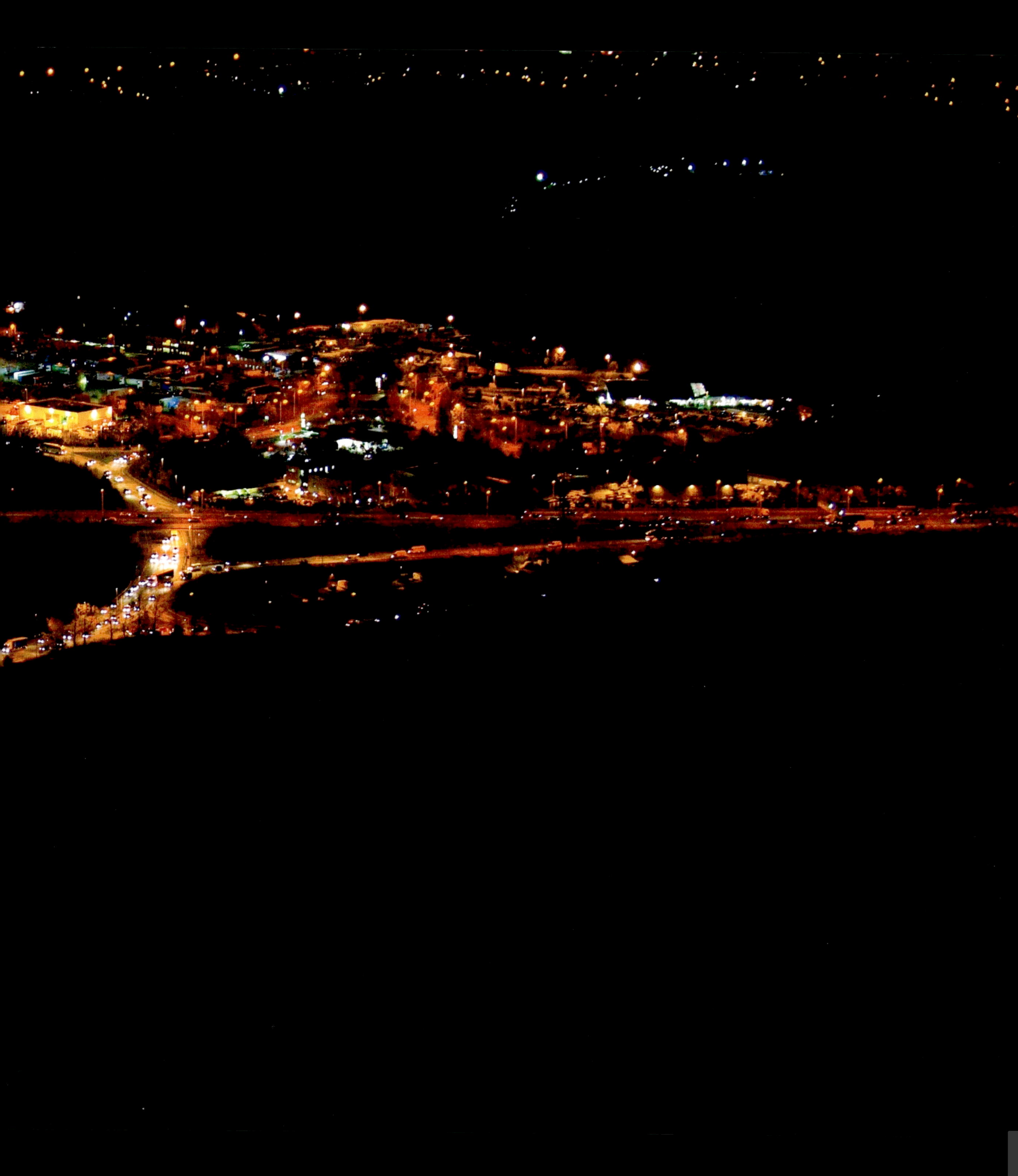

INTRODUCTION

Jason Hawkes's extraordinary photographs of London after dark provide a remarkable insight into not only the look, but also the life of the city today. Even a few decades ago, they would have been technically impossible, since the helicopter, the digital camera and the computer are the essential tools of his art.

It is nearly a century and a half since the first aerial photograph of England was taken, by Henry Negretti, the Italian-born optician, instrument-maker and photographer, one of whose prime commissions was to record the reconstruction of the Crystal Palace (1851) in the south London suburb of Sydenham. He took off from there in a balloon in 1863 and photographed the Thames estuary, but somehow neglected to take pictures of London en route. Nine years later Cecil Shadbolt took the earliest surviving aerial photographs of London from a balloon more than 600 metres above Docklands, his camera strapped to the side of the balloon car. (Shadbolt died in 1892, in a balloon crash at the Crystal Palace.) Exposing heavy photographic plates while airborne was not easy, but by the late 1880s George Eastman of Kodak had invented roll film and produced small, portable cameras ideally suited to aerial photography. In the 1890s Griffith Brewer, a pioneer of powered flight in Britain and the Wright brothers' agent in this country, published aerial views of London in the popular press (although none of them, it appears, was taken by night).

The Great War of 1914–18 transformed the aircraft from an expensive toy into a deadly weapon of war, and in 1917 the first extensive aerial survey of London was carried out along the Thames, from Isleworth to the Royal Docks, by the Royal Flying Corps. Within a decade or so the age of commercial air travel had dawned, and views of the world from above ceased to be a novelty. In the second half of the twentieth century, aerial views of London proliferated, recording the expansion, reconstruction and redevelopment of the capital. Today, dramatic images of London from above are taken from satellites: Google Earth presents three-dimensional images of buildings and panoramic views of streets across the globe. By night, the London region, sprawling into once-rural Hertfordshire,

Kent, Surrey and Essex, reads from space as a vast amoeba of artificial light, only gradually fading as ever-expanding suburbia gives way to countryside.

Flying into Heathrow at night from the east, millions of travellers experience the great panorama of Docklands, the towers of Canary Wharf (profligately lit around the clock, it seems) and the Dome (now O2); followed by the City, with Richard Rogers' Lloyd's building a distinctive landmark thanks to an inspirational lighting scheme; then Westminster and the final run over west London, with the Albert Hall a marker by Hyde Park. Modern lighting has created a London that would be unrecognizable to Negretti, Shadbolt or Brewer. Street lights have turned main roads into ribbons of light. The first electric street lights in Britain were installed on Holborn Viaduct and along parts of the Embankment in the late 1870s, and from then gas lights slowly began to disappear from London's streets. The dark recesses of Victorian London lost their sinister charm. Electric traffic lights were introduced in the late 1920s, and neon signs soon afterwards.

Roads and streets emerge from Hawkes's photographs as the bones of London, the skeleton on which the buildings are hung. Large tracts – Soho and Seven Dials, much of the City – retain the intense and irregular urban form through which the Victorians carved new thoroughfares: Southwark Street, Victoria Street, Holborn Viaduct and (at the beginning of the twentieth century) Kingsway. John Nash's Regent Street, a model for later 'metropolitan improvements', forms the boundary between smart Mayfair and the loucher confines of Soho, leading purposefully towards the Mall and Westminster. Beyond is London's greatest historic throughfare, the Thames, now left largely to tourists. The river was the focus for aerial photographs of London from the 1860s onwards. A century or more ago, large stretches of the river that had escaped the 'embanking' projects of the engineer Joseph Bazalgette were virtually inaccessible, walled off behind a line of wharves, docks and warehouses. Today's night-time views show a riverside that is not only part of the public domain but also a magnet for Londoners and visitors alike. From

Butler's Wharf in the east to Westminster Bridge and beyond, via More London, Bankside and the London Eye, the south side of the Thames is thronged with people by day and night. From Tower Bridge, itself strikingly illuminated, there are marvellous views of the City, with Norman Foster's 30 St Mary Axe (the 'Gherkin') a prominent landmark, and the new Heron Tower rapidly rising to overtop every other City building.

Roads remain the points of reference in views of London after dark, but there are spaces where lights are few: these black holes in the townscape are London's parks, foremost among them the great expanse of Hyde Park and Kensington Gardens, with George Gilbert Scott's Albert Memorial another Victorian landmark now brilliantly lit. (In one view, Hyde Park is animated by an open-air concert.) To the north, Regent's Park and Primrose Hill form another void in the city, with the vast expanses of Hampstead Heath beyond. South London is punctuated by a series of commons, which define the edge of the Victorian city and are another great legacy of the Victorian vision. Where is the vision in the London that has sprawled beyond the neat suburbs of the inter-war years: a terrain of arterial roads, superstores, drive-in fast-food joints and industrial 'parks'? The virtue of darkness here is to hide the ugliness and the lack of any sense of urban reality, although Hawkes is, remarkably, able to conjure a sense of beauty from the M25.

London has never had the urban coherence imposed on central Paris, for example, by Baron Haussmann. The occasional grand gesture aside – the Mall, for instance, or the cultural quarter of South Kensington ('Albertopolis') – it is a city created by private enterprise rather than royal edict. Once every half century or so, however, London embraces a big idea, and a whole area is transformed as a result. The Festival of Britain in 1951 created the South Bank as a cultural Mecca around the Royal Festival Hall. Today the former railway yards and derelict factory sites of Stratford, which developed in the nineteenth century as an industrial town in its own right, are being recast as the site for the 2012 Olympic Games. A scene of activity by day and night, it is the largest of innumerable building sites spread across London. It seems no recession can lessen the constant pressure of change.

Jason Hawkes's photographs present the big picture of London, from the intricate heartlands of the City and the West End to the further reaches of outer suburbia. But the photographs equally illuminate the details of London life. A red carpet on Leicester Square awaits the arrival of the stars for a film premiere. The courtyard of Somerset House, for long no more than a car park for tax inspectors, has become another of London's living rooms. Players move across football grounds. Hawkes's camera zooms in to give us a view into the British Museum's Great Court, where visitors can be seen walking below Norman Foster's billowing glazed roof, with the former Reading Room a solid object at the centre of the space. Along the Euston Road, the line of railway termini forms a clear boundary between central and north London; the renewed Victorian vault of St Pancras, relieved of a century and a half of grime generated by steam and diesel traction, is a symbol of the rebirth of rail travel. Euston, in contrast, is a dark mass, its platforms sunk below a raft of 1960s concrete. Modern lighting is frequently pilloried as a polluter of the night sky, and empty office floors brilliantly lit at midnight reflect an arrogant disregard of urgent environmental issues. But the more sensitive lighting of London's great public monuments – St Paul's, Westminster Abbey, Big Ben, Nelson's Column – merely underlines their role as symbols of the identity of London. Any great city by night is a thrilling place, a great subject for colour postcards of the Empire State Building, the Eiffel Tower, the Colosseum or other defining landmarks. Hawkes gives us not the obviously picturesque London seen on countless postcards, but London as it really is. He gives us a record of the extraordinary visual and social diversity of a great world city in the first decade of the twenty-first century.

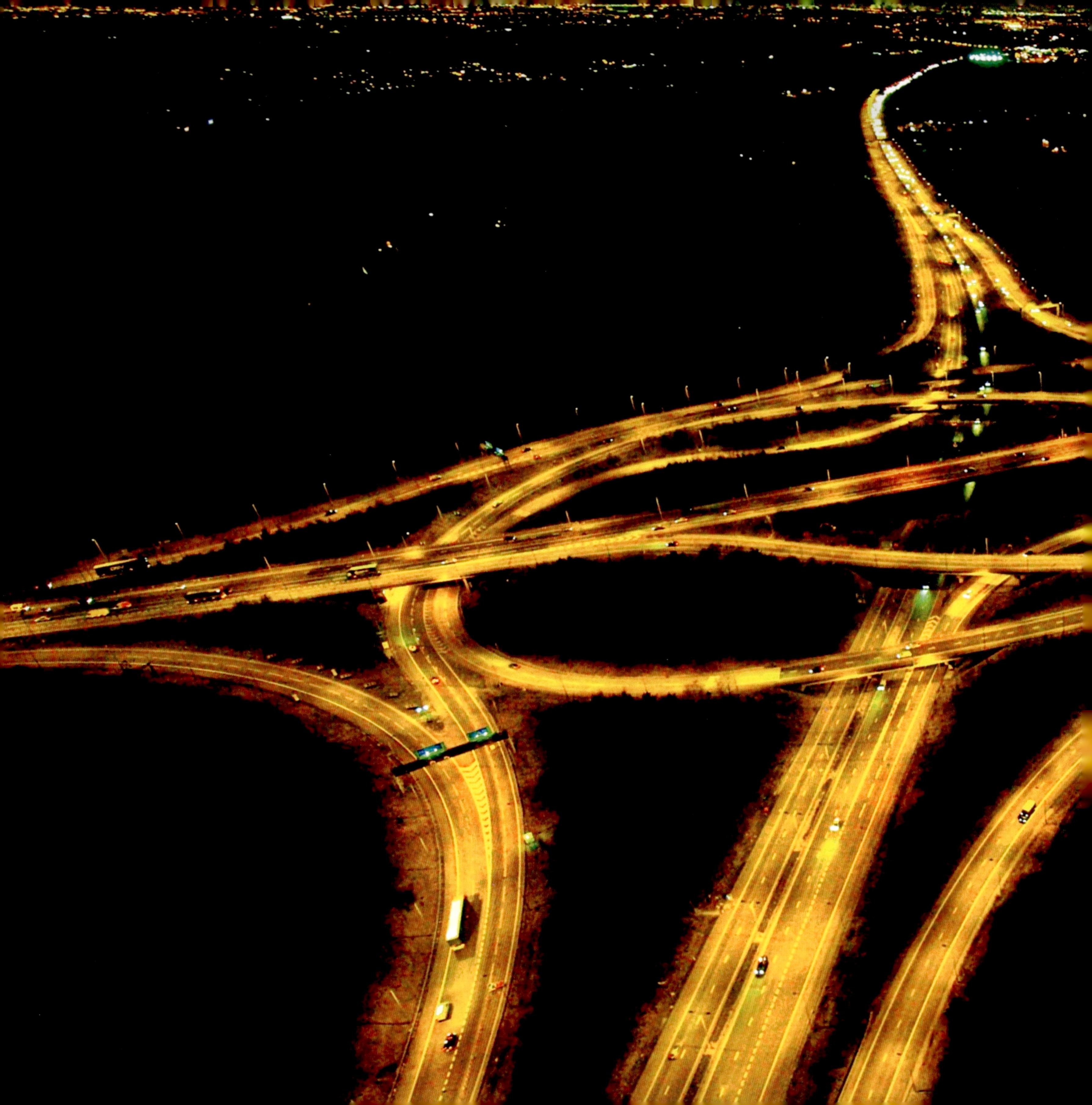

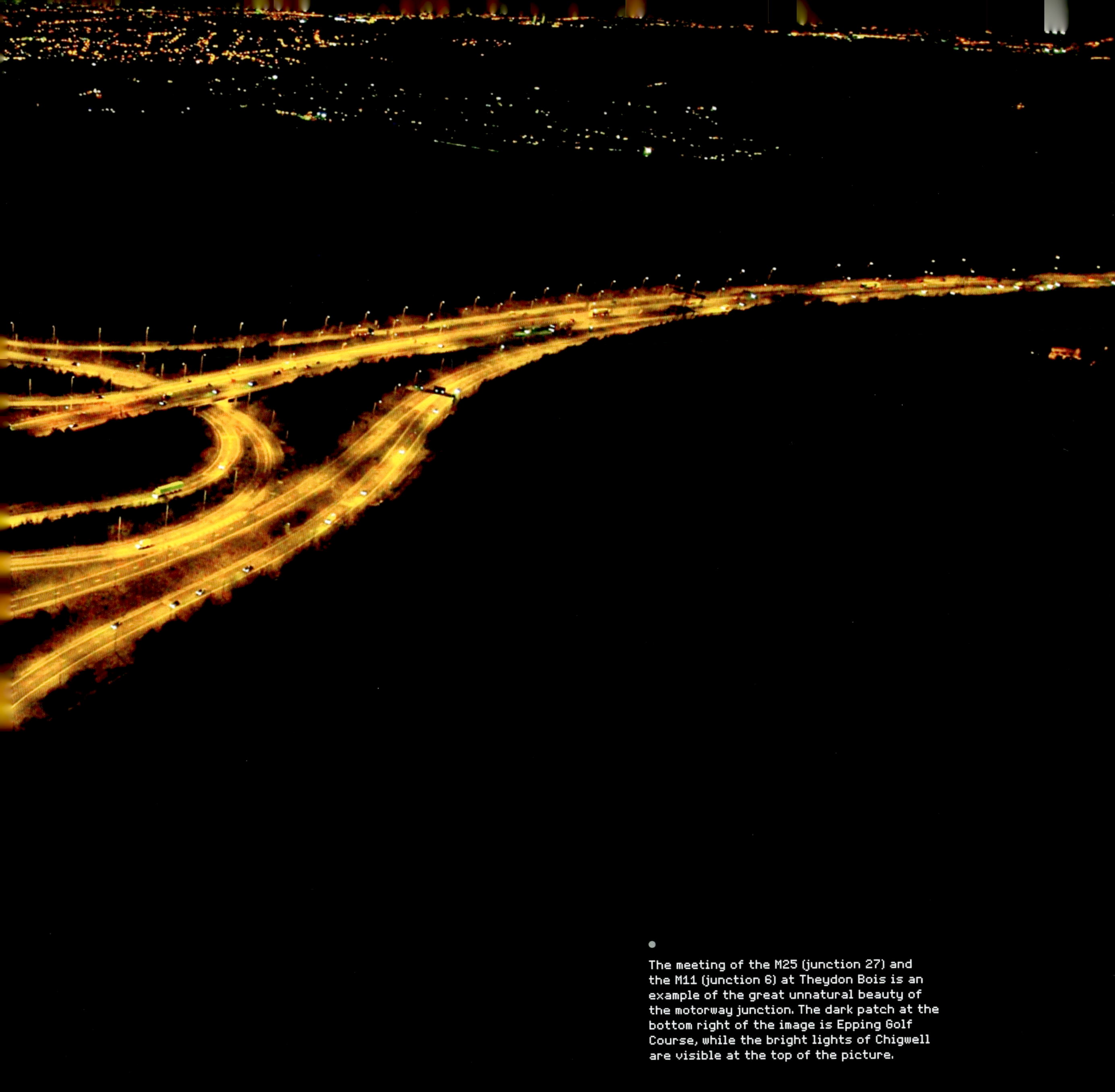

The meeting of the M25 (junction 27) and
the M11 (junction 6) at Theydon Bois is an
example of the great unnatural beauty of
the motorway junction. The dark patch at the
bottom right of the image is Epping Golf
Course, while the bright lights of Chigwell
are visible at the top of the picture.

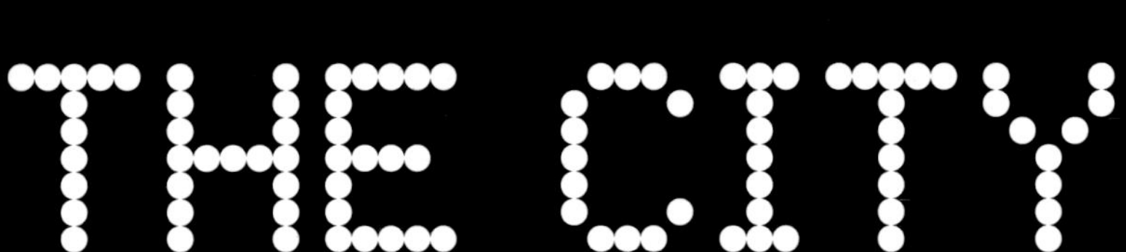

THE CITY

The City of London wears its history lightly. By night, as by day, it is dominated by the office towers and slabs that reflect its role as a global business centre. Before the Second World War, the steeples of Christopher Wren's City churches still provided the principal vertical accents. Those that survived the war are now mostly boxed in by post-1945 commercial development. Yet St Paul's, standing on a site where there has been a cathedral for 1400 years, still emerges – even more clearly after dark – as the best-known symbol of London, recognized across the globe. Only one recent building, Norman Foster's distinctive 'Gherkin', challenges the iconic role of St Paul's, although a new generation of tall buildings spearheaded by the Heron Tower promises more sculptural highlights on the skyline.

Bombing, followed by redevelopment, has removed much of the historic fabric of the City; yet the street pattern, which is essentially medieval, has survived both – and before them, the Great Fire of 1666. Such ancient streets as Ludgate Hill, Cheapside and Bishopsgate still form the backbone of the area. Only in a few places has the old streetscape been radically recast. The Barbican is the most dramatic example of comprehensive redevelopment, with buildings linked by a high-level pedestrian route. Planned on similar lines, the 1960s Paternoster Square, just north of St Paul's, has been replaced by a new complex of buildings and a square worthy of its name. Perhaps the most enlightened example of urban planning of recent years in the Square Mile, Broadgate makes use of derelict railway land, together with 'air rights' development over Liverpool Street station, to create a series of public spaces that are more significant for a city starved of open spaces than the office buildings enclosing them. After dark, its central arena remains a lively place, especially in the winter months, when a skating rink – inspired by that at New York's Rockefeller Center – attracts the crowds.

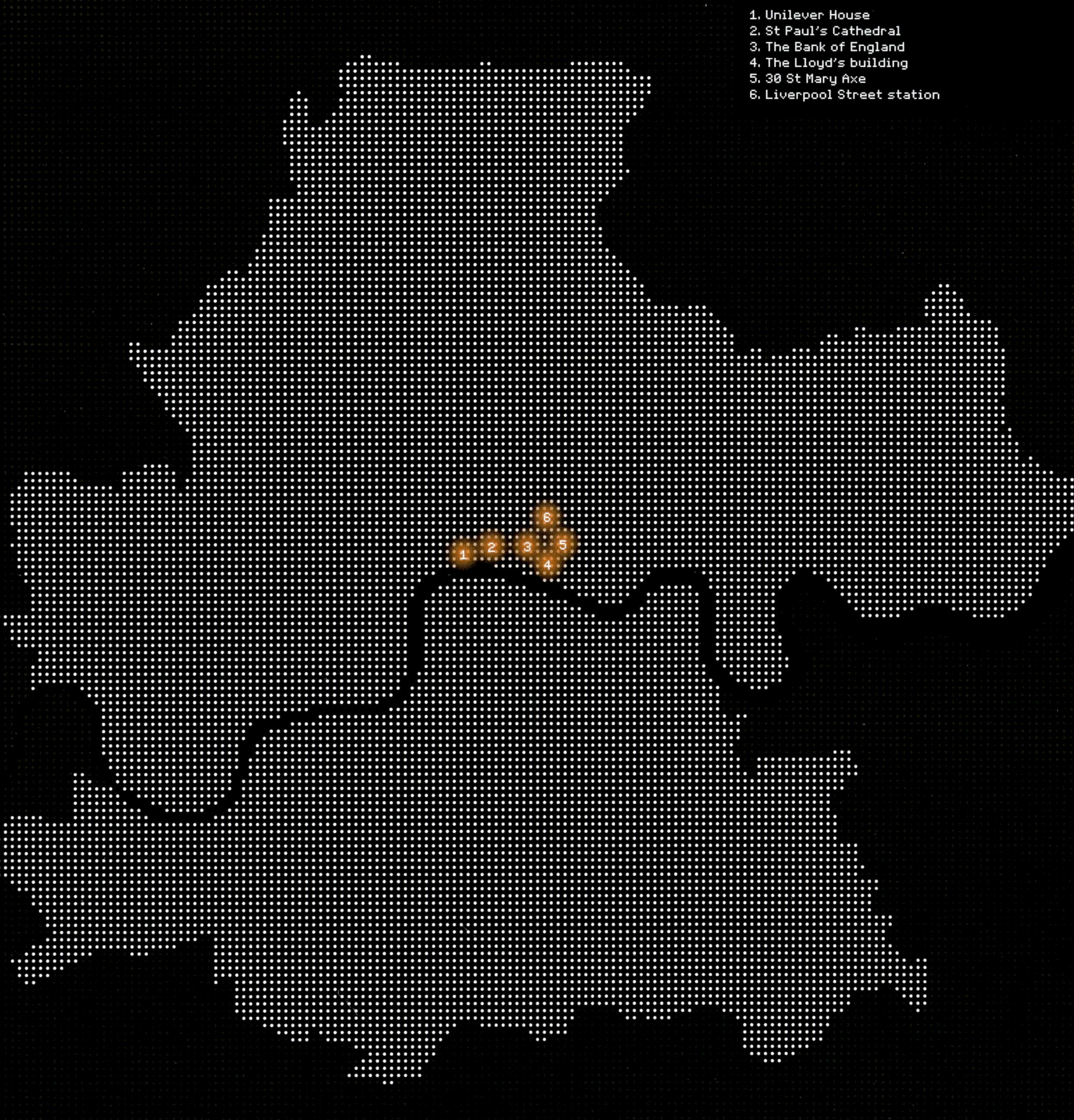

1. Unilever House
2. St Paul's Cathedral
3. The Bank of England
4. The Lloyd's building
5. 30 St Mary Axe
6. Liverpool Street station

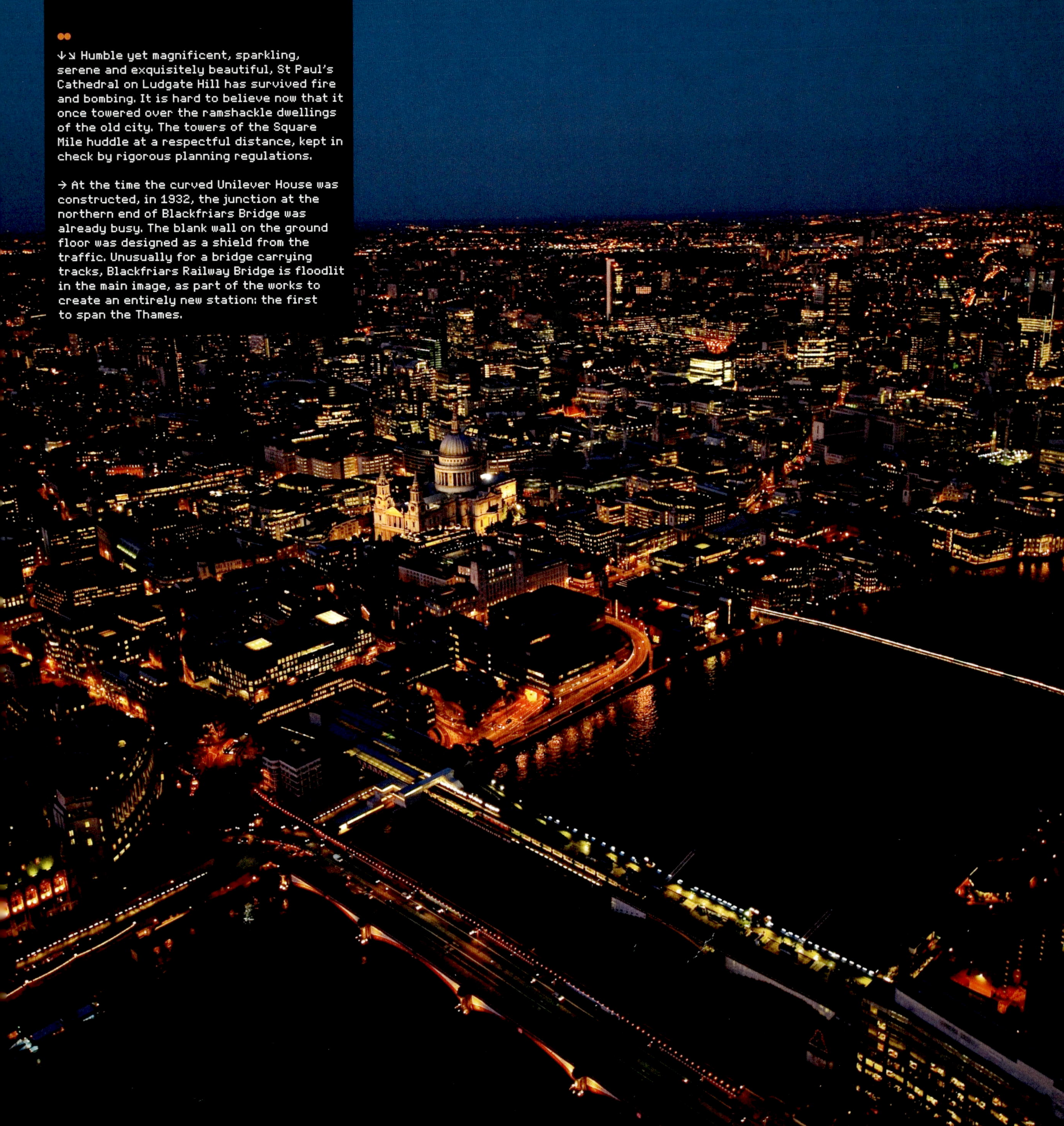

↓↘ Humble yet magnificent, sparkling, serene and exquisitely beautiful, St Paul's Cathedral on Ludgate Hill has survived fire and bombing. It is hard to believe now that it once towered over the ramshackle dwellings of the old city. The towers of the Square Mile huddle at a respectful distance, kept in check by rigorous planning regulations.

→ At the time the curved Unilever House was constructed, in 1932, the junction at the northern end of Blackfriars Bridge was already busy. The blank wall on the ground floor was designed as a shield from the traffic. Unusually for a bridge carrying tracks, Blackfriars Railway Bridge is floodlit in the main image, as part of the works to create an entirely new station: the first to span the Thames.

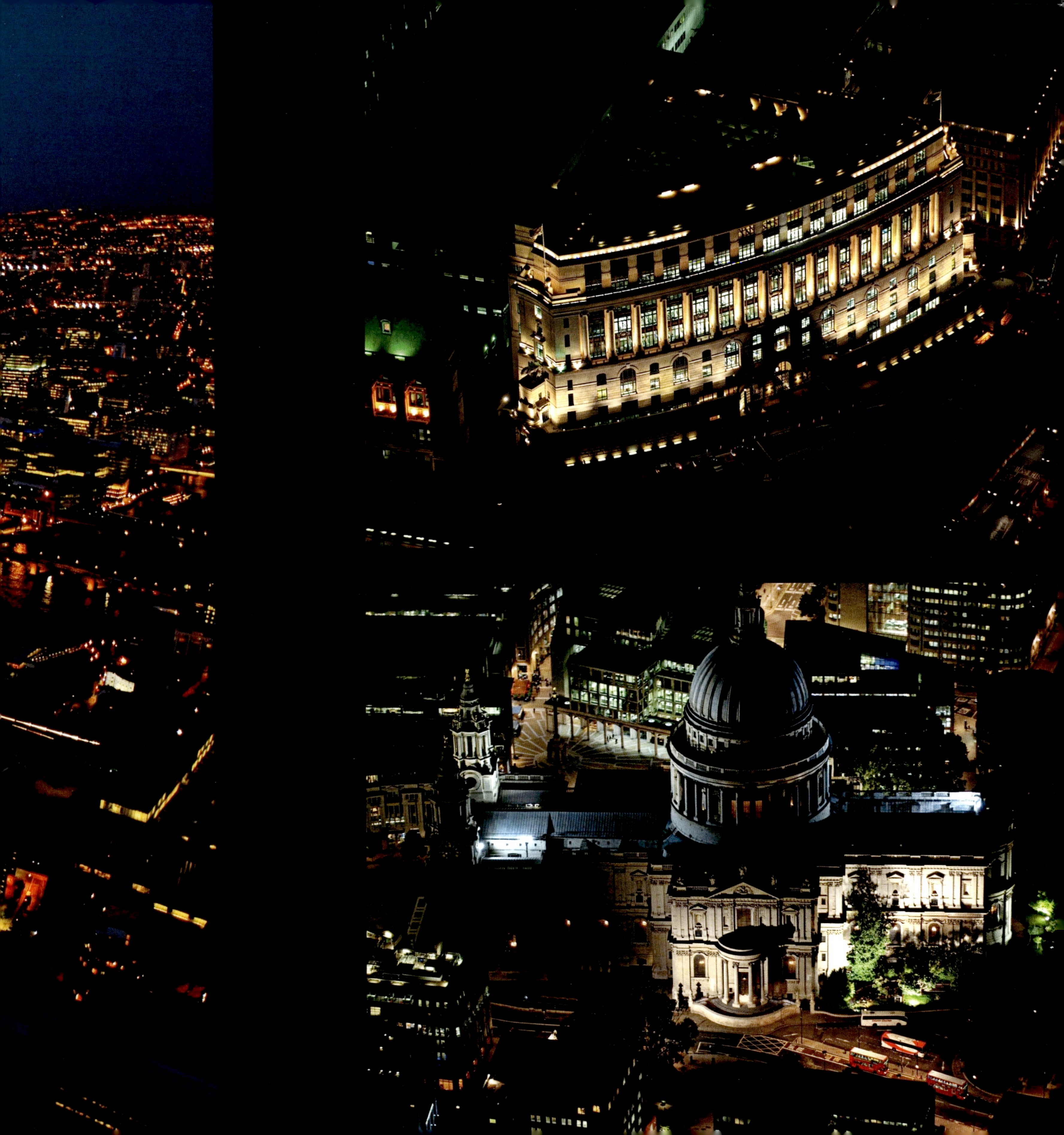

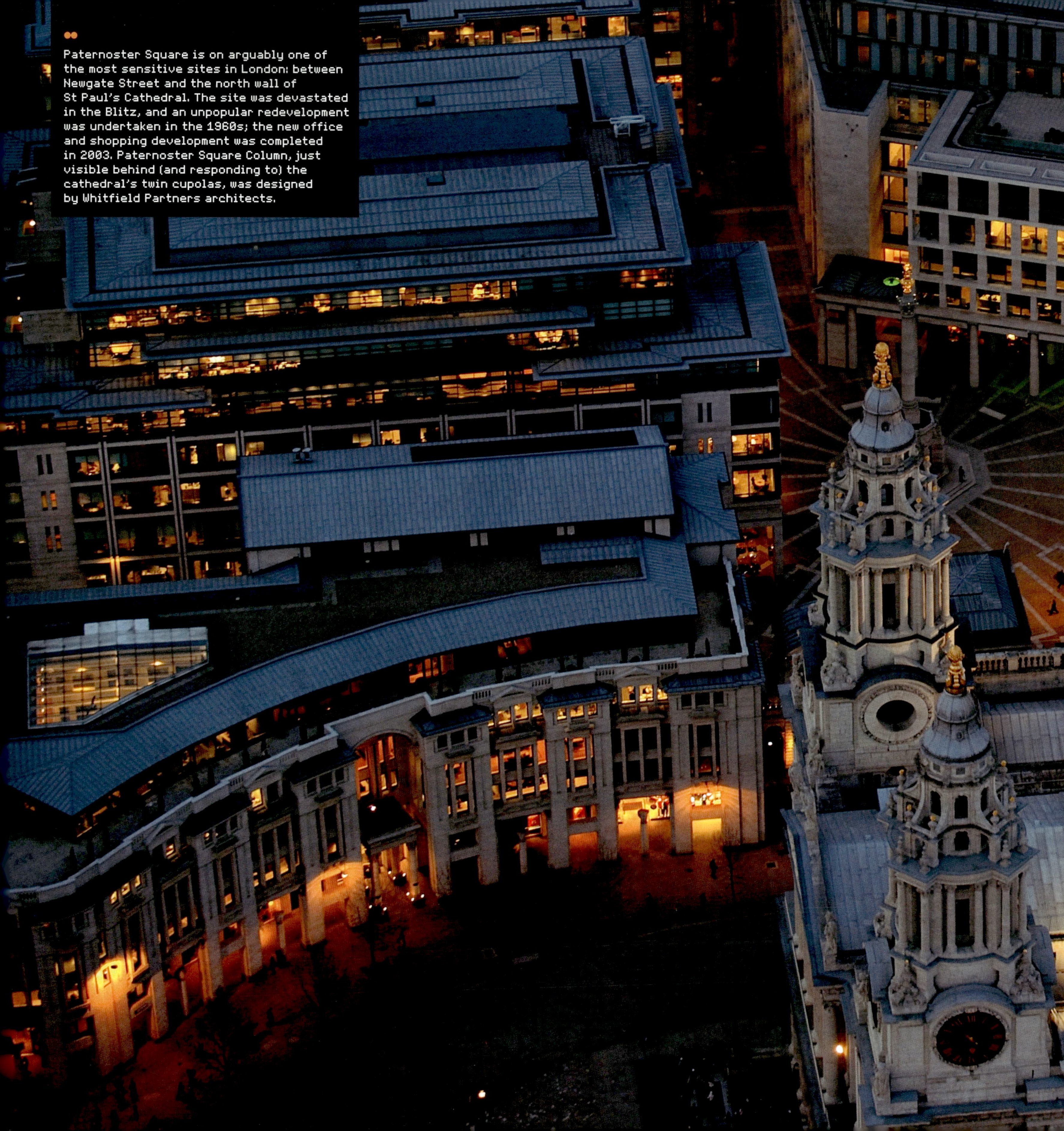

Paternoster Square is on arguably one of
the most sensitive sites in London: between
Newgate Street and the north wall of
St Paul's Cathedral. The site was devastated
in the Blitz, and an unpopular redevelopment
was undertaken in the 1960s; the new office
and shopping development was completed
in 2003. Paternoster Square Column, just
visible behind (and responding to) the
cathedral's twin cupolas, was designed
by Whitfield Partners architects.

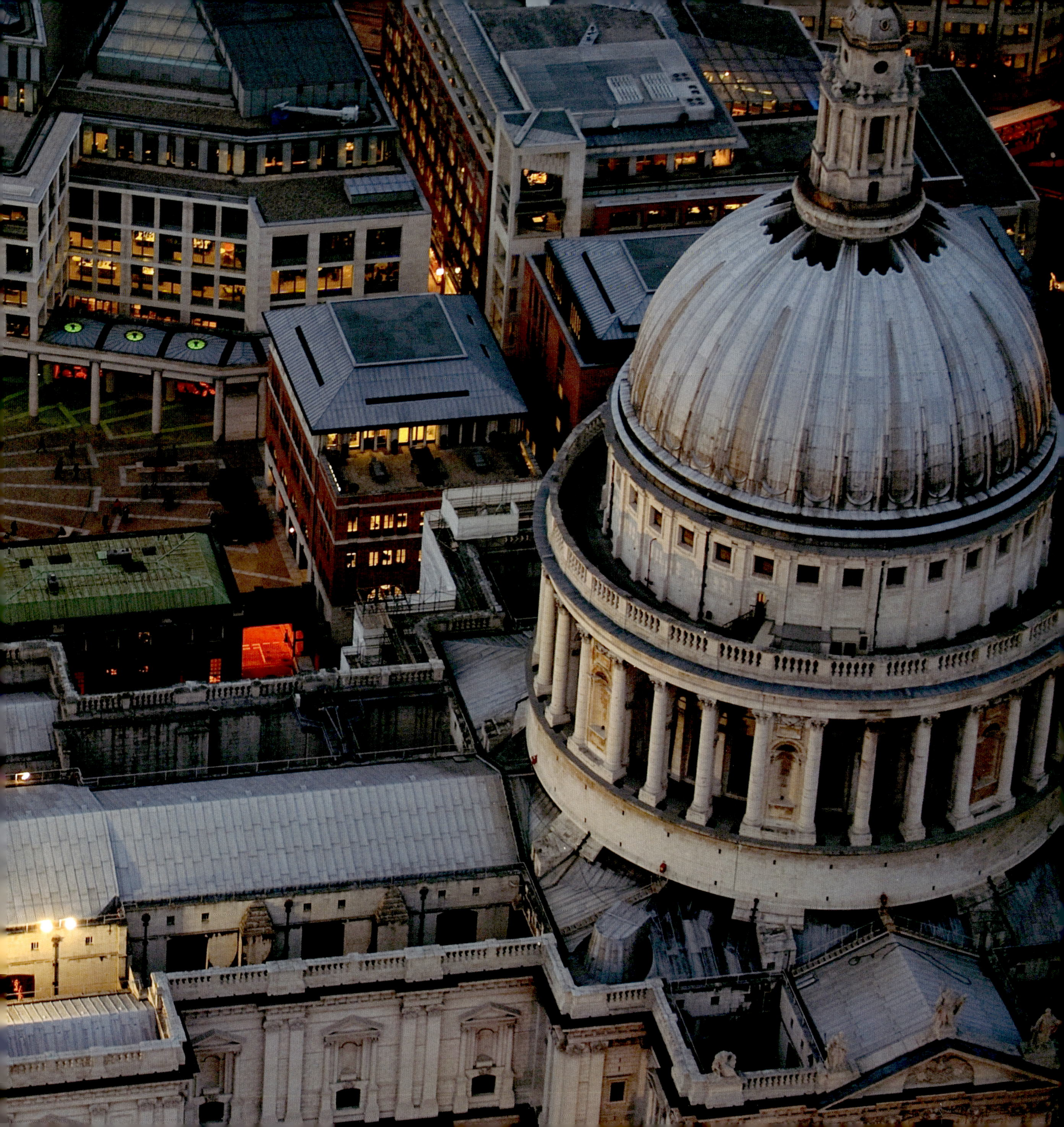

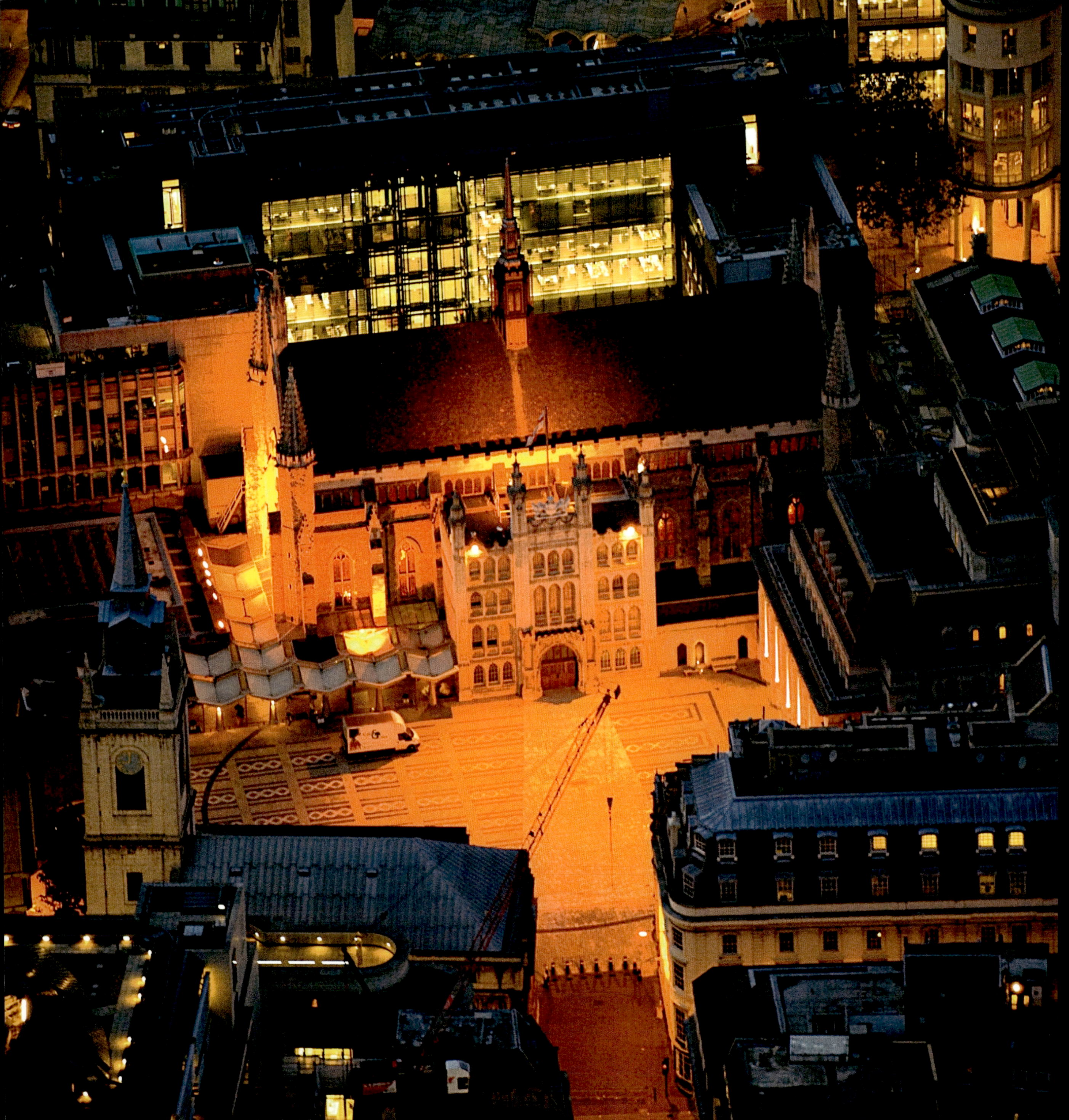

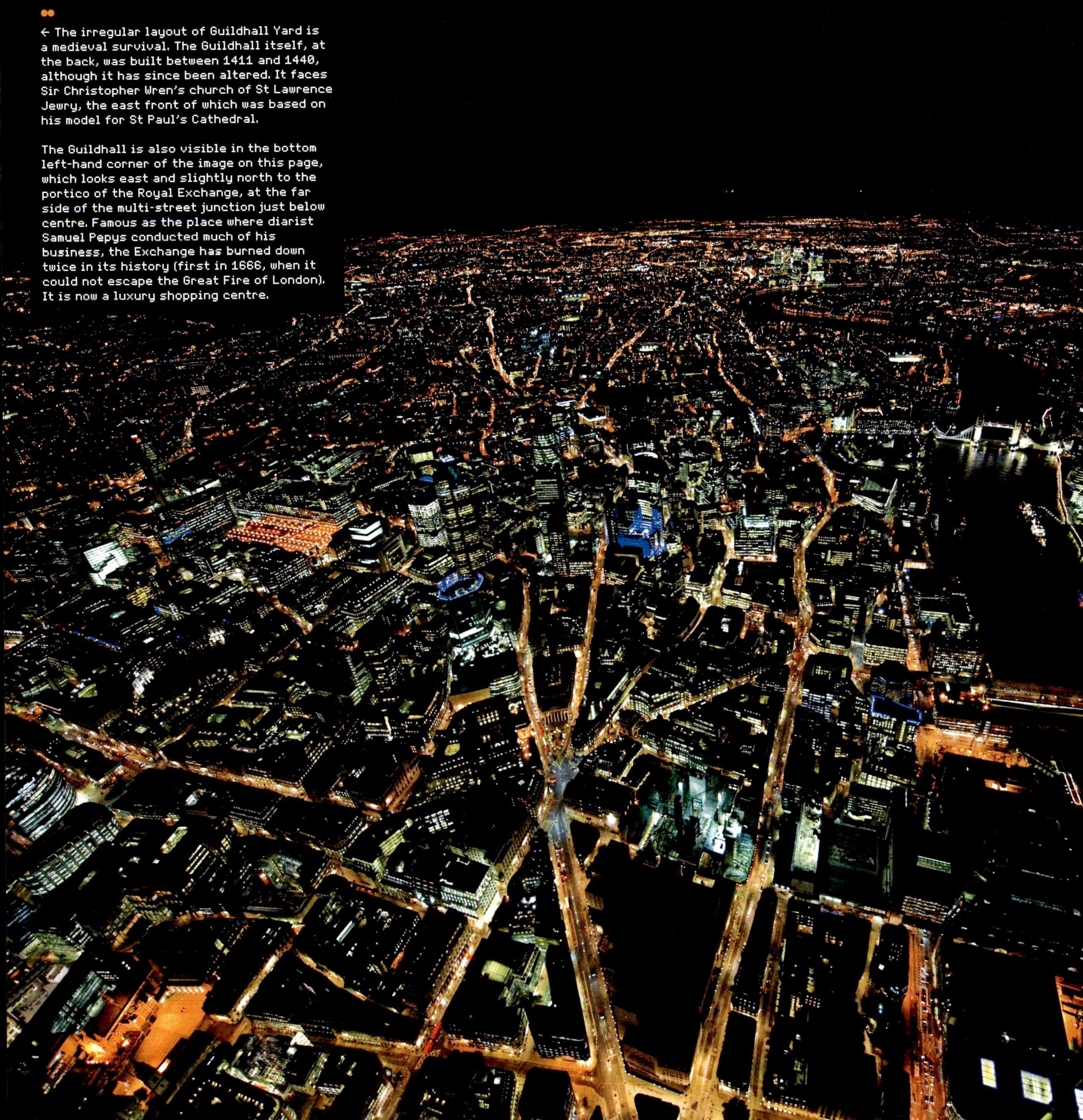
← The irregular layout of Guildhall Yard is a medieval survival. The Guildhall itself, at the back, was built between 1411 and 1440, although it has since been altered. It faces Sir Christopher Wren's church of St Lawrence Jewry, the east front of which was based on his model for St Paul's Cathedral.

The Guildhall is also visible in the bottom left-hand corner of the image on this page, which looks east and slightly north to the portico of the Royal Exchange, at the far side of the multi-street junction just below centre. Famous as the place where diarist Samuel Pepys conducted much of his business, the Exchange has burned down twice in its history (first in 1666, when it could not escape the Great Fire of London). It is now a luxury shopping centre.

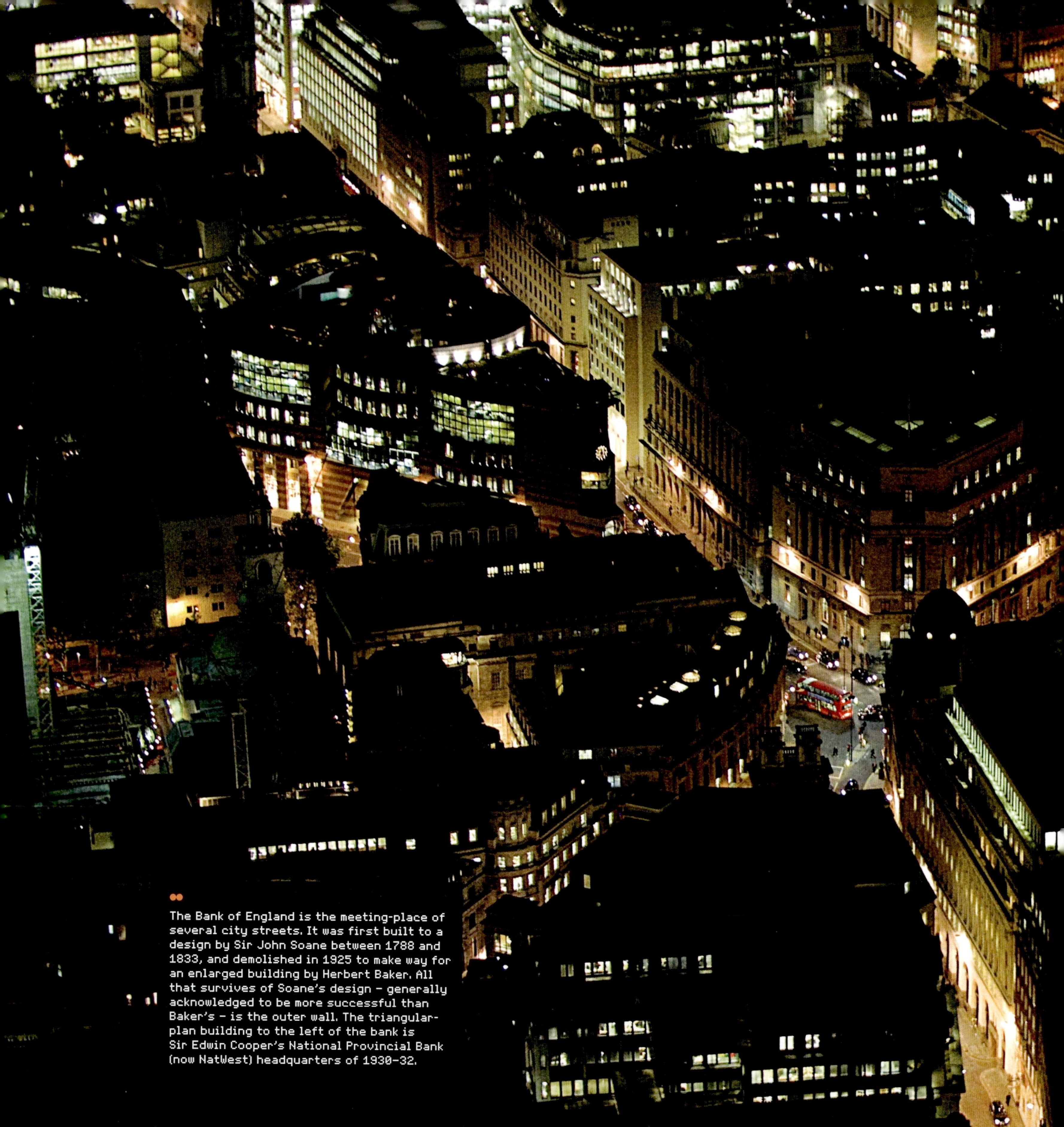

The Bank of England is the meeting-place of several city streets. It was first built to a design by Sir John Soane between 1788 and 1833, and demolished in 1925 to make way for an enlarged building by Herbert Baker. All that survives of Soane's design – generally acknowledged to be more successful than Baker's – is the outer wall. The triangular-plan building to the left of the bank is Sir Edwin Cooper's National Provincial Bank (now NatWest) headquarters of 1930–32.

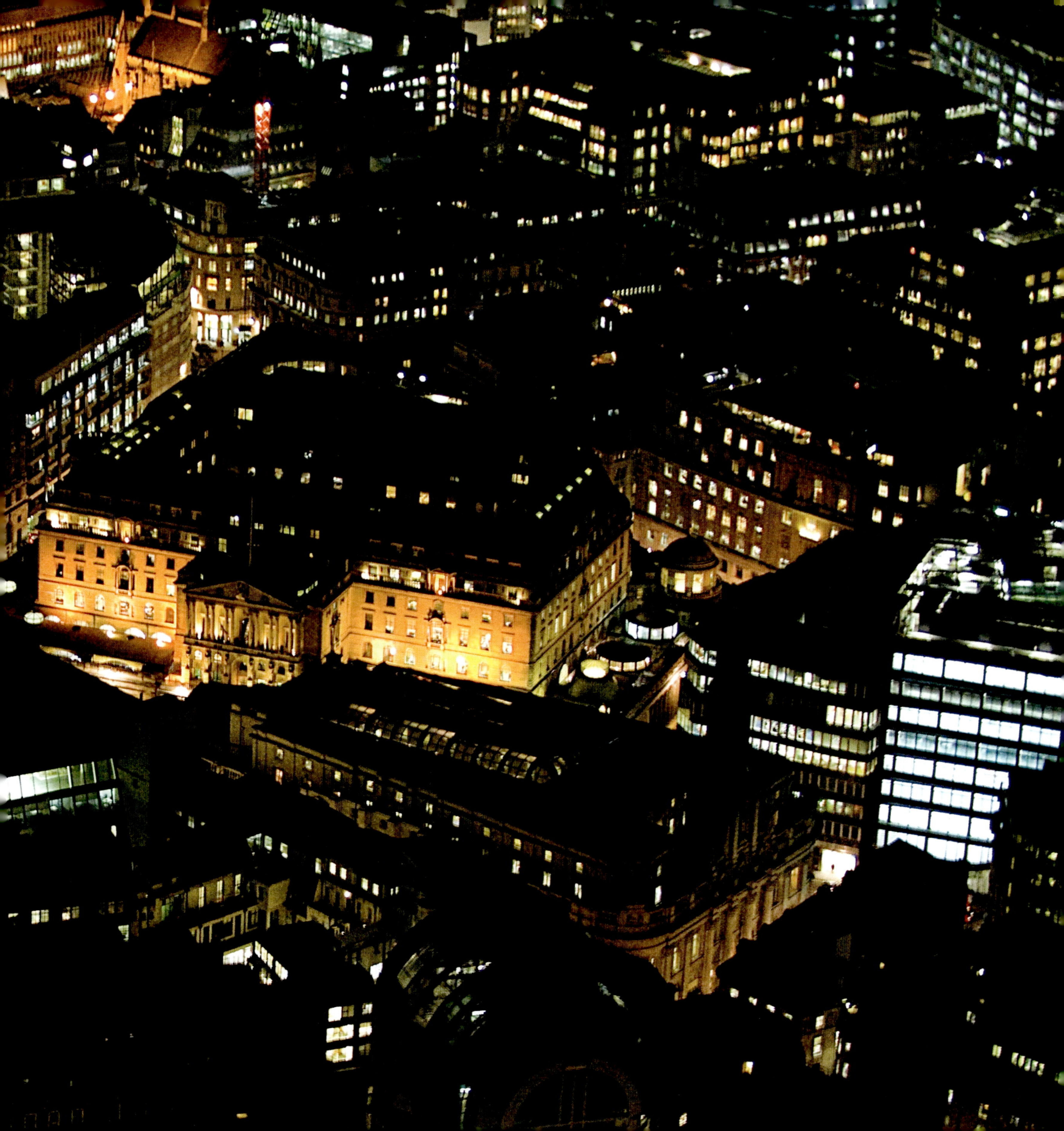

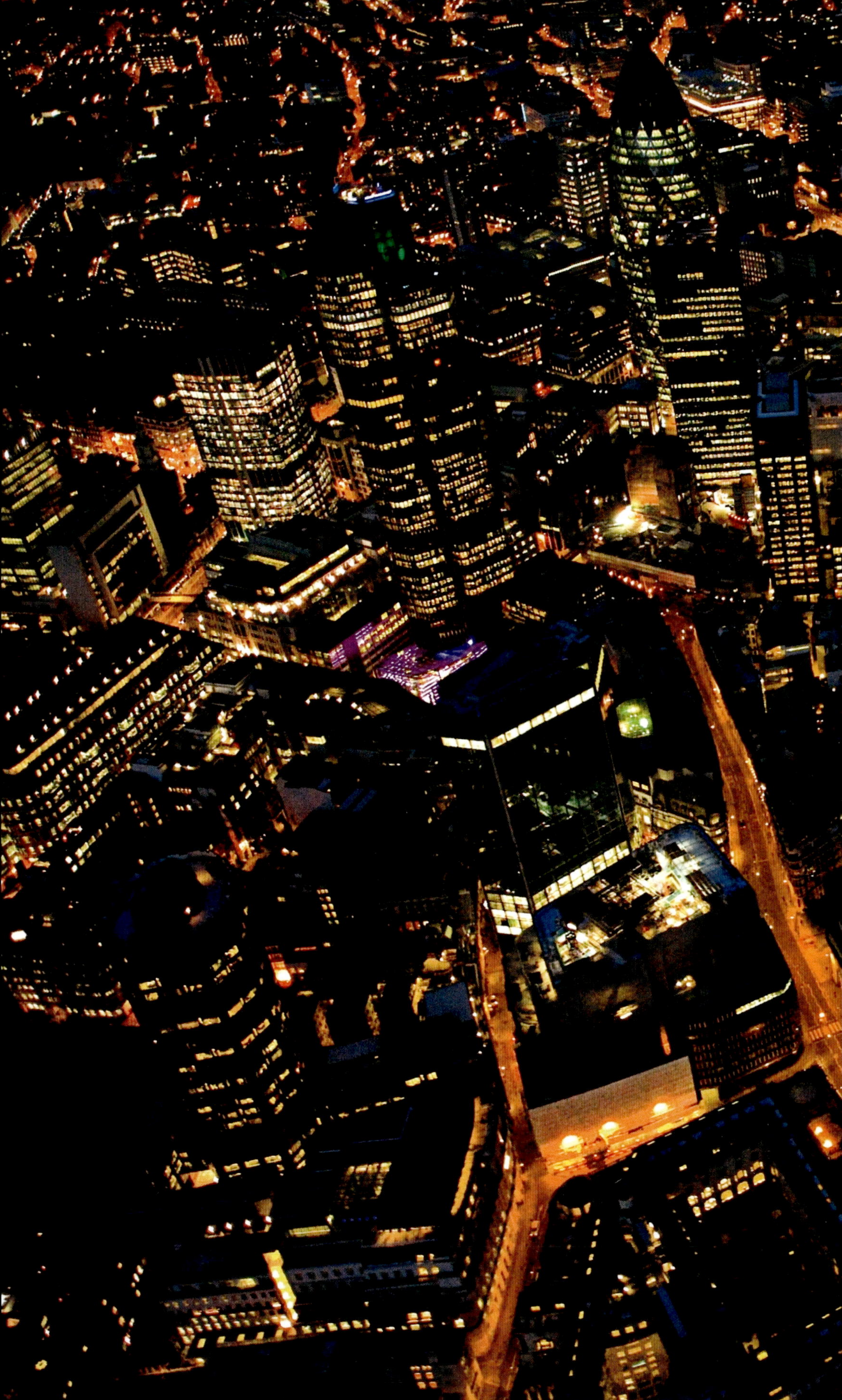

An unusual angle over St Paul's Cathedral brings the east-west streets of the City into sharp prominence. Under construction next to the Bank of England (left foreground), on the site of the former Stock Exchange, is 60 Threadneedle Street, a speculative office building in gleaming steel by Eric Parry Architects.

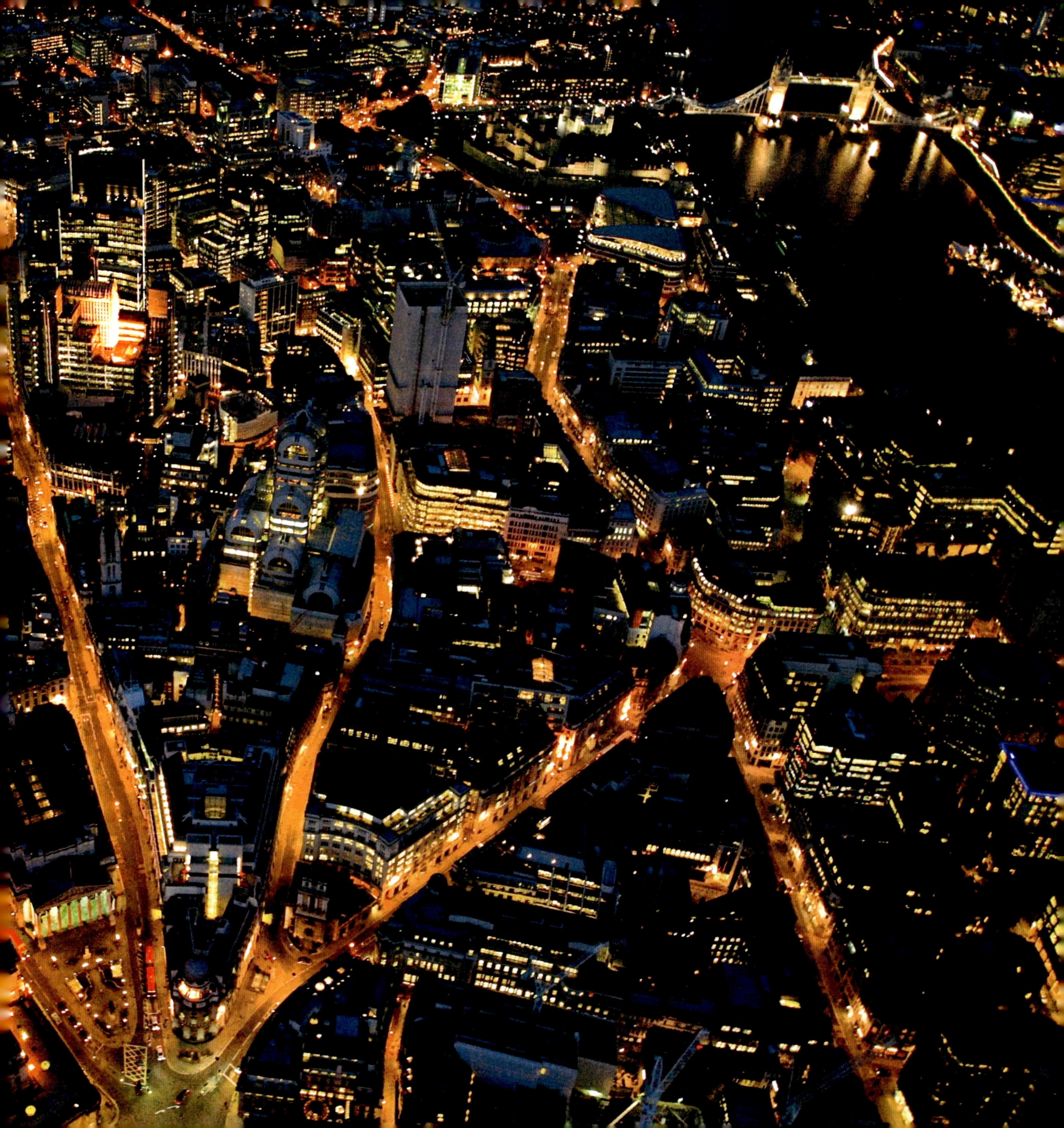

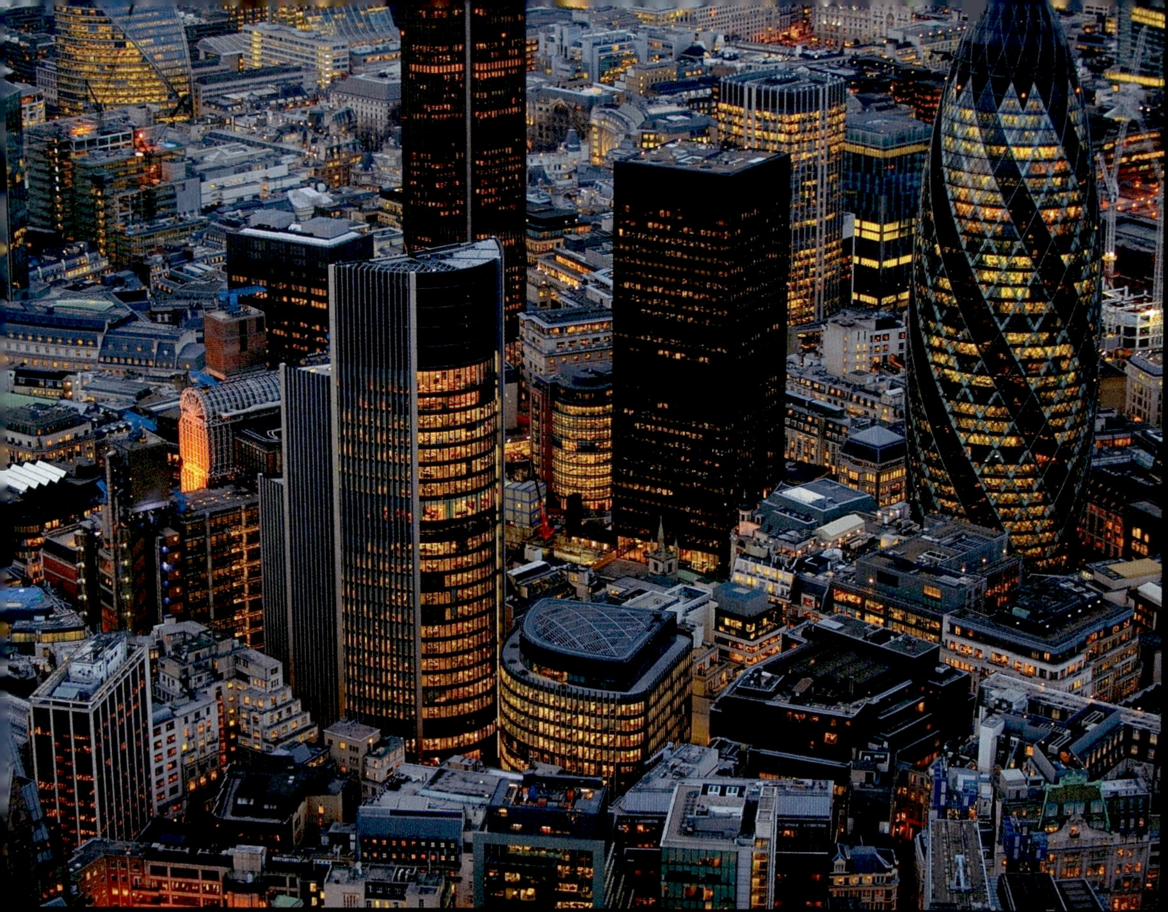

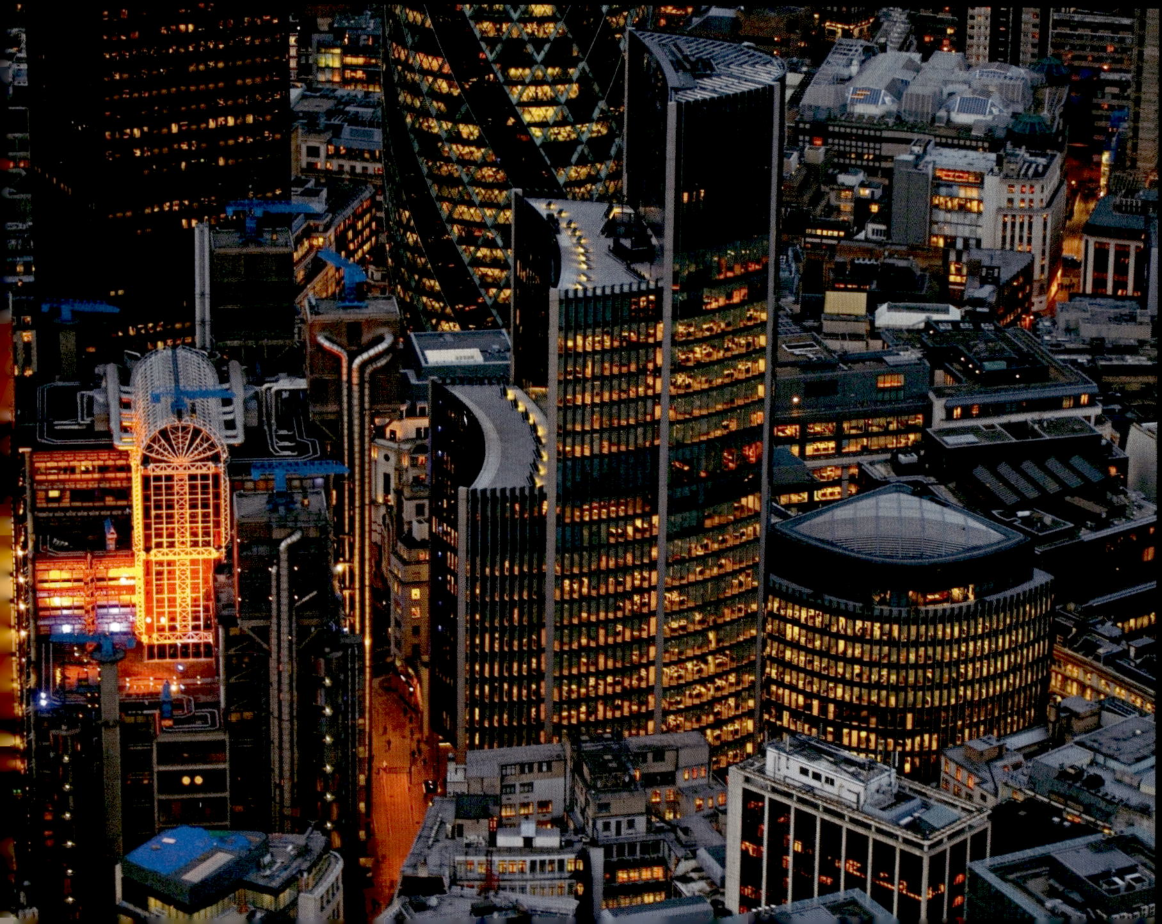

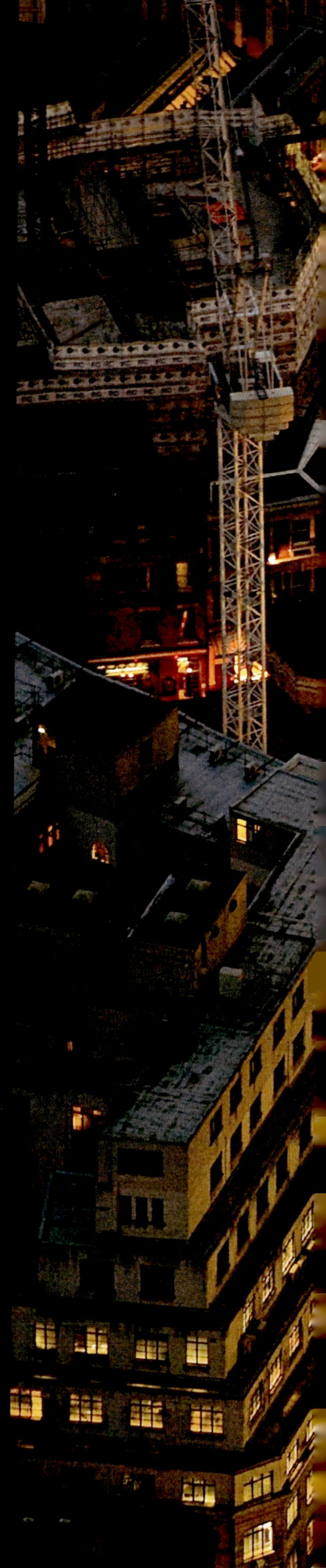

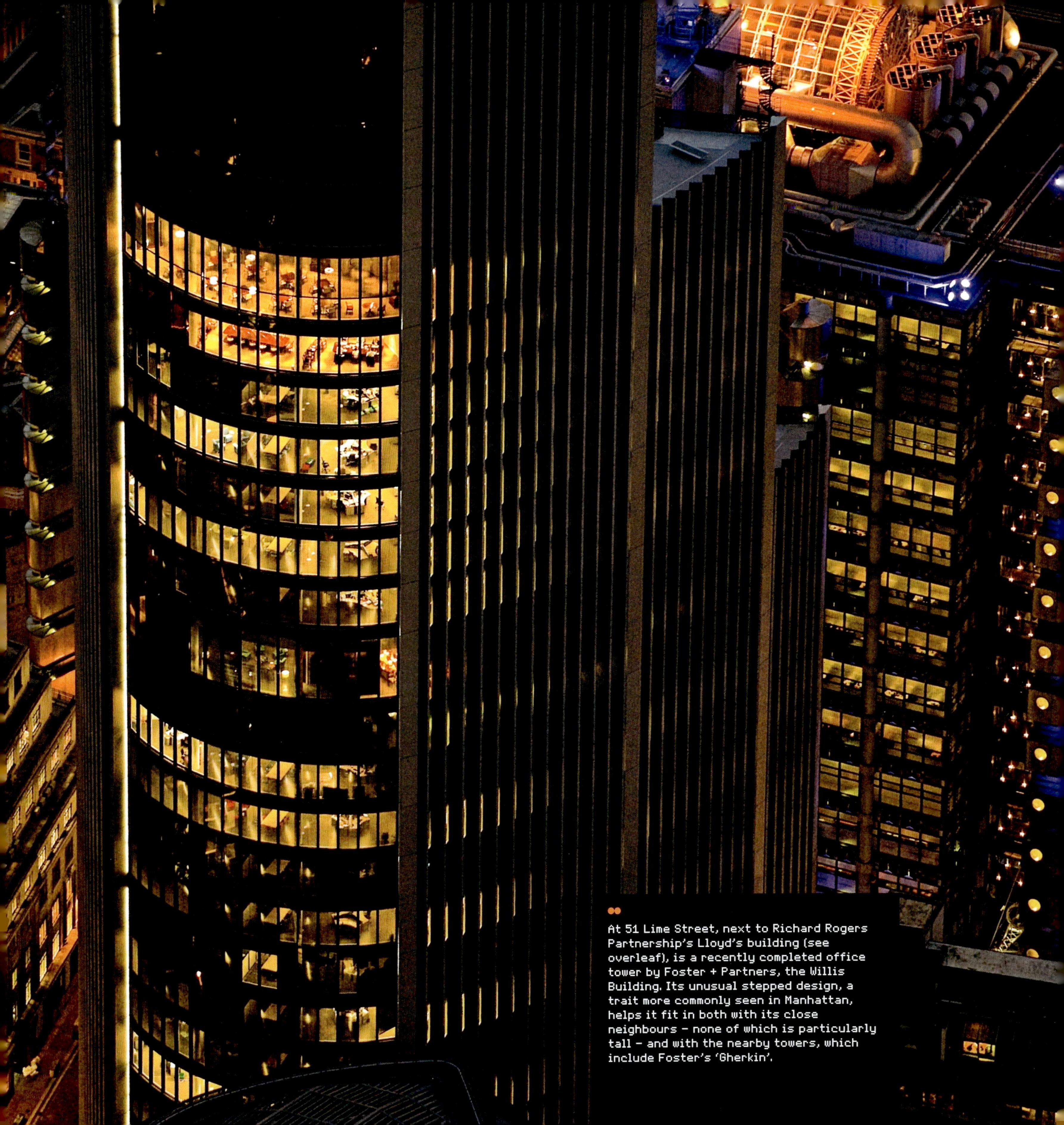

At 51 Lime Street, next to Richard Rogers Partnership's Lloyd's building (see overleaf), is a recently completed office tower by Foster + Partners, the Willis Building. Its unusual stepped design, a trait more commonly seen in Manhattan, helps it fit in both with its close neighbours – none of which is particularly tall – and with the nearby towers, which include Foster's 'Gherkin'.

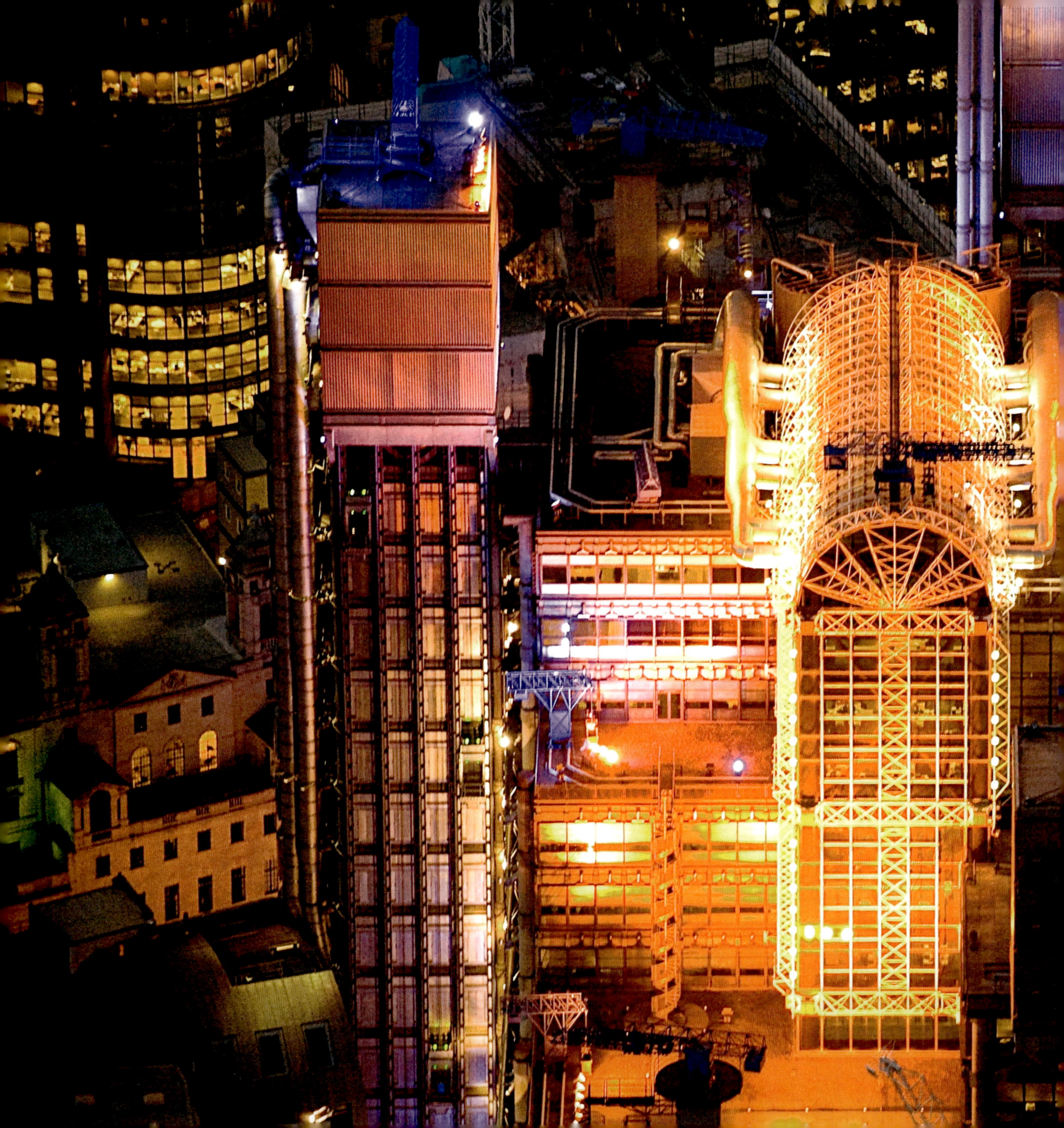

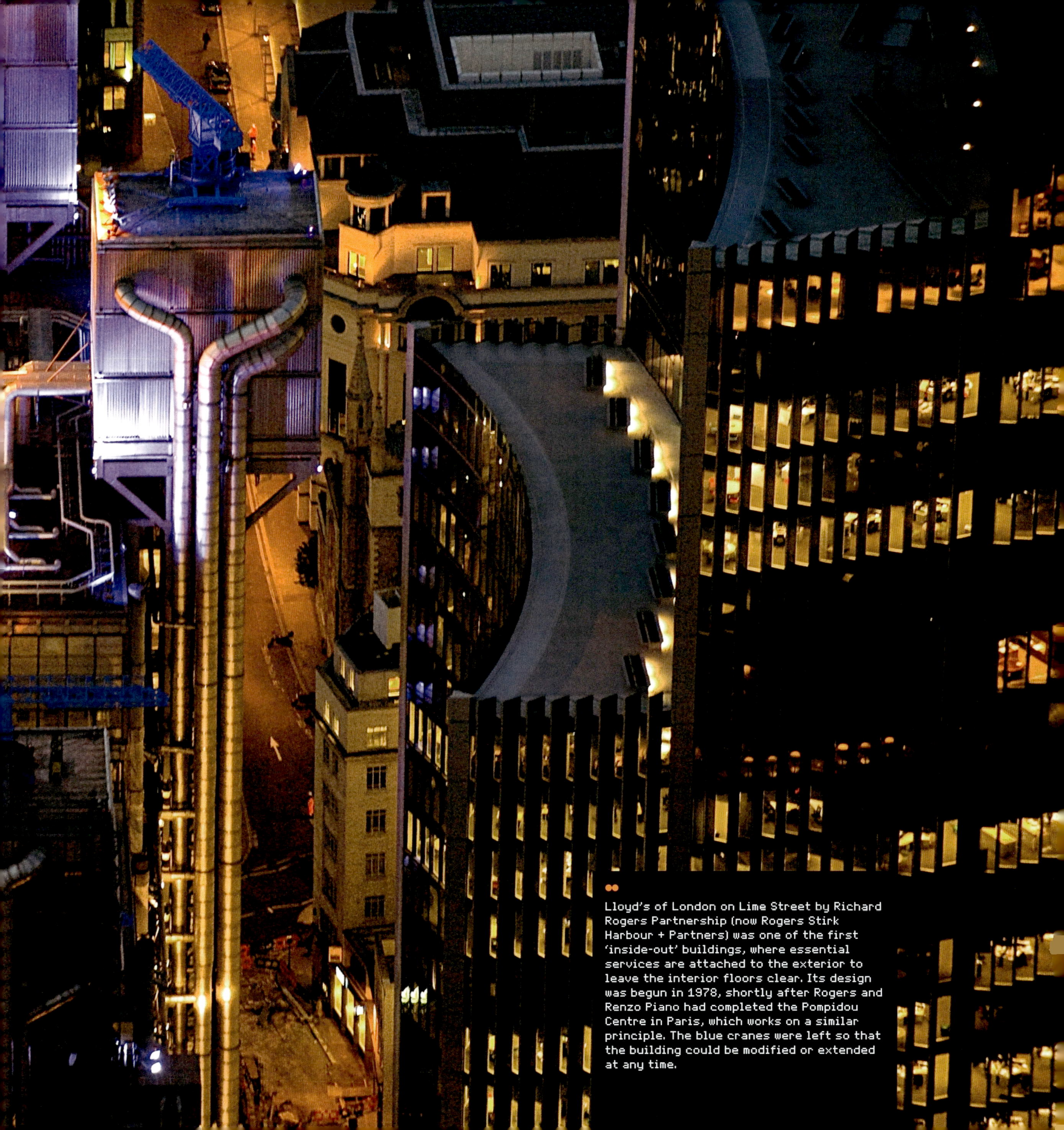

Lloyd's of London on Lime Street by Richard
Rogers Partnership (now Rogers Stirk
Harbour + Partners) was one of the first
'inside-out' buildings, where essential
services are attached to the exterior to
leave the interior floors clear. Its design
was begun in 1978, shortly after Rogers and
Renzo Piano had completed the Pompidou
Centre in Paris, which works on a similar
principle. The blue cranes were left so that
the building could be modified or extended
at any time.

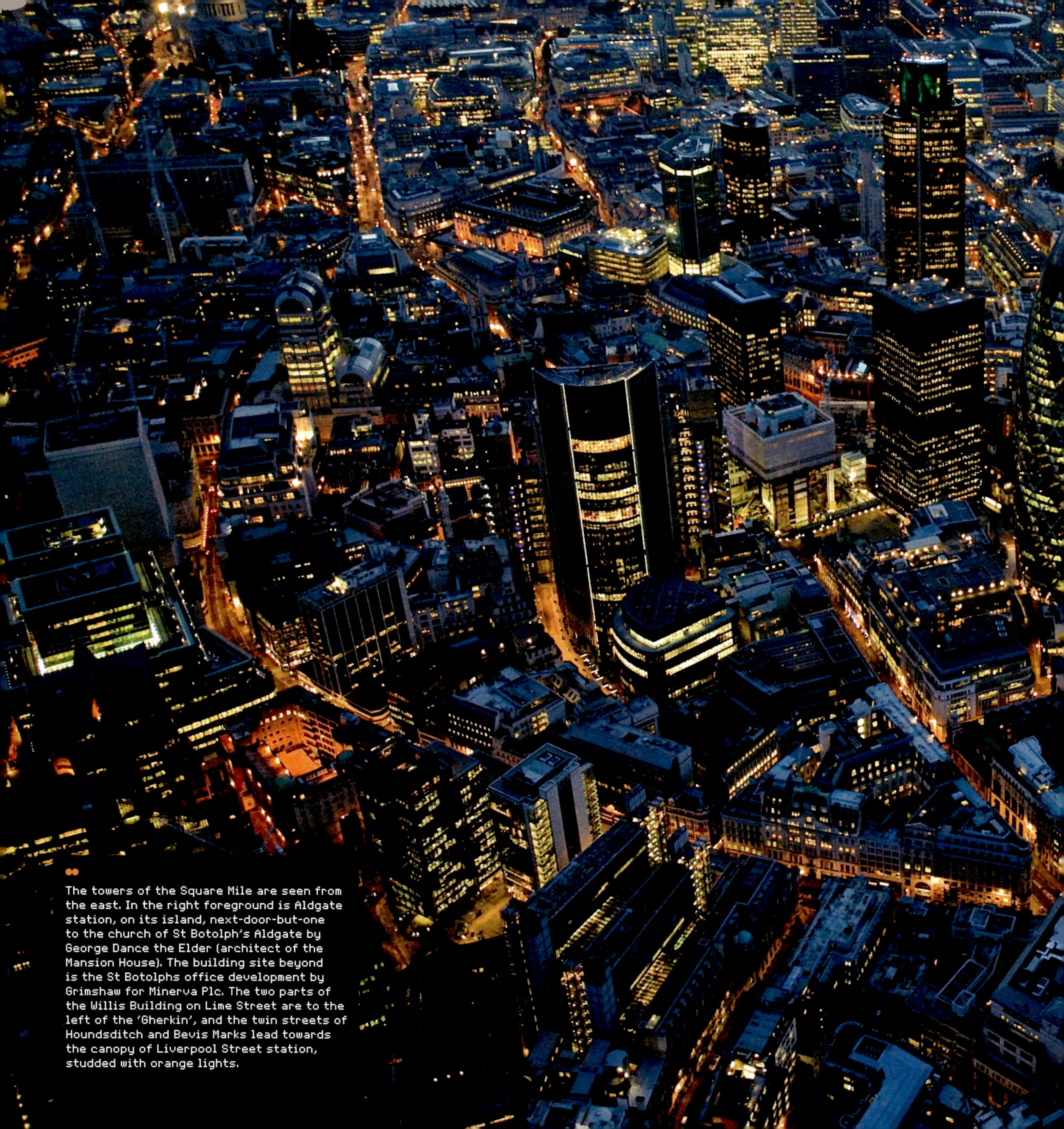

The towers of the Square Mile are seen from the east. In the right foreground is Aldgate station, on its island, next-door-but-one to the church of St Botolph's Aldgate by George Dance the Elder (architect of the Mansion House). The building site beyond is the St Botolphs office development by Grimshaw for Minerva Plc. The two parts of the Willis Building on Lime Street are to the left of the 'Gherkin', and the twin streets of Houndsditch and Bevis Marks lead towards the canopy of Liverpool Street station, studded with orange lights.

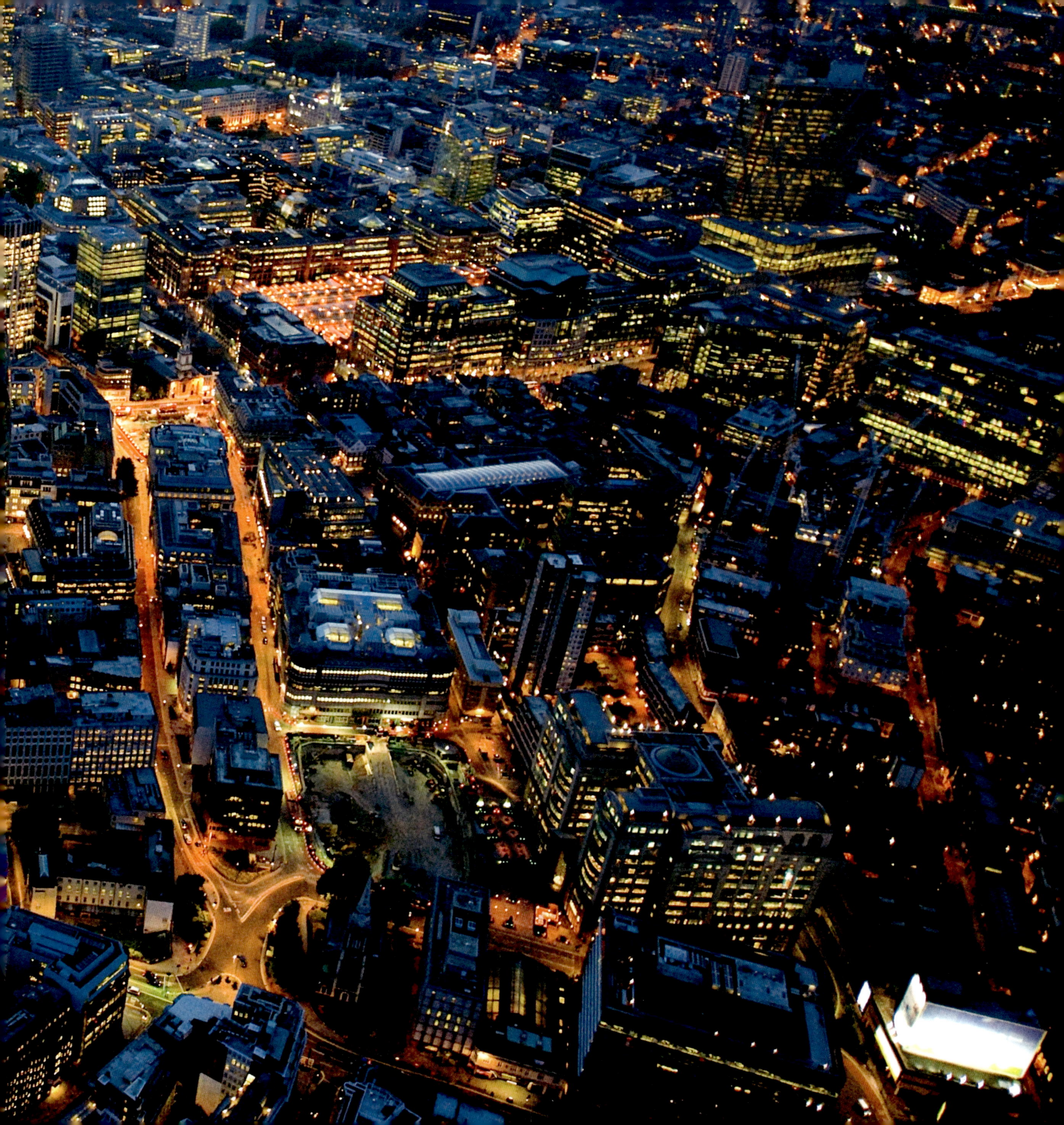

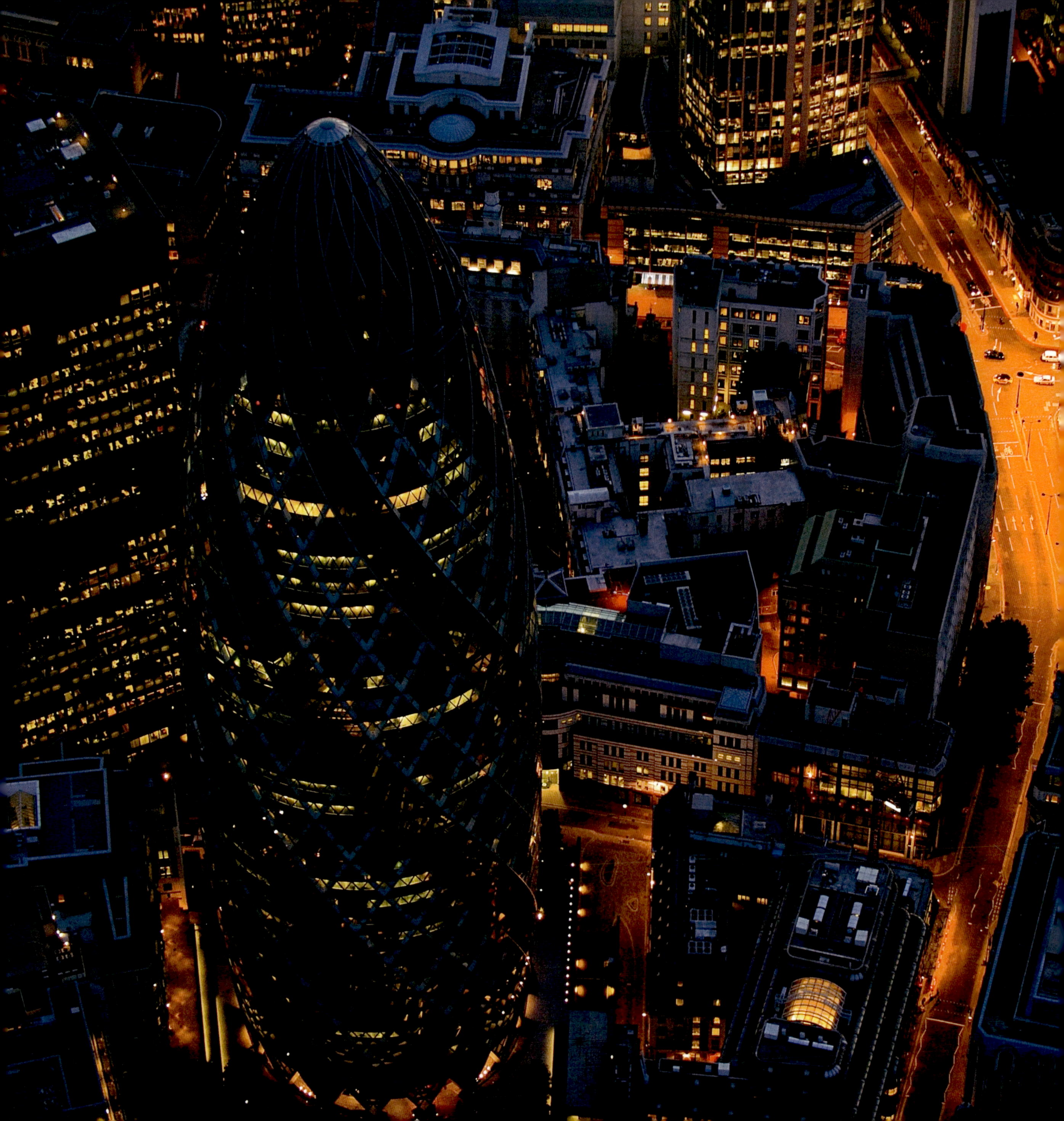

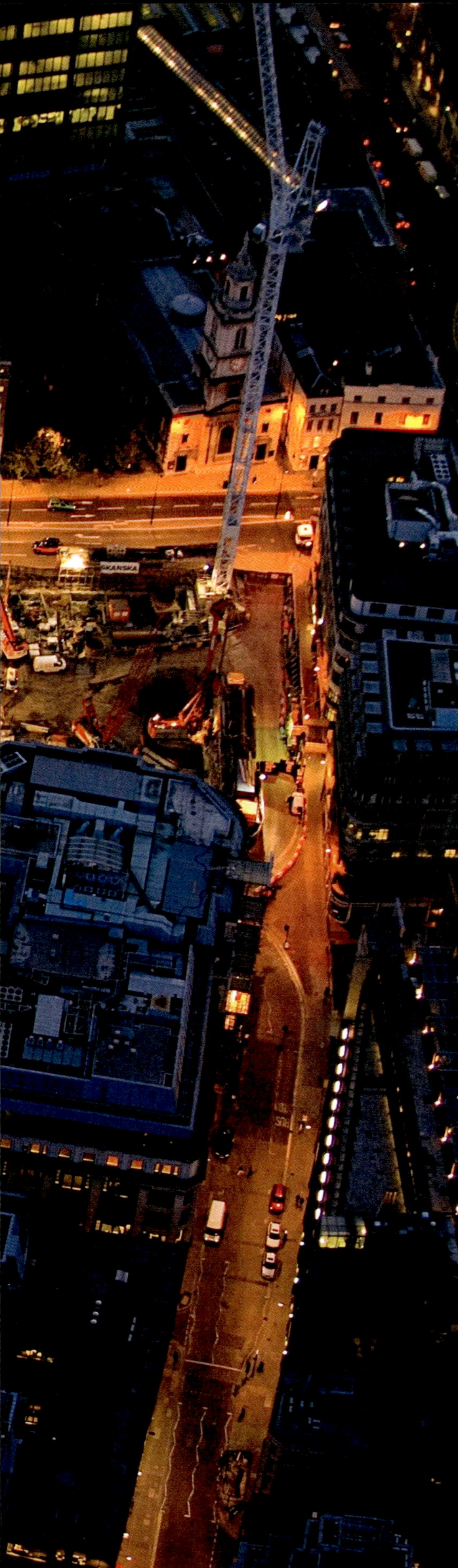

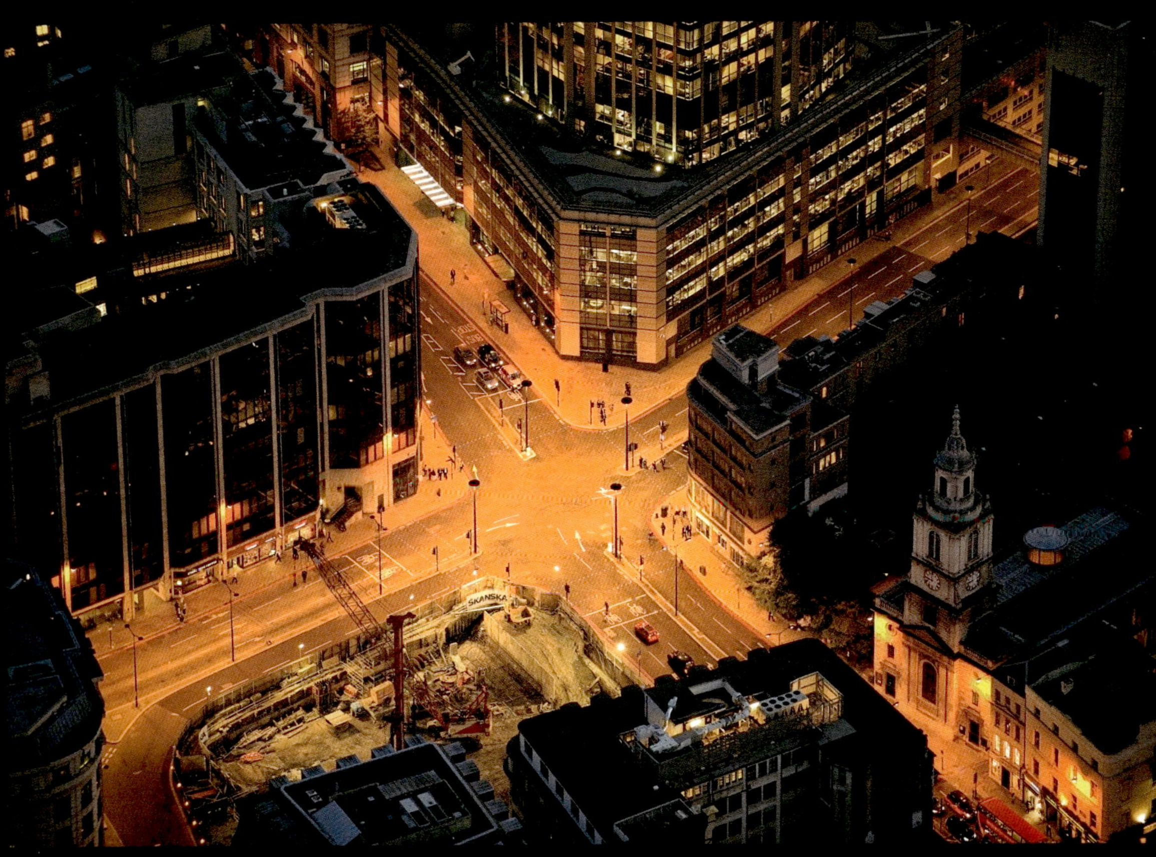

← The forty-storey tower at 30 St Mary Axe, by Foster + Partners, was built on the site of the Baltic Exchange, which was destroyed by an IRA bomb in 1992. Known as the 'Gherkin' and with tenants including reinsurance firm Swiss Re and law practice Kirkland & Ellis, it is an example of progressive office design. The tower's curvy design is more aerodynamic than traditional orthogonal towers, resulting in less turbulence at street level.

↑ This crossroads presents an ever-changing picture. The building site is that of the Heron Tower (110 Bishopsgate, designed by Kohn Pedersen Fox), which when finished will be just over 200 metres tall, towering over the nearby church of St Botolph's. The handsome white building next-but-one to the church is the White Hart inn, the original building of which dated from 1480. Coaching inns were once plentiful on Bishopsgate, to serve those travelling north.

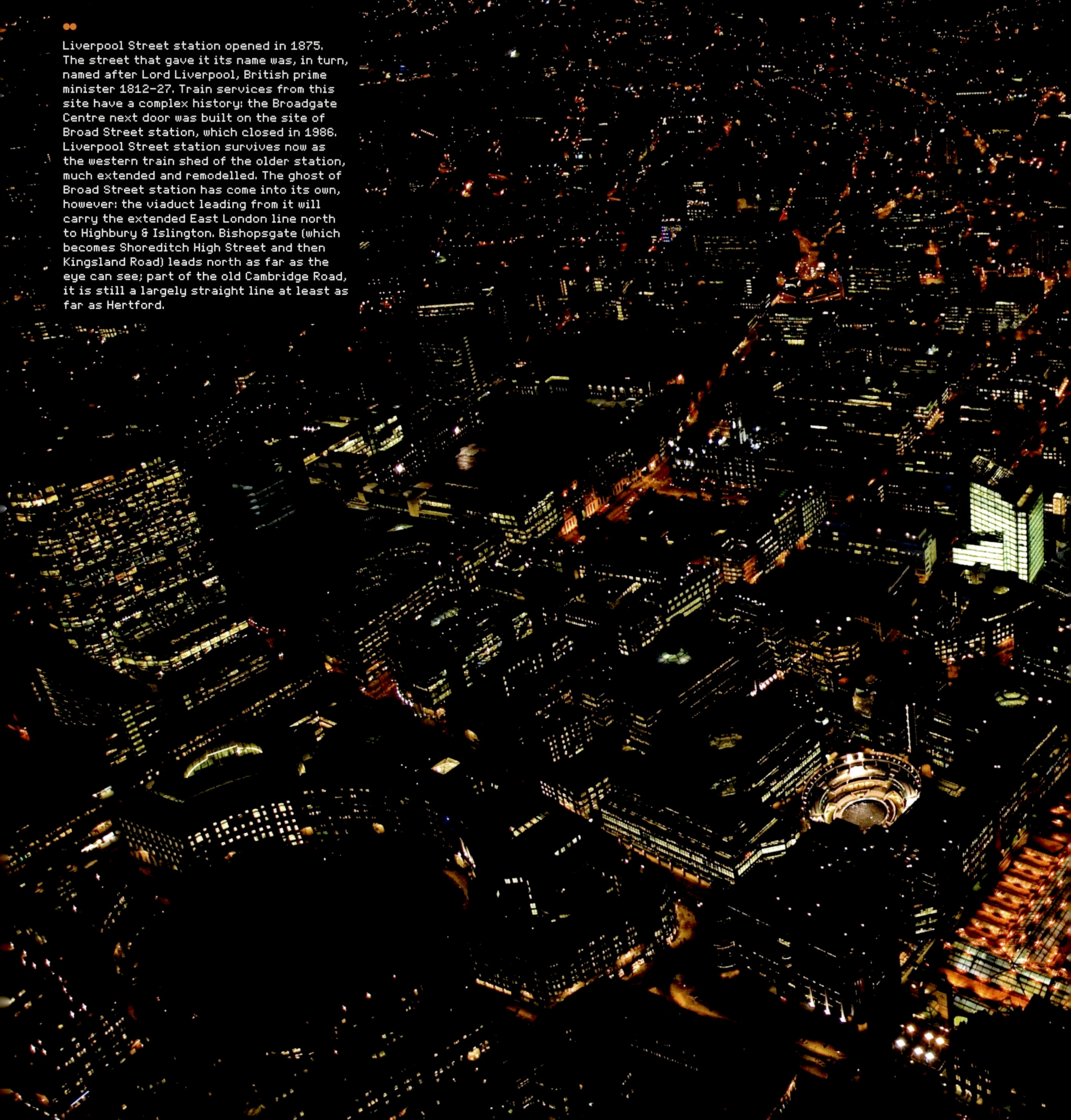

Liverpool Street station opened in 1875. The street that gave it its name was, in turn, named after Lord Liverpool, British prime minister 1812-27. Train services from this site have a complex history: the Broadgate Centre next door was built on the site of Broad Street station, which closed in 1986. Liverpool Street station survives now as the western train shed of the older station, much extended and remodelled. The ghost of Broad Street station has come into its own, however: the viaduct leading from it will carry the extended East London line north to Highbury & Islington. Bishopsgate (which becomes Shoreditch High Street and then Kingsland Road) leads north as far as the eye can see; part of the old Cambridge Road, it is still a largely straight line at least as far as Hertford.

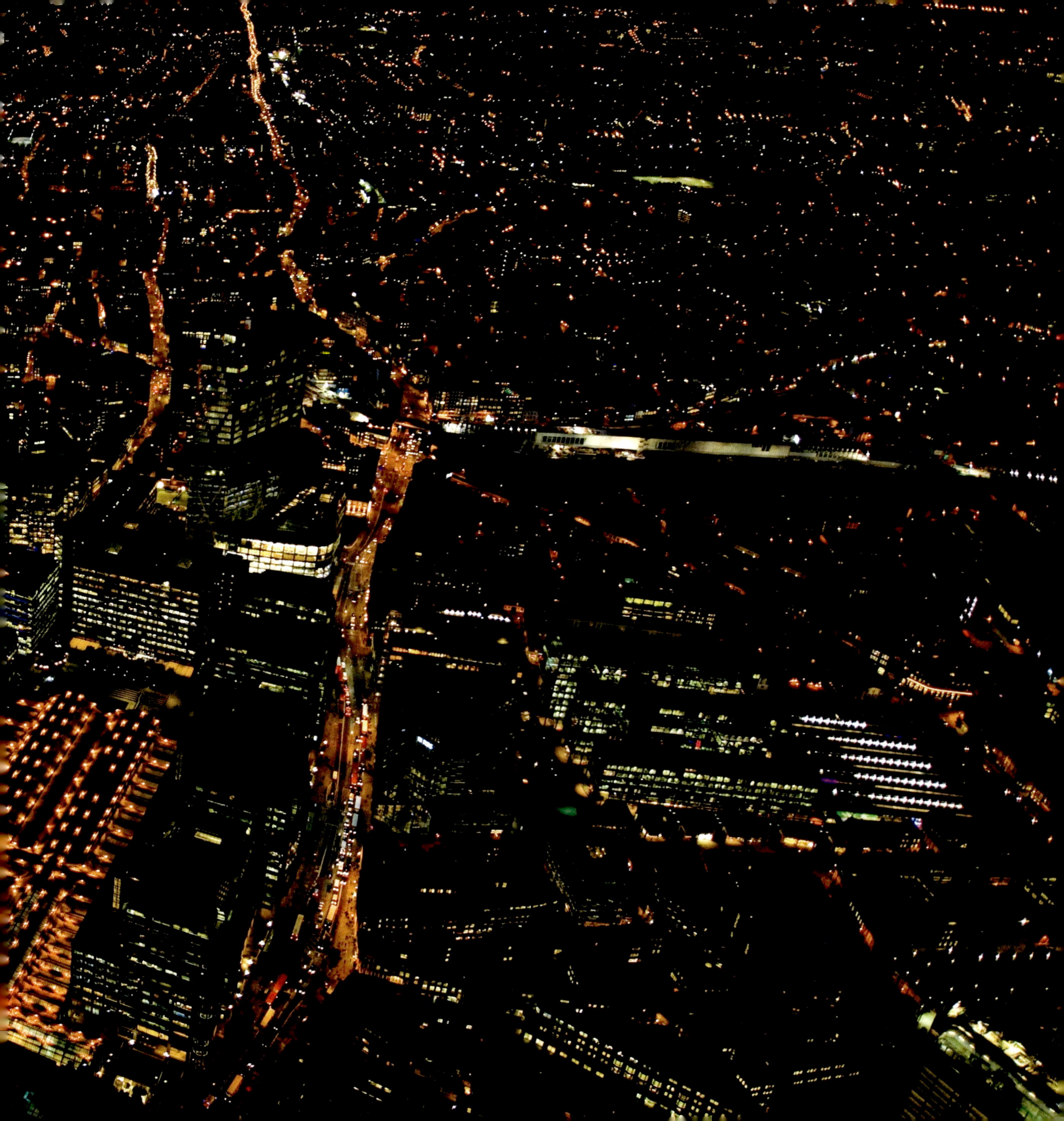

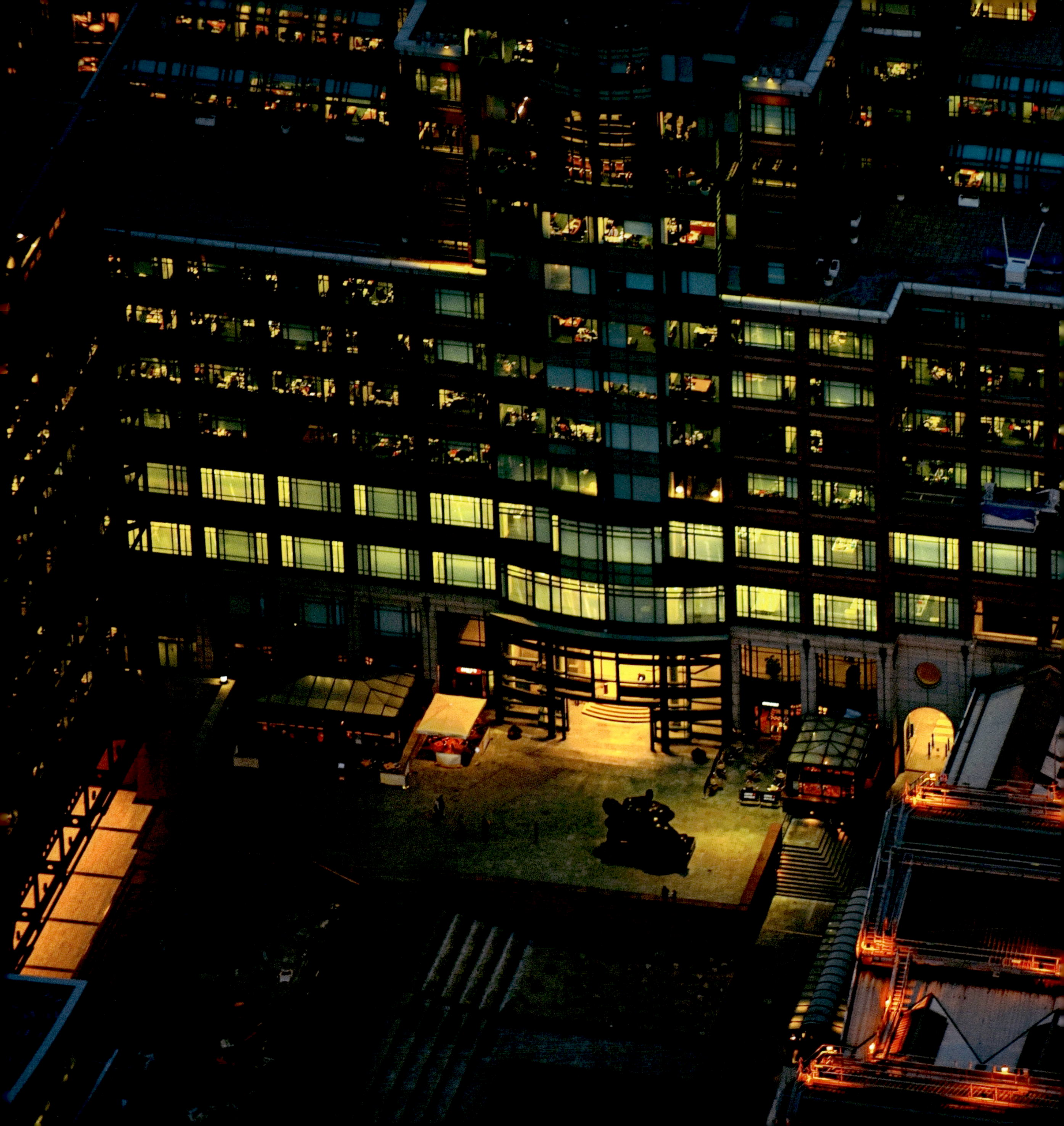

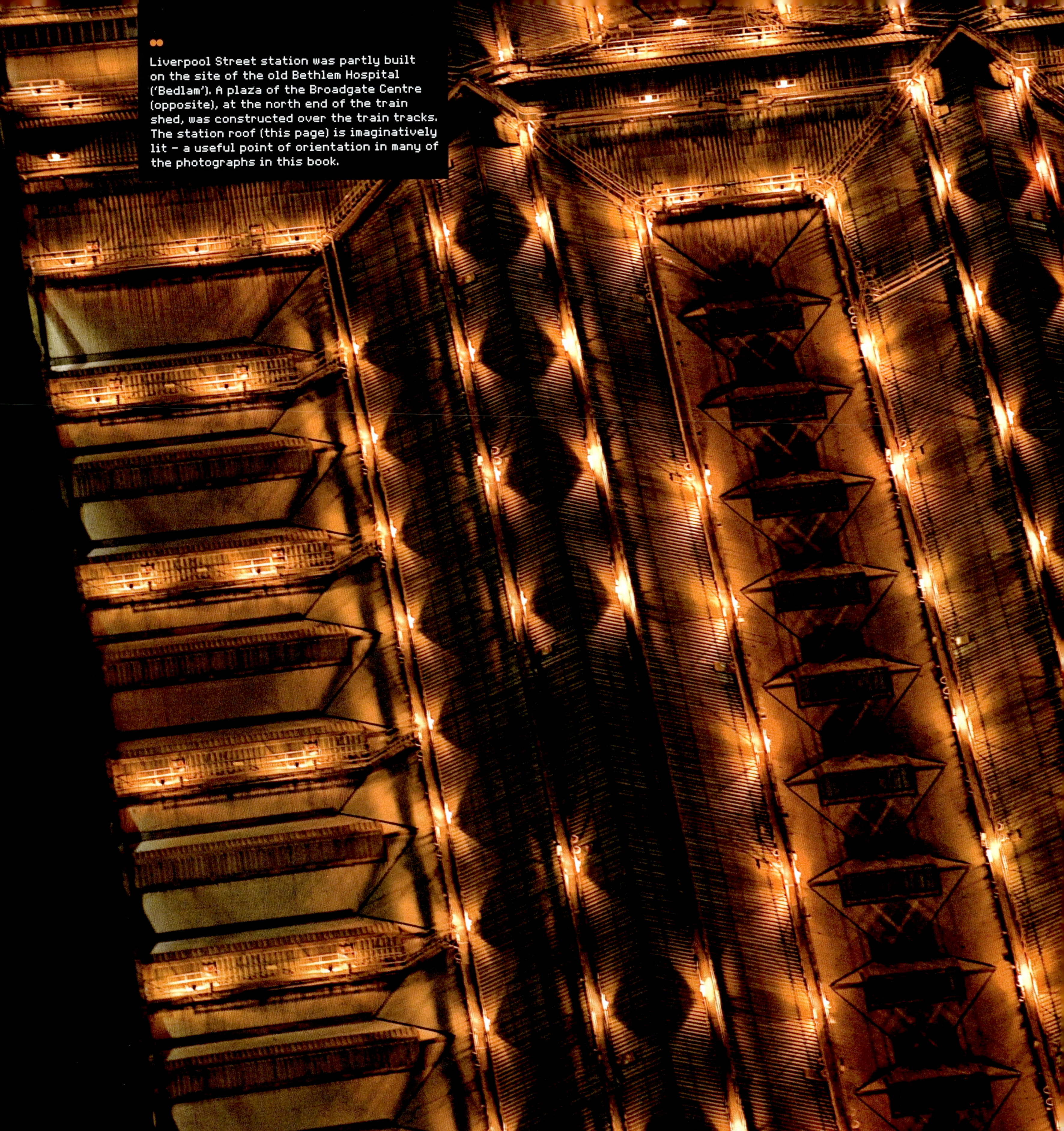

Liverpool Street station was partly built
on the site of the old Bethlem Hospital
('Bedlam'). A plaza of the Broadgate Centre
(opposite), at the north end of the train
shed, was constructed over the train tracks.
The station roof (this page) is imaginatively
lit – a useful point of orientation in many of
the photographs in this book.

The award-winning Broadgate development, which was designed by Arup with Skidmore, Owings & Merrill and completed in 1991, focuses on a central plaza, an enlightened and popular piece of public space. In winter (below) its ice rink – less well known than that of Somerset House, for example – is gratifyingly empty during the day, although office workers on their lunch breaks cluster to watch for mishaps. In summer the plaza hosts outdoor events (opposite).

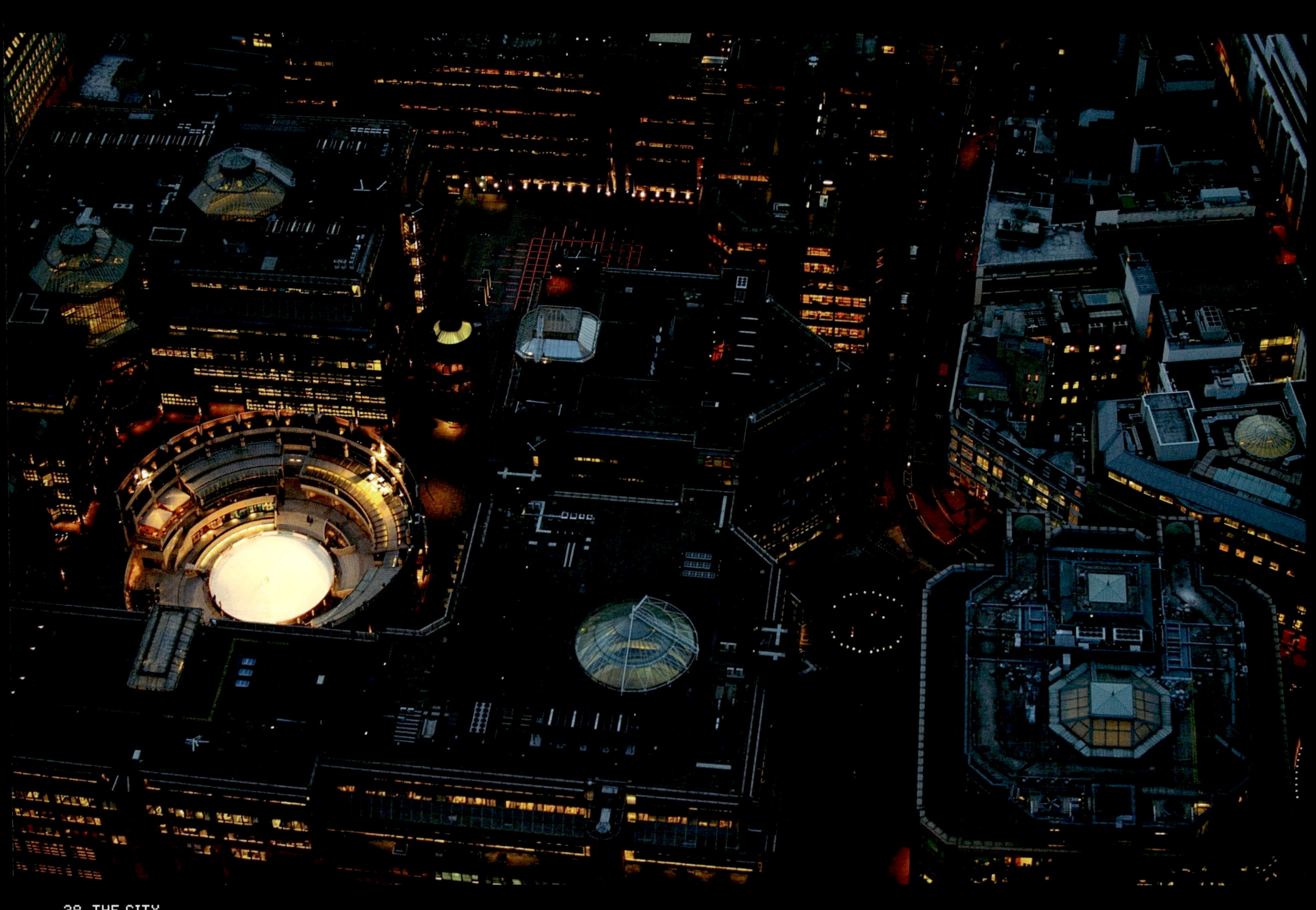

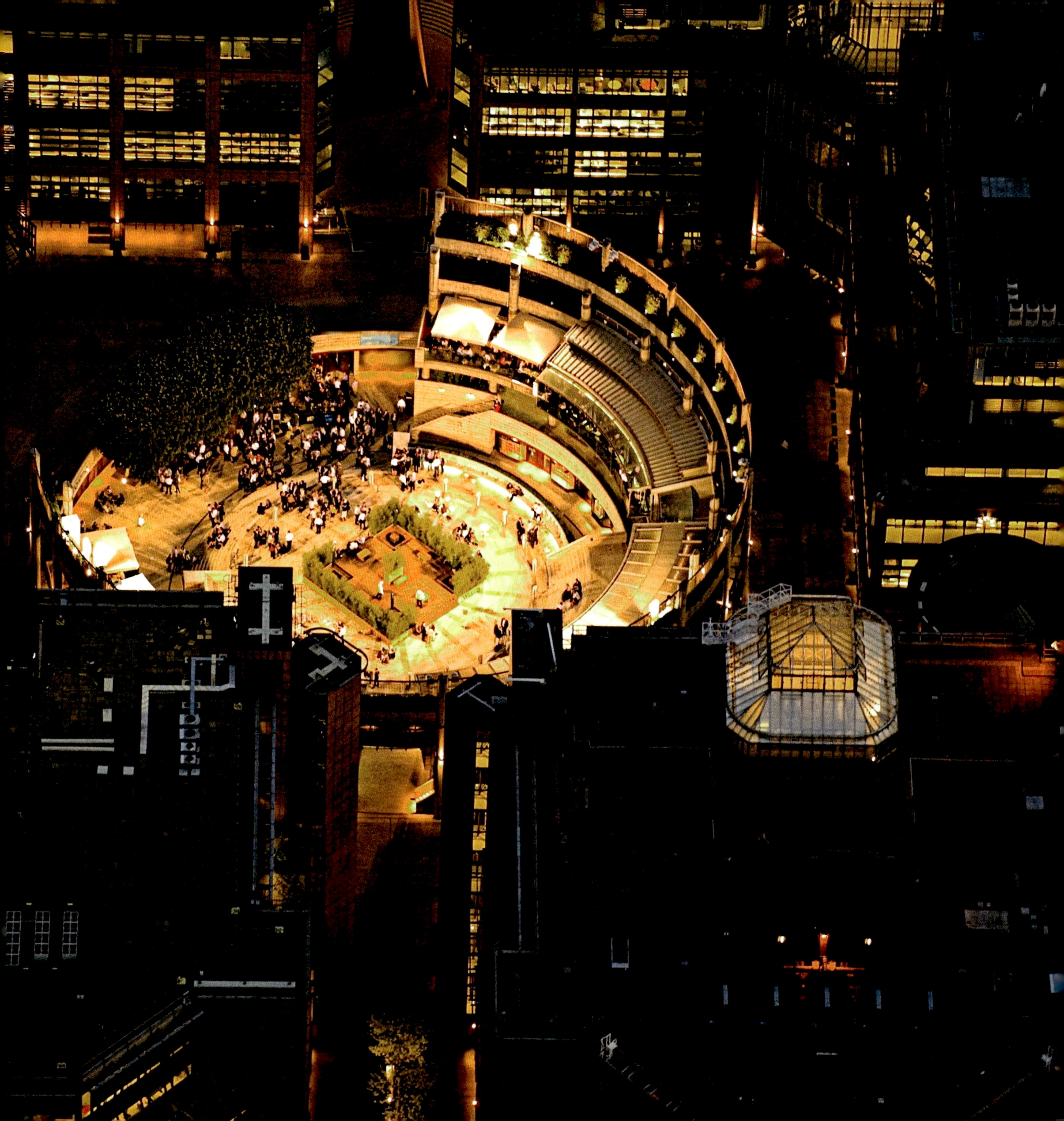

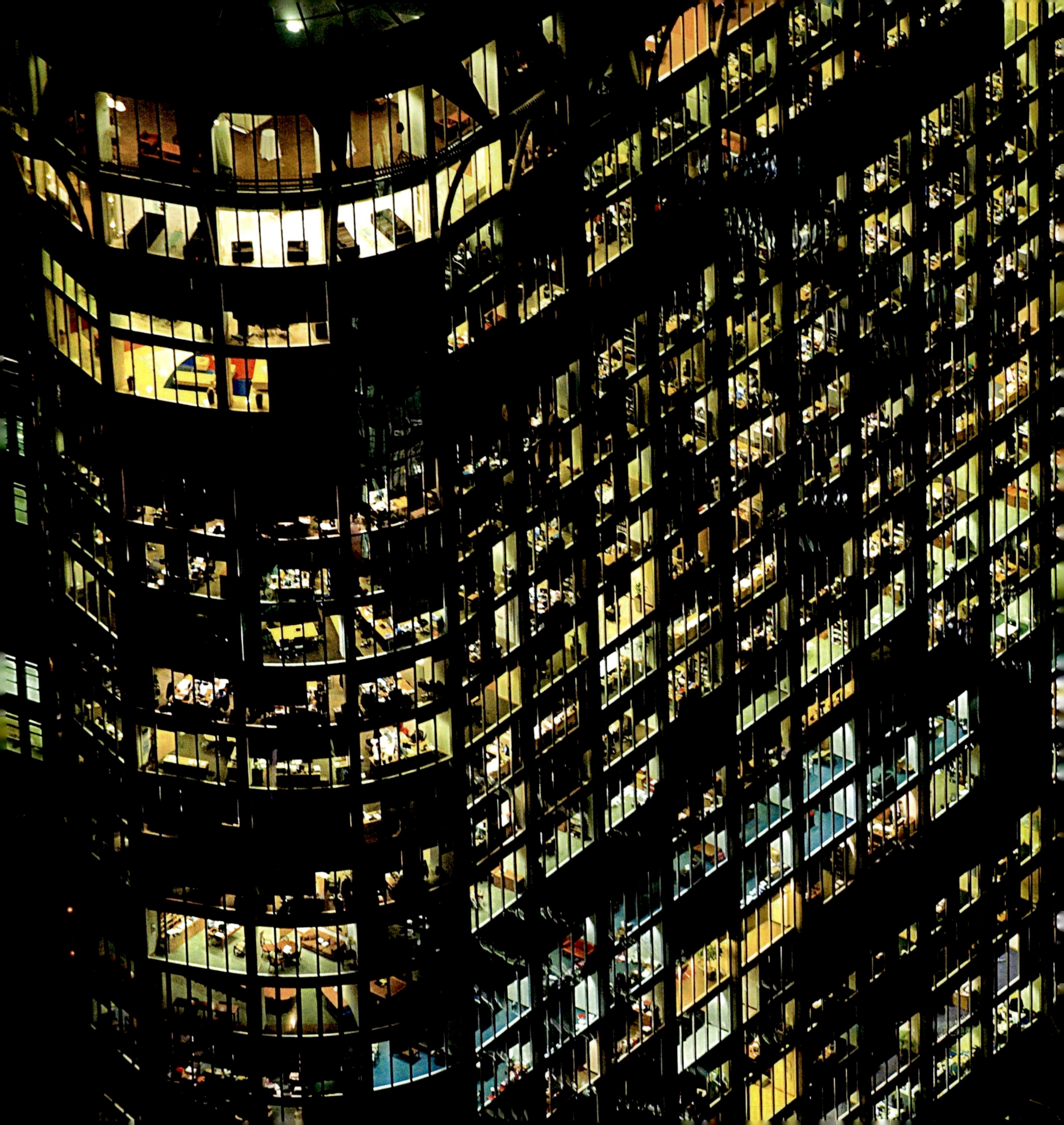

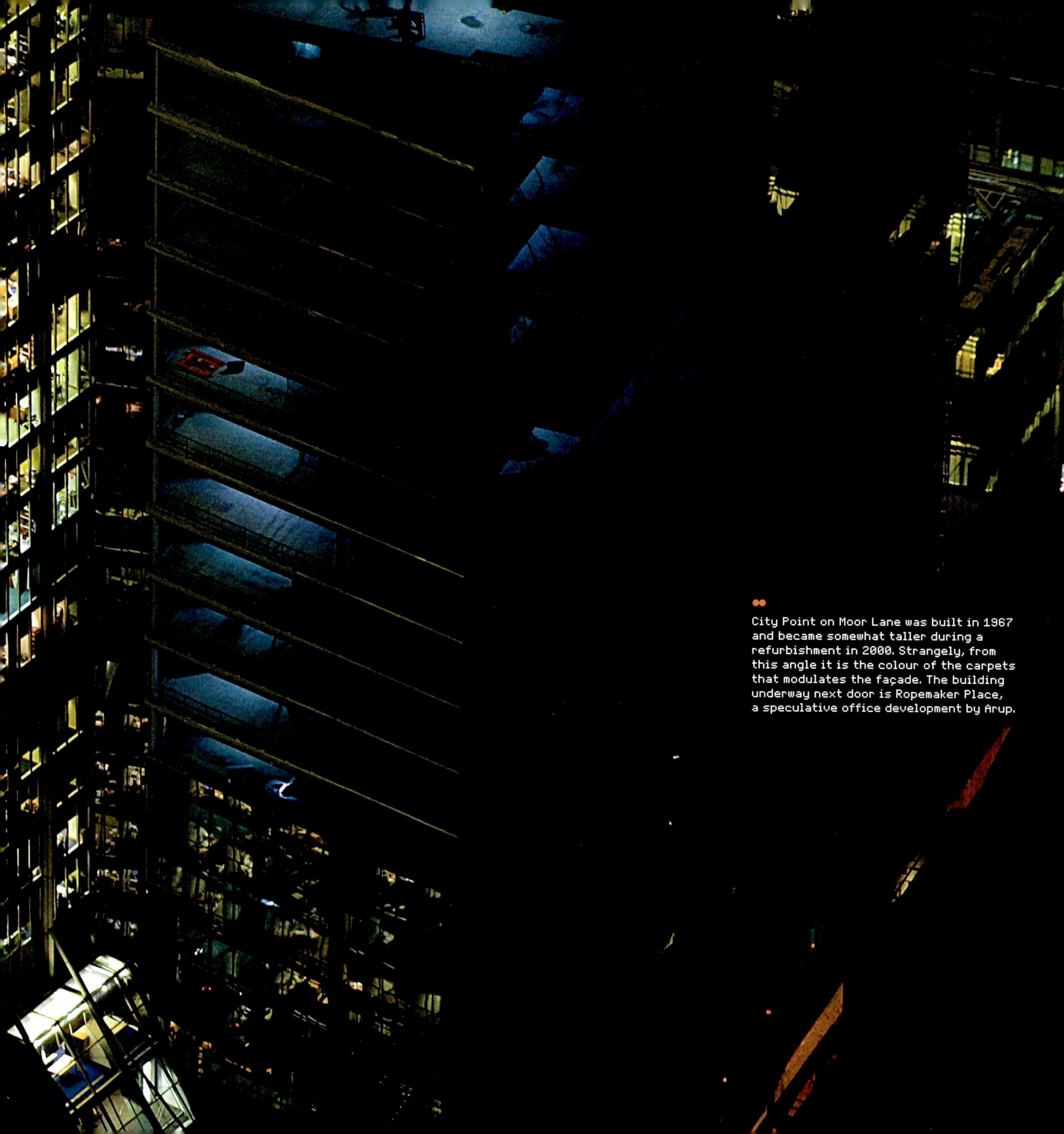

City Point on Moor Lane was built in 1967
and became somewhat taller during a
refurbishment in 2000. Strangely, from
this angle it is the colour of the carpets
that modulates the façade. The building
underway next door is Ropemaker Place,
a speculative office development by Arup.

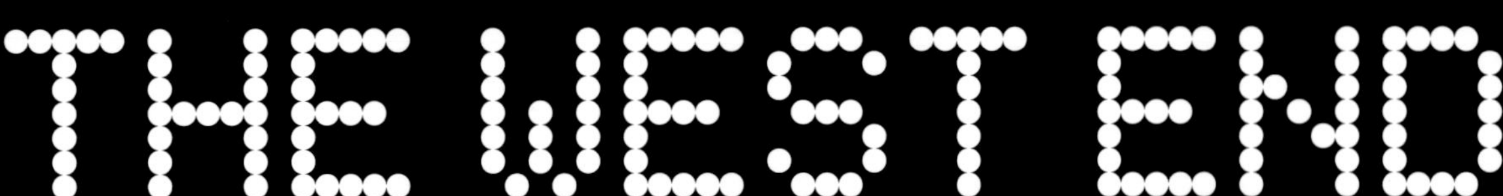# THE WEST END

For most visitors, the West End is London. Oxford Street and Regent Street, Parliament Square and Whitehall, Piccadilly Circus and Trafalgar Square, Covent Garden and Soho: the London of shops, restaurants, theatres and clubs generates most of the city's tourist income. At ground level, the West End can be a dispiriting place. The packed pavements of Oxford Street, for example, and the seedy – and, late at night, even slightly threatening – confines of Leicester Square have no obvious charm. Trafalgar Square has sacrificed much of its public dignity to become a raucous 'events' venue.

Yet there is charm, even calm, to be found in the West End. A swathe of parkland links Piccadilly with Parliament Square. The regular street grid of Mayfair and Marylebone is punctuated by garden squares (some of them defiantly private), and between Baker Street and Edgware Road the scale, if not always the built fabric, of Georgian London remains intact. The impact of John Nash's planning visions remains apparent in the great progression of spaces along Portland Place and Regent Street to the Mall.

There are, indeed, few really tall buildings in the West End, and those there are – the BT Tower, Centre Point, the Millbank Tower – are mostly characterful enough to assume the role of landmarks, although New Zealand House is an ill-mannered interloper into Pall Mall. Vested interests made sure that the Victorian railway builders were never allowed to penetrate the heart of London: Charing Cross is as close as they came; Paddington is safely consigned to the northern margins. Major roads define the edges of the West End; Park Lane to the west and Marylebone Road/Euston Road to the north form very real barriers. Currently they are little more than urban motorways, although they could be tamed as expansive boulevards in the manner of Paris's Champs-Elysées. Seething with life and activity, and never anything less than cosmopolitan, the West End encapsulates the character of London as a world city.

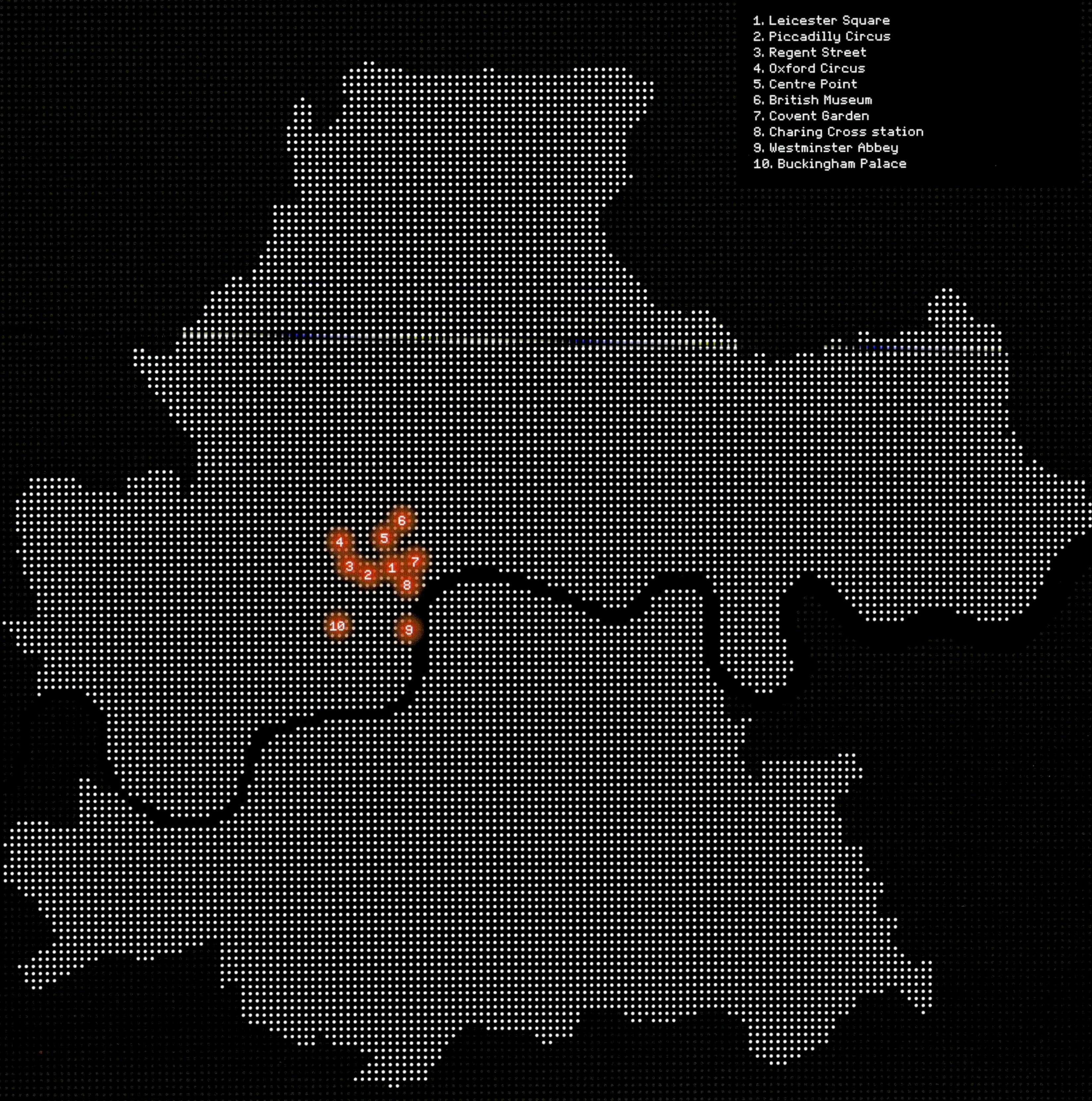

1. Leicester Square
2. Piccadilly Circus
3. Regent Street
4. Oxford Circus
5. Centre Point
6. British Museum
7. Covent Garden
8. Charing Cross station
9. Westminster Abbey
10. Buckingham Palace
4
5
6
3
2
1
7
8
10
9

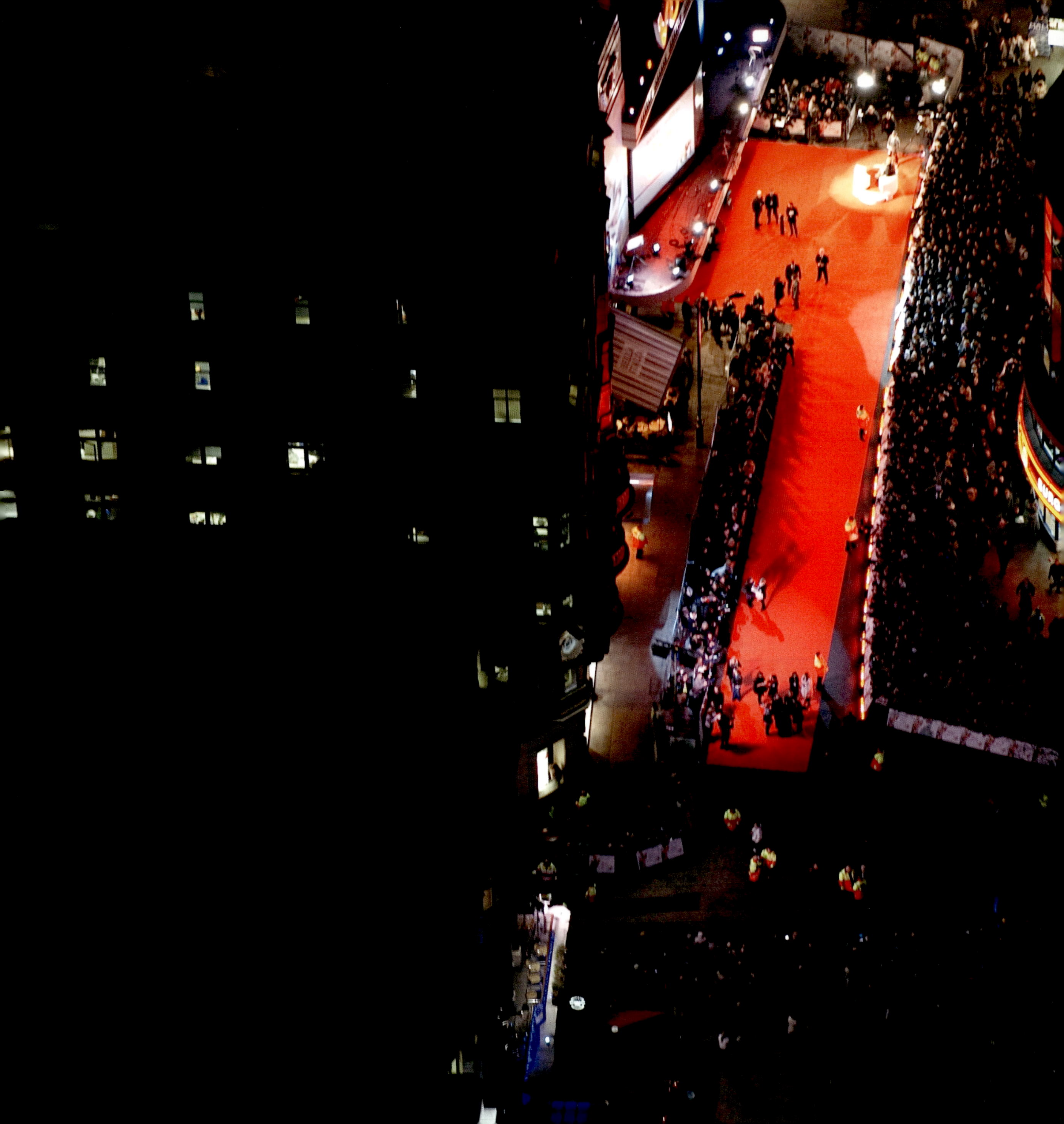

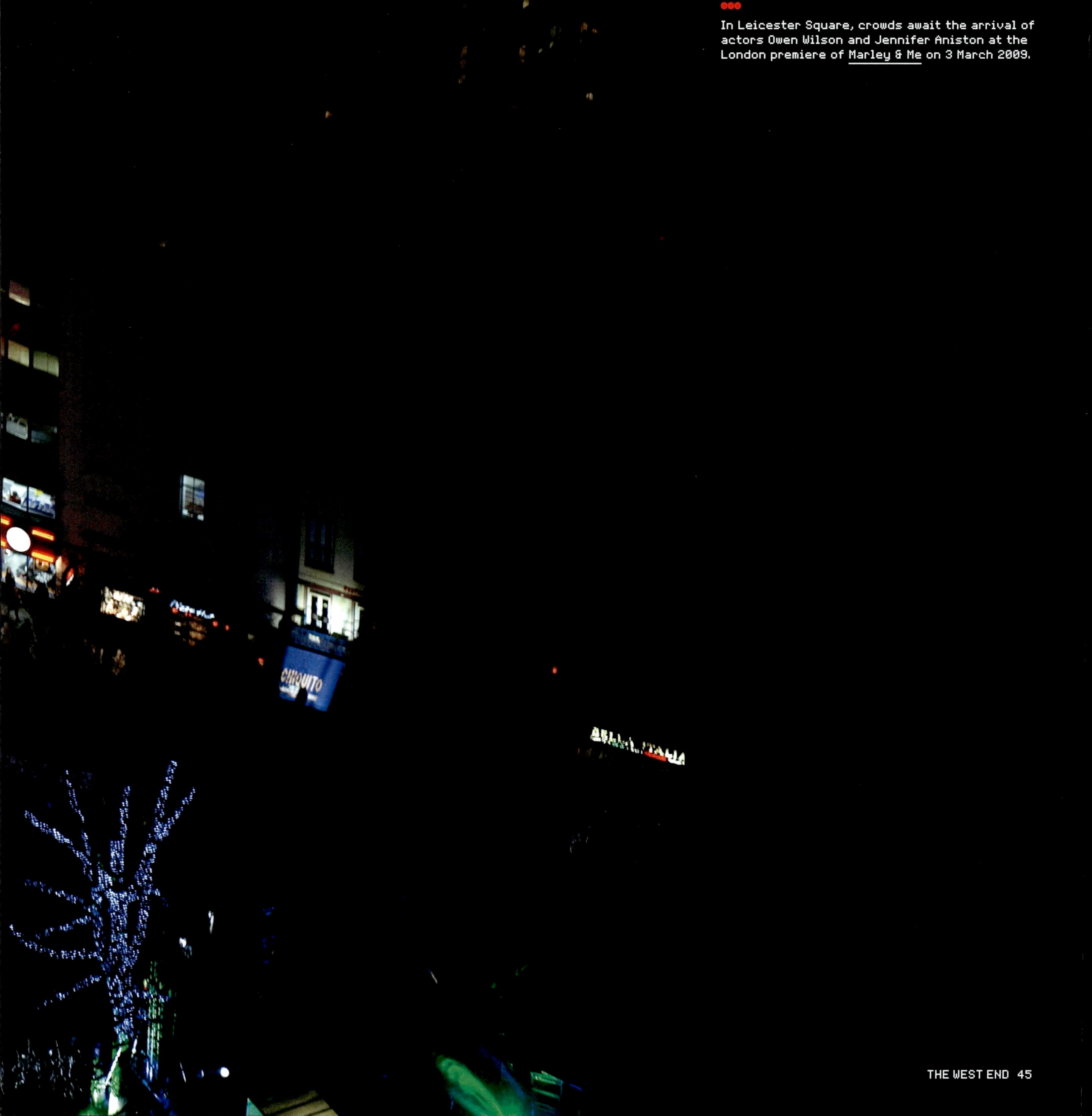

In Leicester Square, crowds await the arrival of
actors Owen Wilson and Jennifer Aniston at the
London premiere of <u>Marley & Me</u> on 3 March 2009.

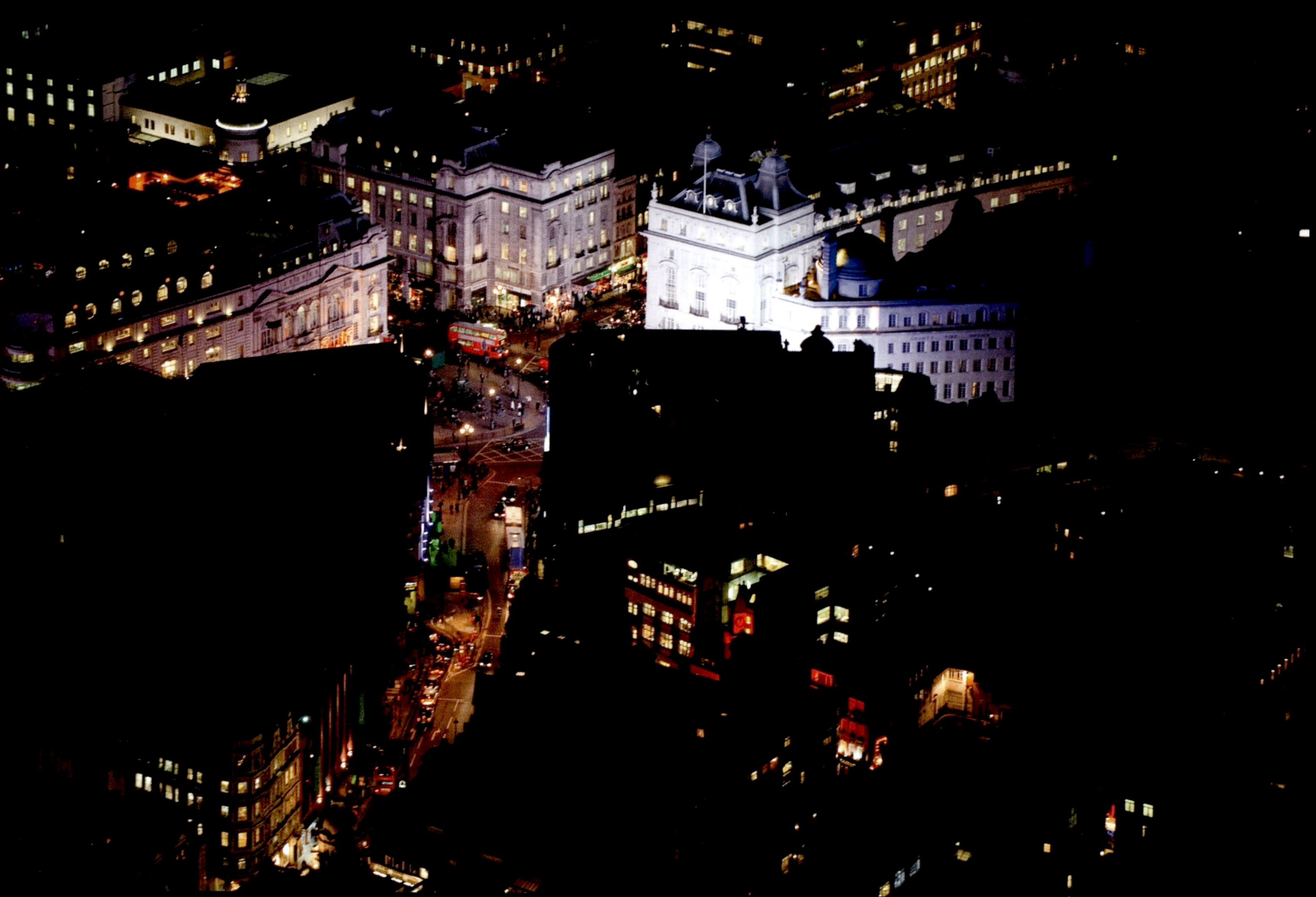

● ● ●

The sweep of Shaftesbury Avenue leads the eye
past the Trocadero into Piccadilly Circus. Now
a hectic and incoherent junction, the latter
was at one time a proper 'circus': the three
large, brightly lit buildings here, although now
remodelled or even rebuilt, originally had one
concave corner each. The fourth quarter of the
circus was demolished in the late nineteenth
century to make way for Shaftesbury Avenue.

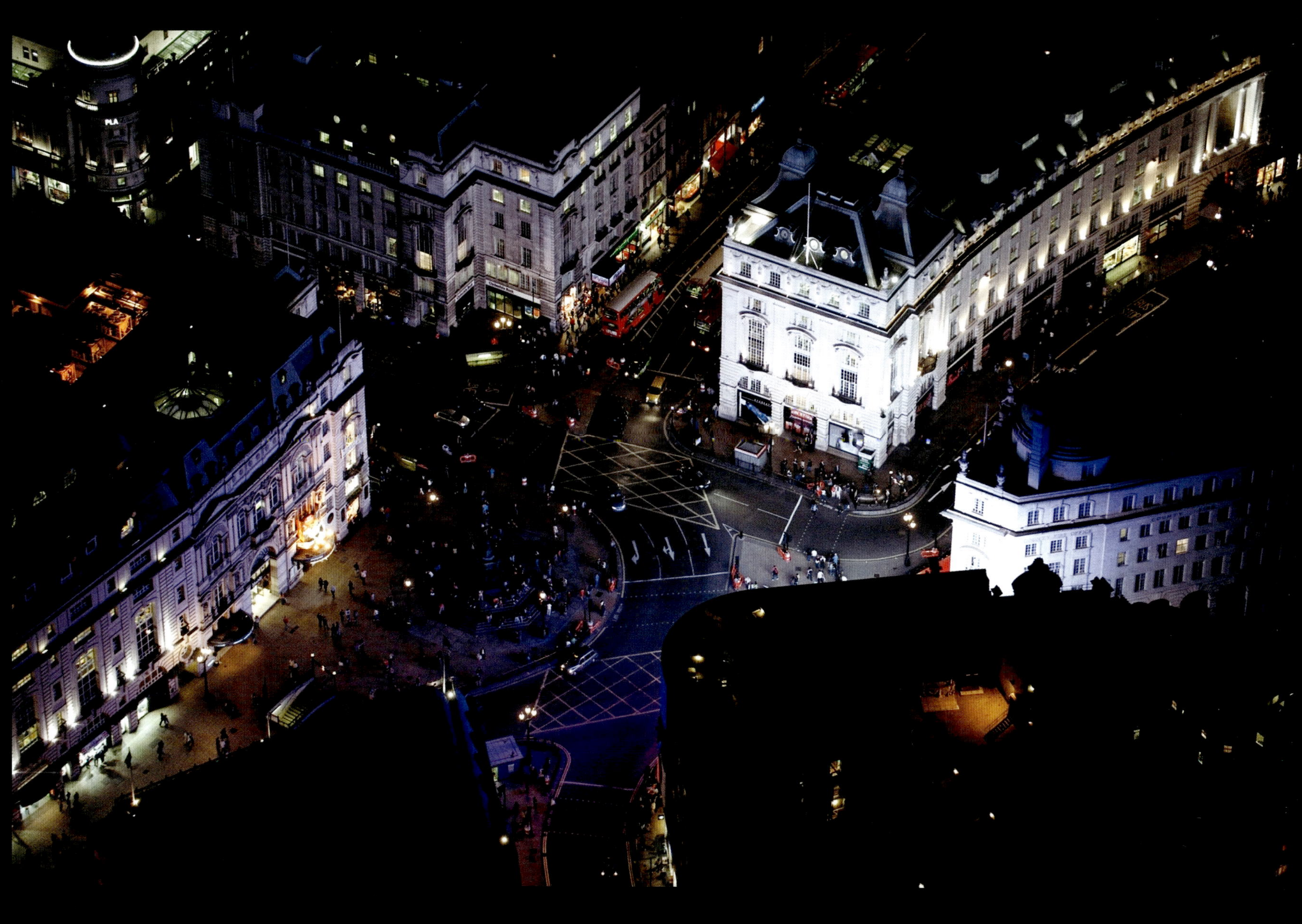

Piccadilly Circus has been known since the
first years of the twentieth century for its
illuminated advertisements. The Sanyo sign is
the oldest currently in place, dating from the
late 1980s. The entrance to the Tube at the
very bottom of the picture gives no indication
of the extent of the subterranean whirligig
that is Piccadilly Circus station.

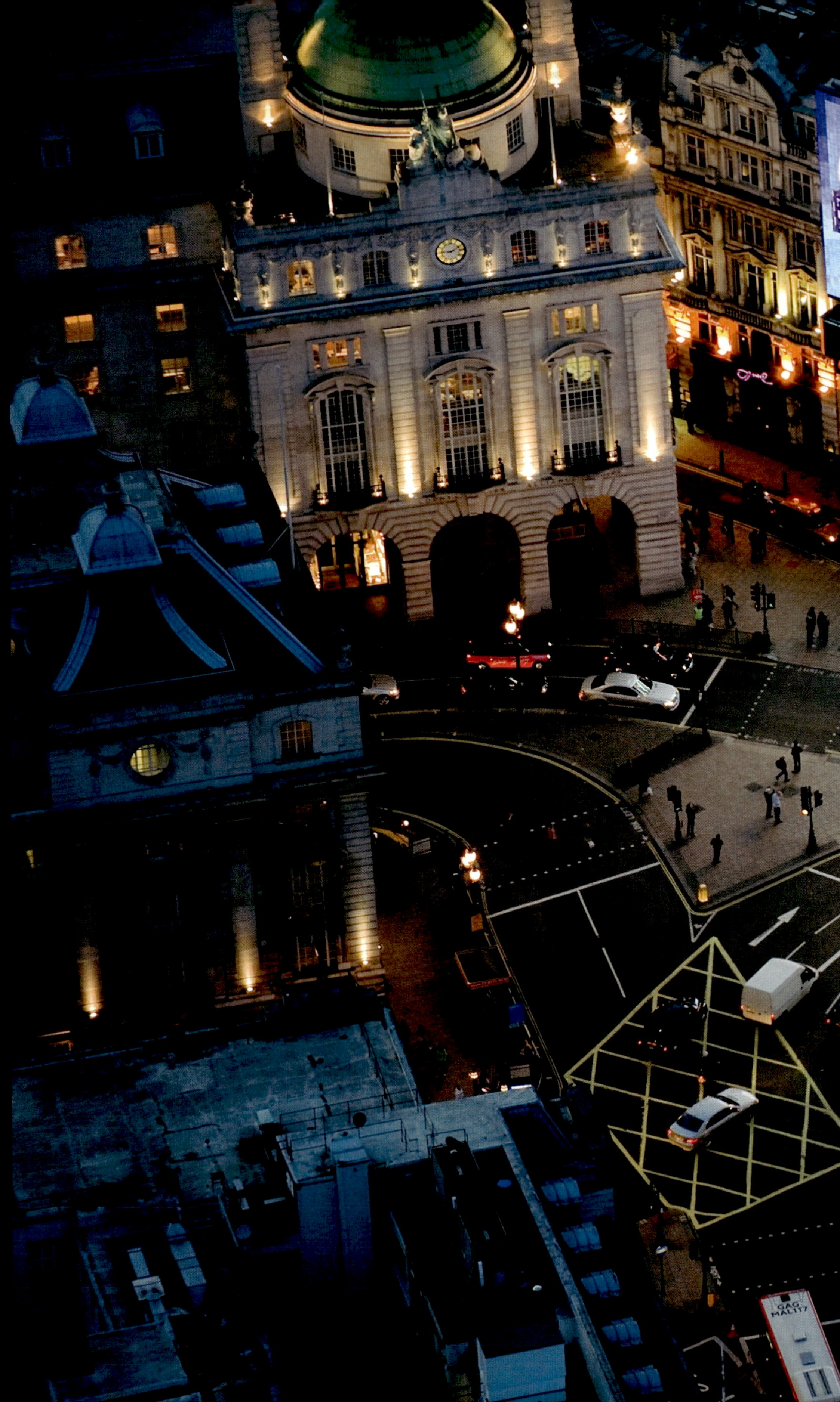

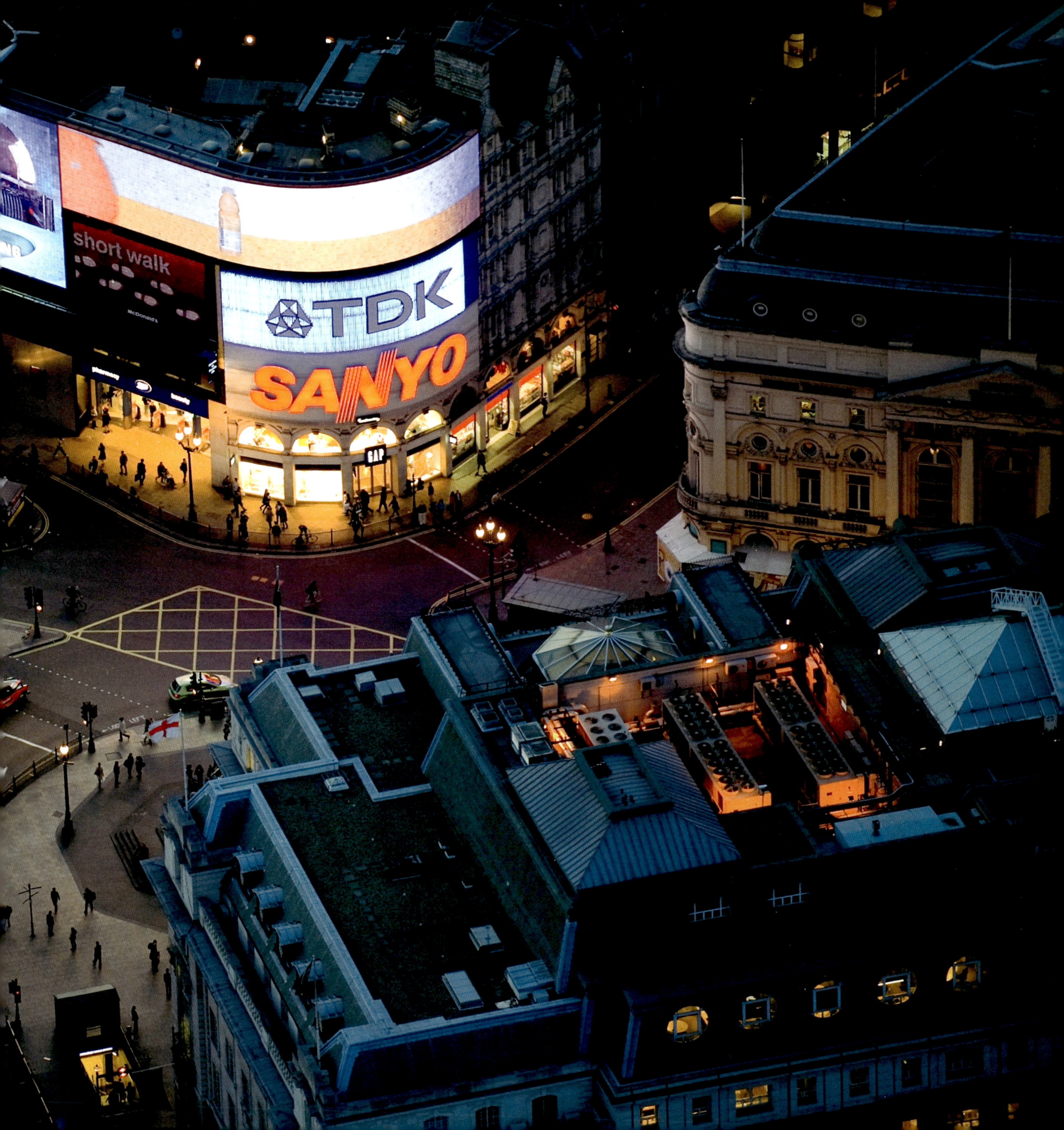

short walk
McDonald's
TDK
SANYO
GAP

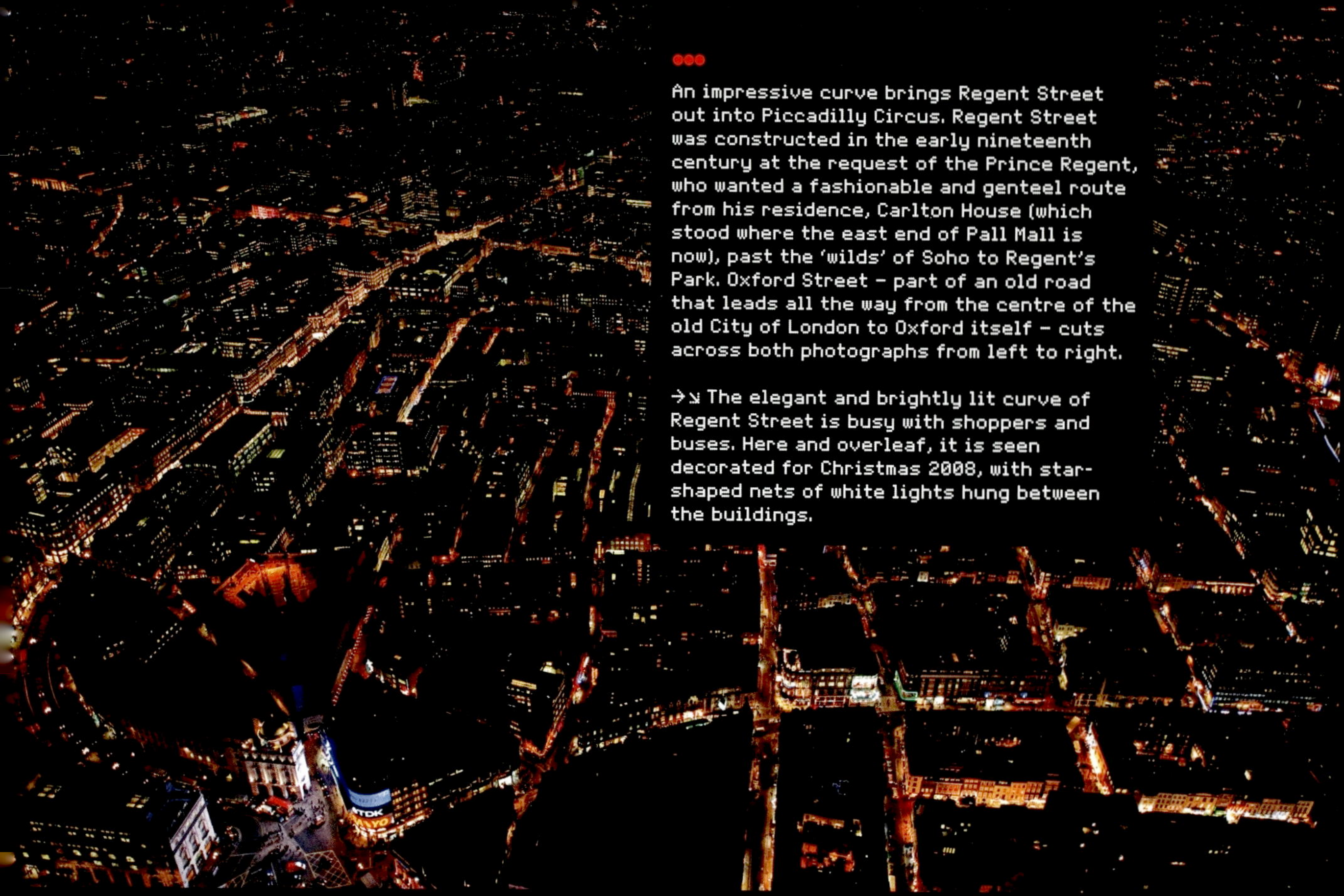

●●●

An impressive curve brings Regent Street
out into Piccadilly Circus. Regent Street
was constructed in the early nineteenth
century at the request of the Prince Regent,
who wanted a fashionable and genteel route
from his residence, Carlton House (which
stood where the east end of Pall Mall is
now), past the 'wilds' of Soho to Regent's
Park. Oxford Street – part of an old road
that leads all the way from the centre of the
old City of London to Oxford itself – cuts
across both photographs from left to right.

→↘ The elegant and brightly lit curve of
Regent Street is busy with shoppers and
buses. Here and overleaf, it is seen
decorated for Christmas 2008, with star-
shaped nets of white lights hung between
the buildings.

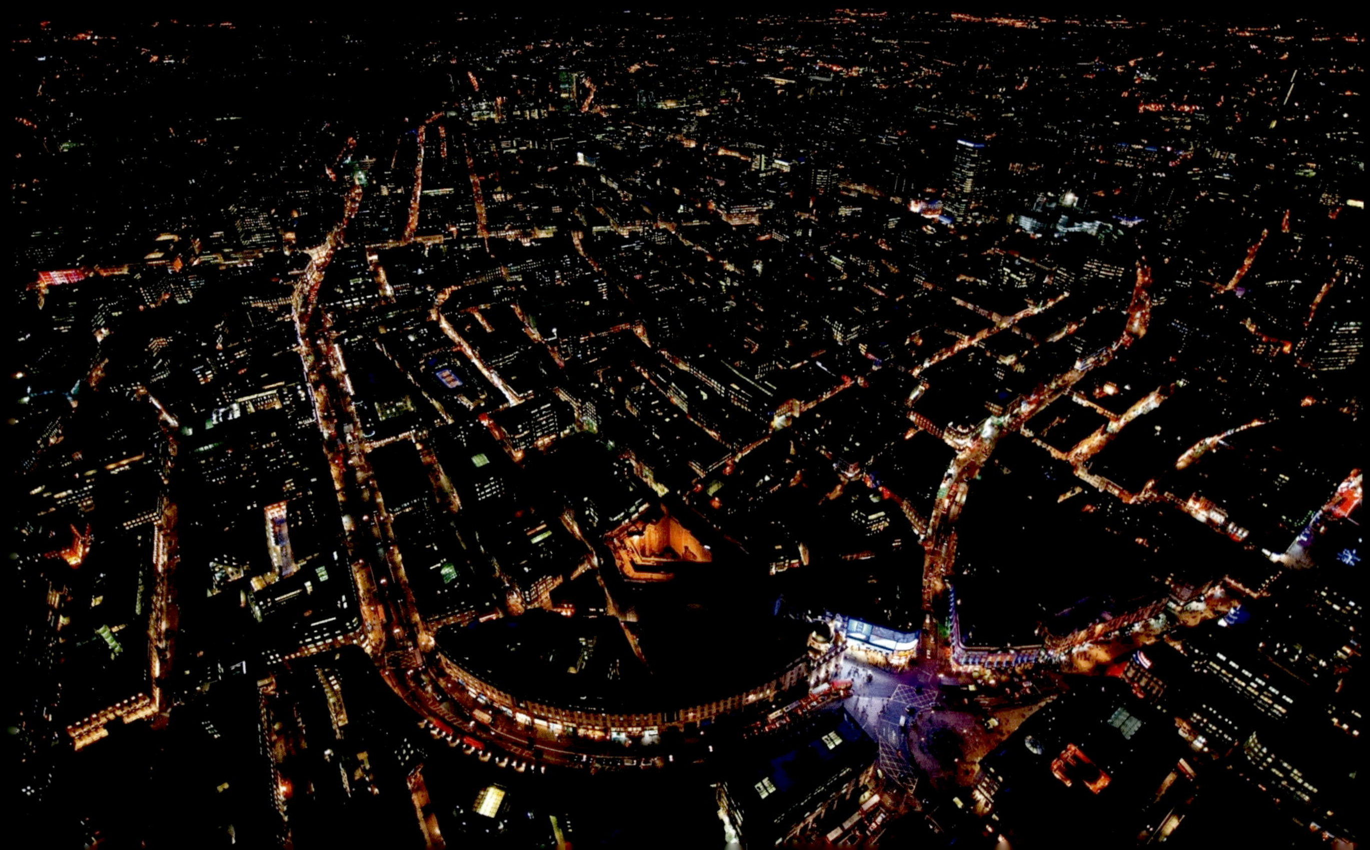

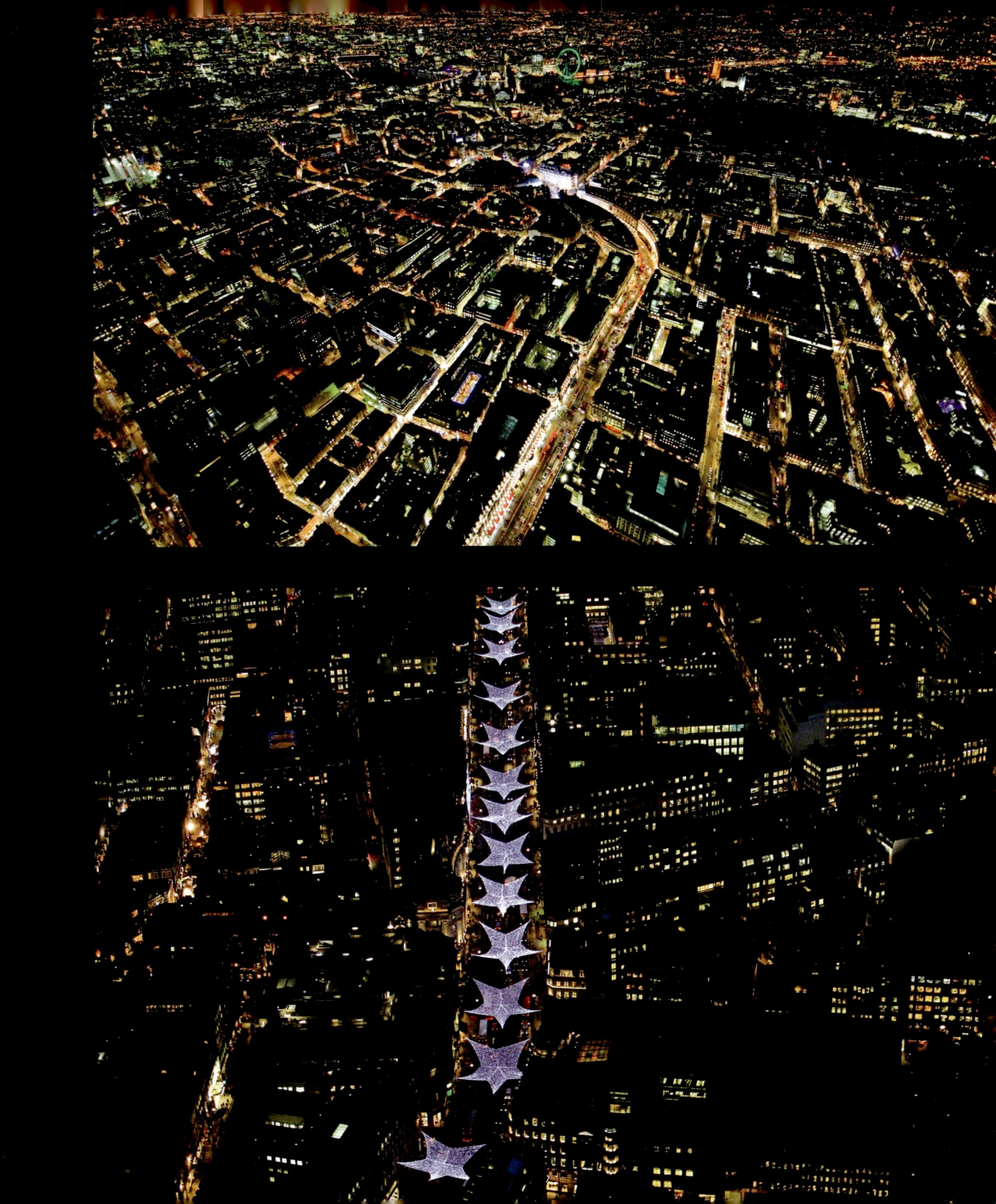

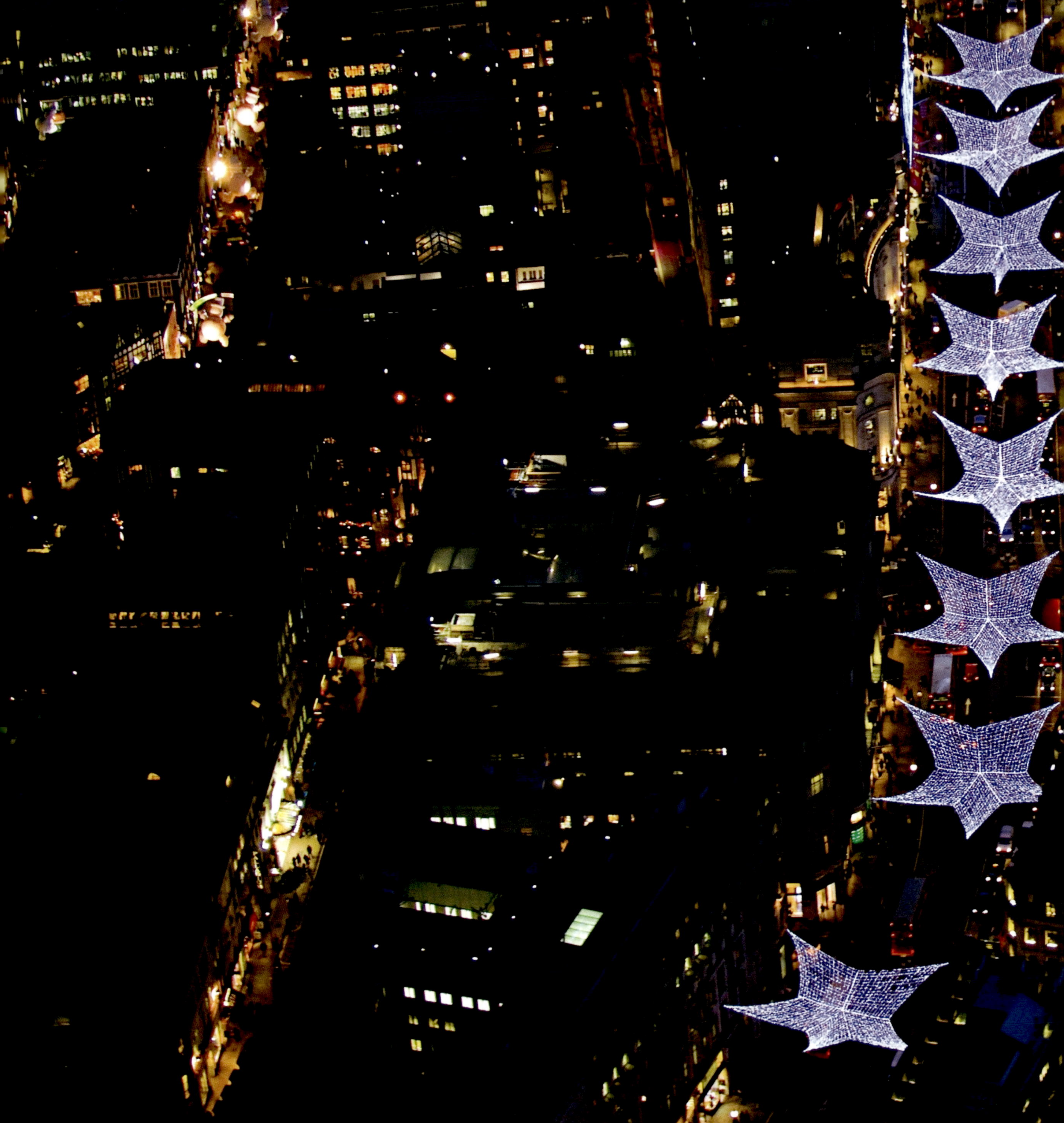

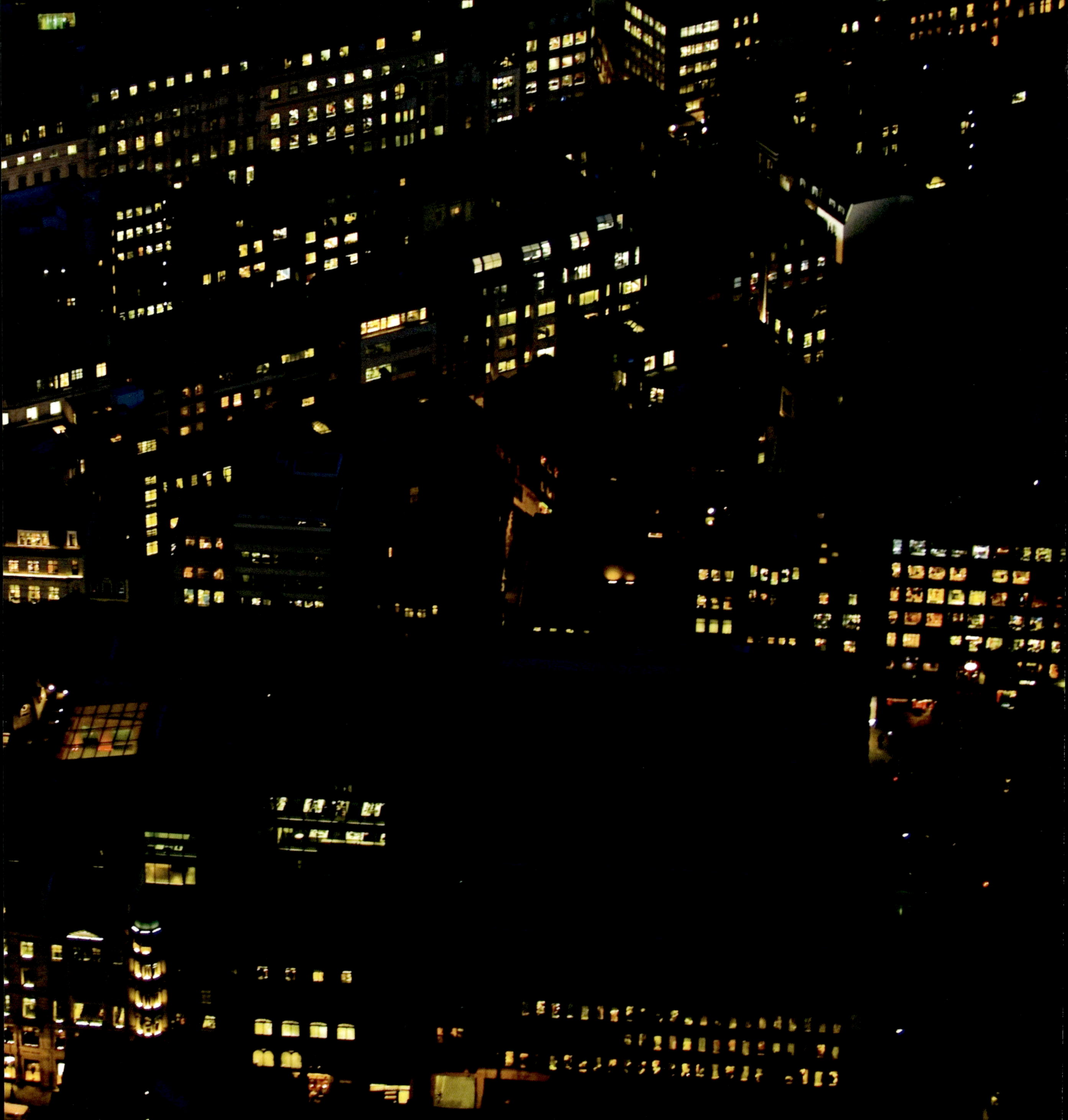

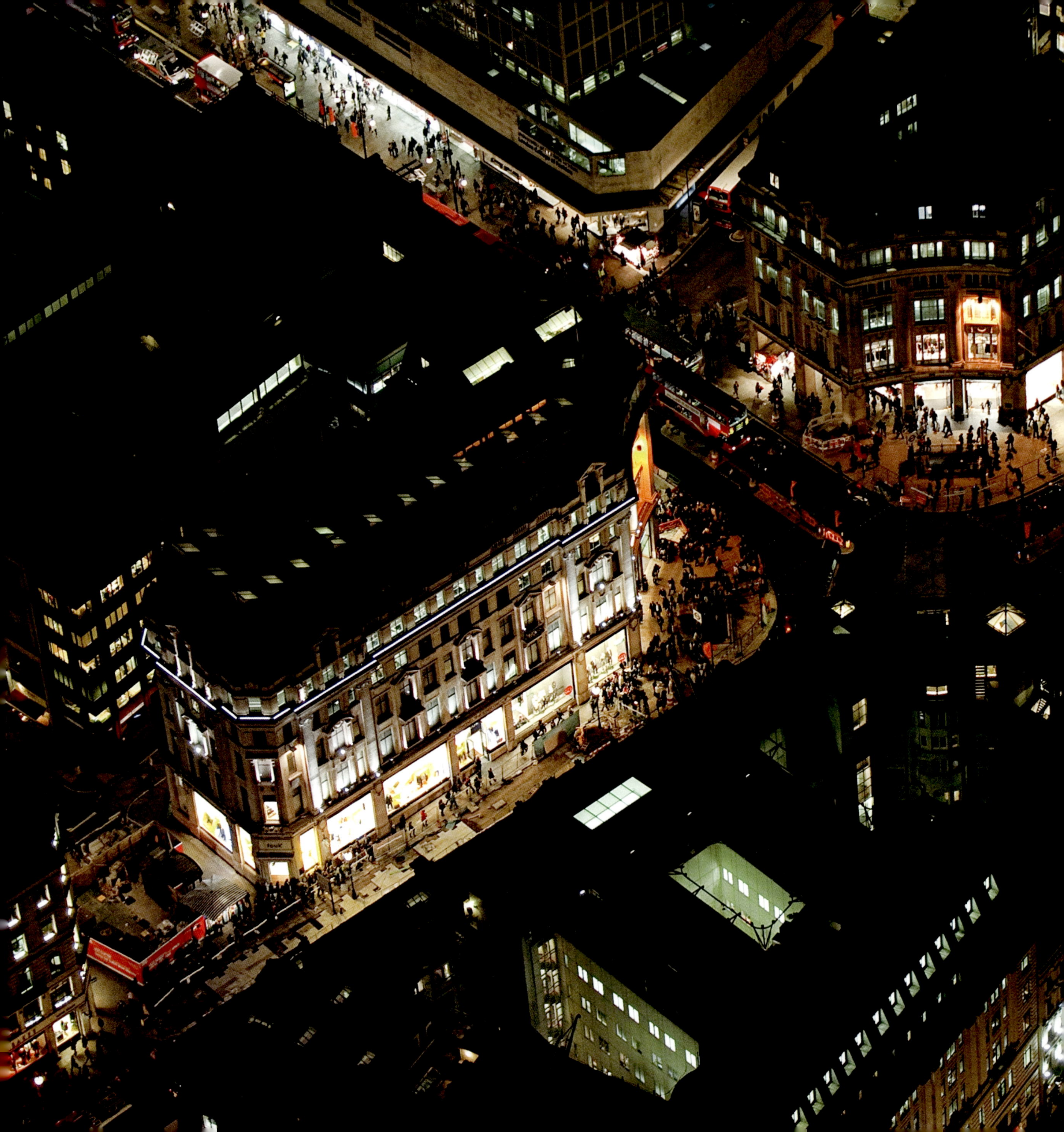

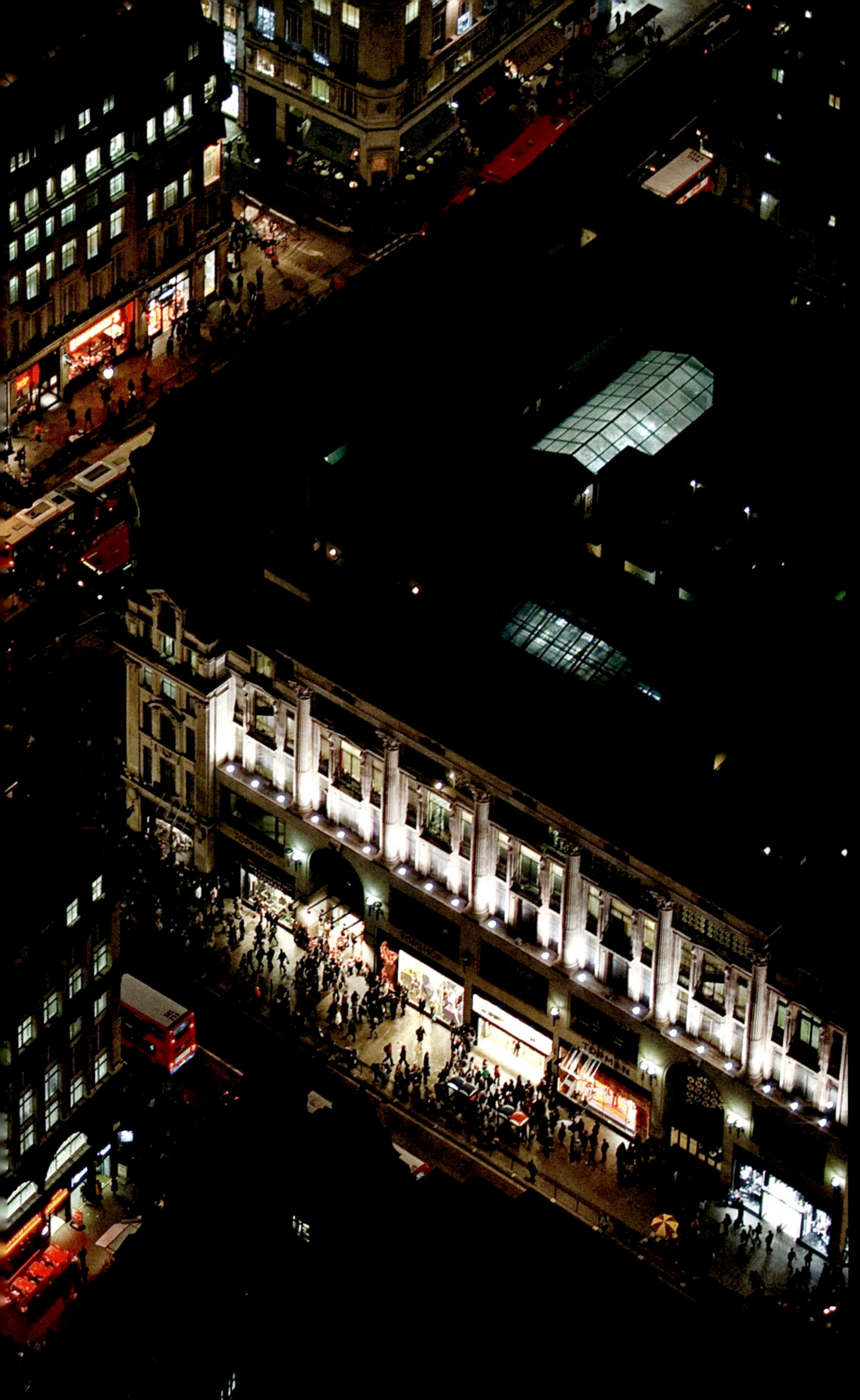

Oxford Circus is shopping Mecca for teenage girls, with both H&M and Topshop's flagship store. Unlike Piccadilly Circus, it still has its curved building profiles, making it an elegant intersection.

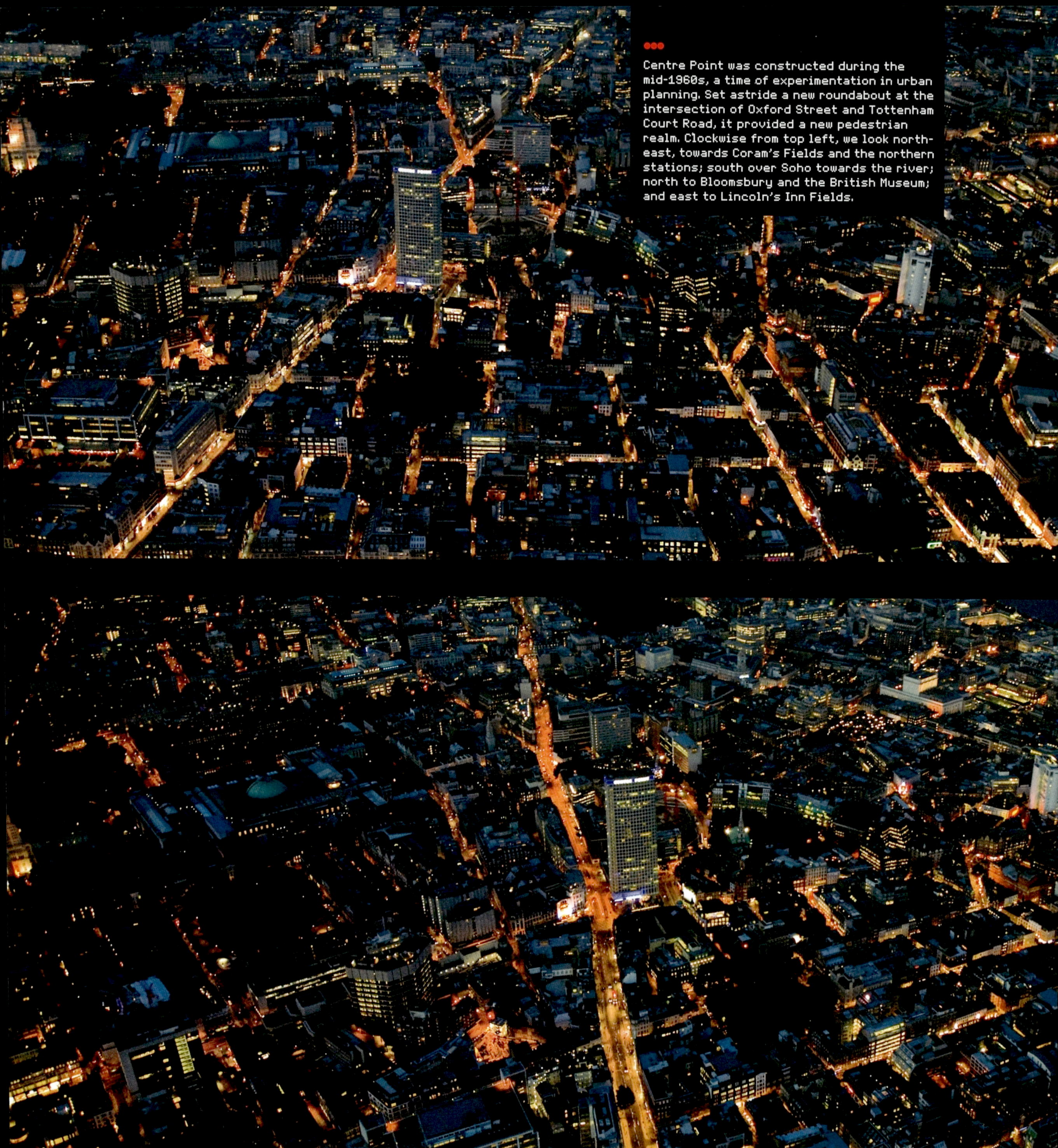

Centre Point was constructed during the mid-1960s, a time of experimentation in urban planning. Set astride a new roundabout at the intersection of Oxford Street and Tottenham Court Road, it provided a new pedestrian realm. Clockwise from top left, we look north-east, towards Coram's Fields and the northern stations; south over Soho towards the river; north to Bloomsbury and the British Museum; and east to Lincoln's Inn Fields.

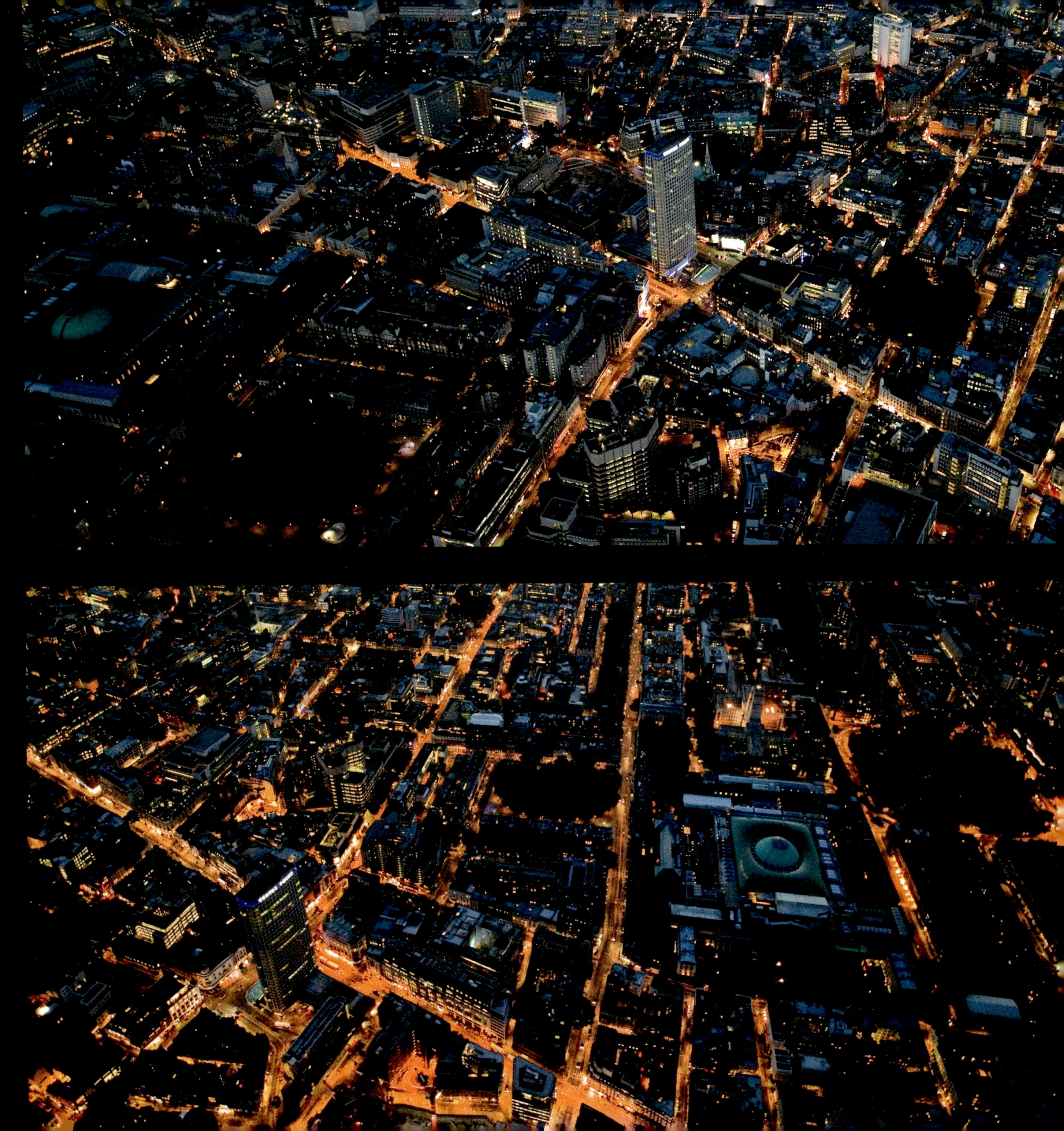

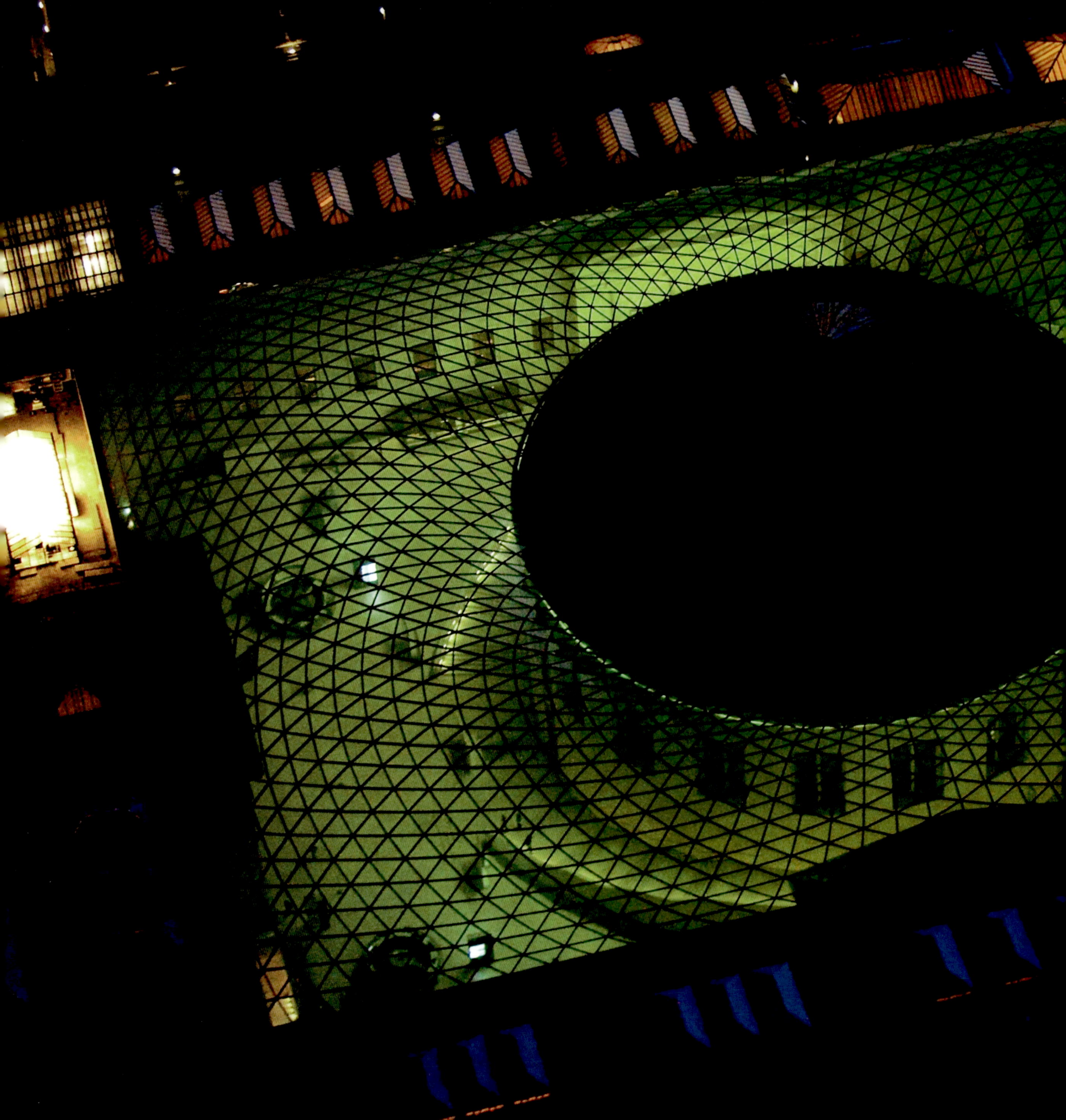

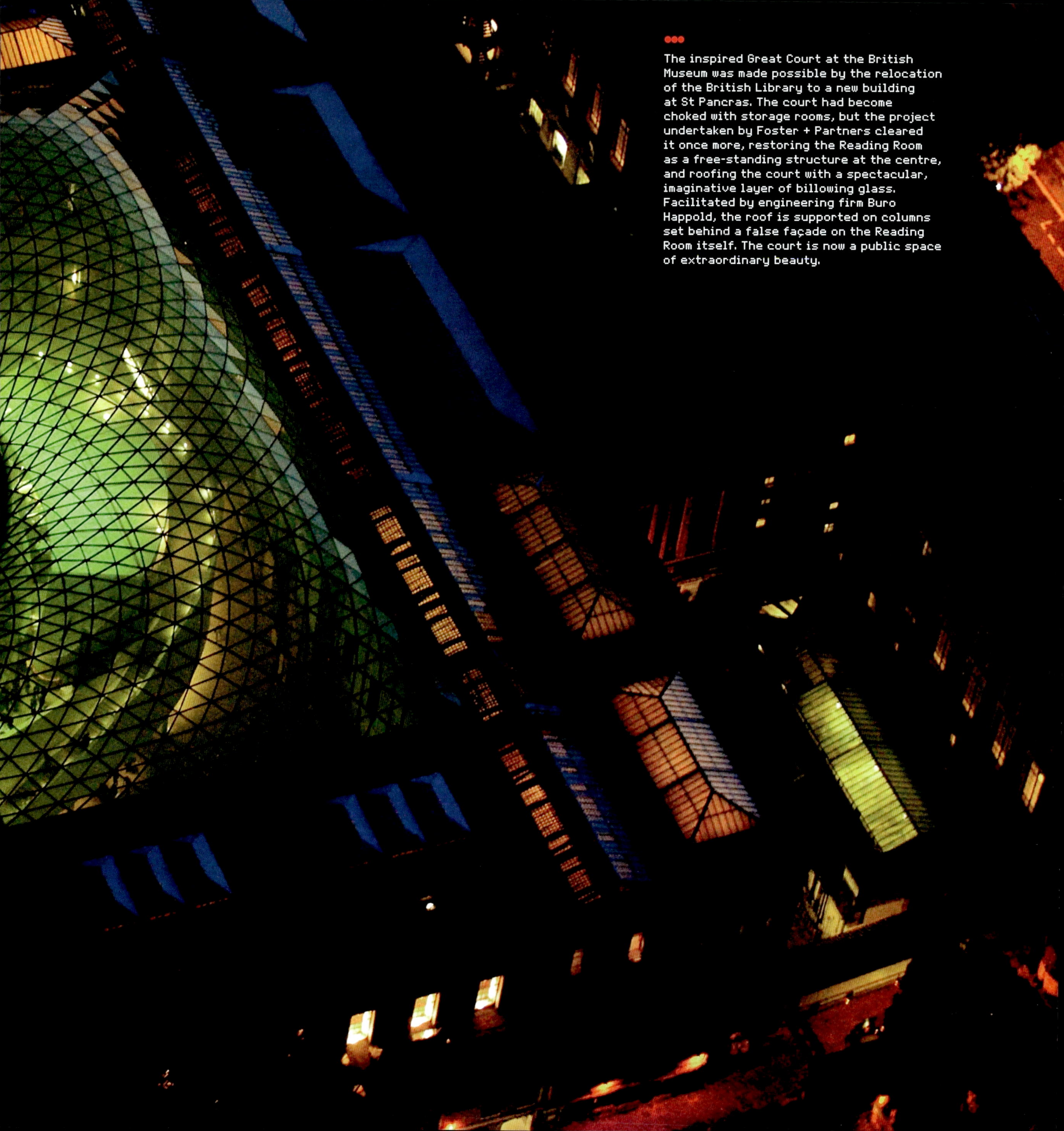

The inspired Great Court at the British Museum was made possible by the relocation of the British Library to a new building at St Pancras. The court had become choked with storage rooms, but the project undertaken by Foster + Partners cleared it once more, restoring the Reading Room as a free-standing structure at the centre, and roofing the court with a spectacular, imaginative layer of billowing glass. Facilitated by engineering firm Buro Happold, the roof is supported on columns set behind a false façade on the Reading Room itself. The court is now a public space of extraordinary beauty.

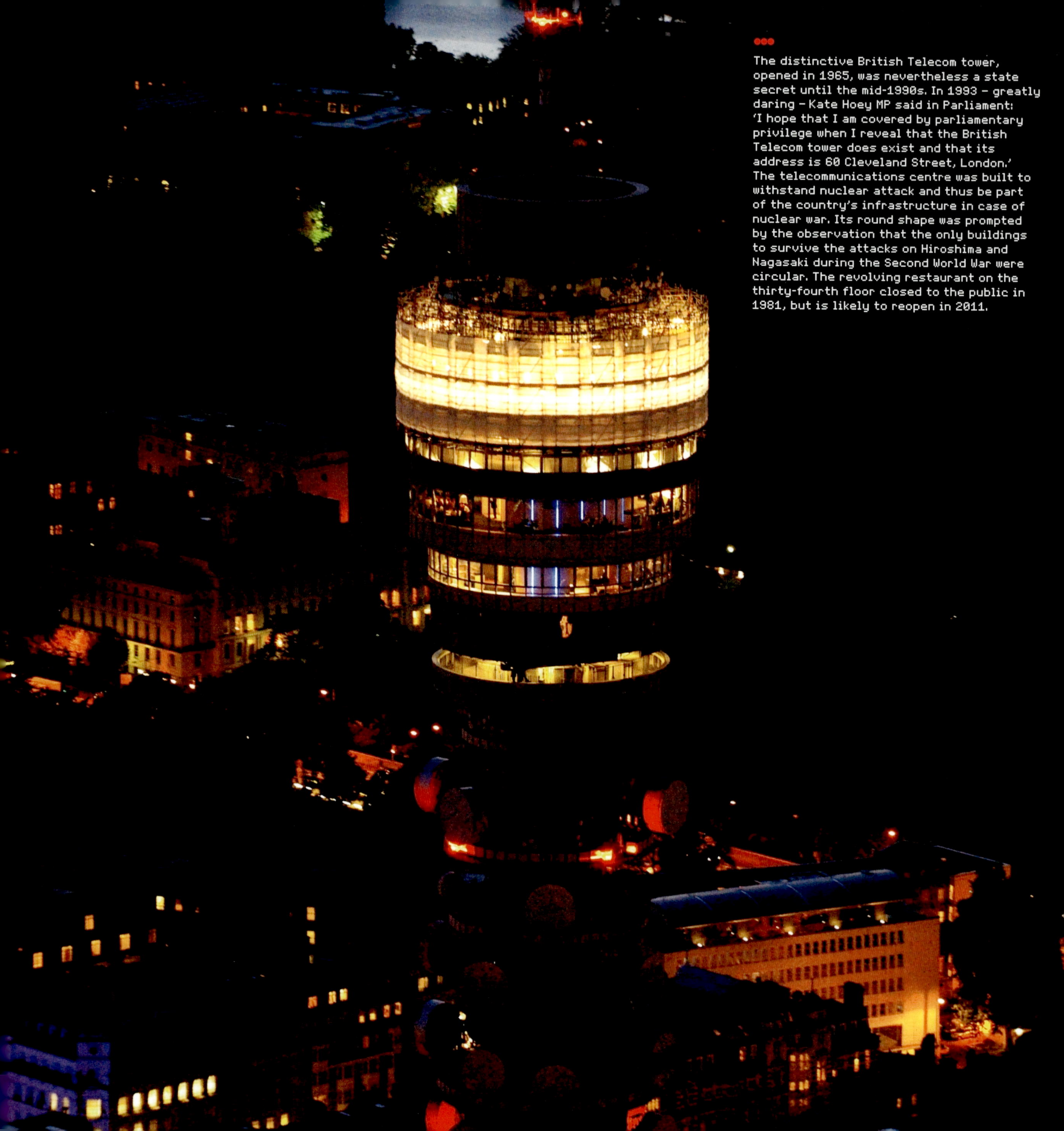

●●●
The distinctive British Telecom tower, opened in 1965, was nevertheless a state secret until the mid-1990s. In 1993 – greatly daring – Kate Hoey MP said in Parliament: 'I hope that I am covered by parliamentary privilege when I reveal that the British Telecom tower does exist and that its address is 60 Cleveland Street, London.' The telecommunications centre was built to withstand nuclear attack and thus be part of the country's infrastructure in case of nuclear war. Its round shape was prompted by the observation that the only buildings to survive the attacks on Hiroshima and Nagasaki during the Second World War were circular. The revolving restaurant on the thirty-fourth floor closed to the public in 1981, but is likely to reopen in 2011.

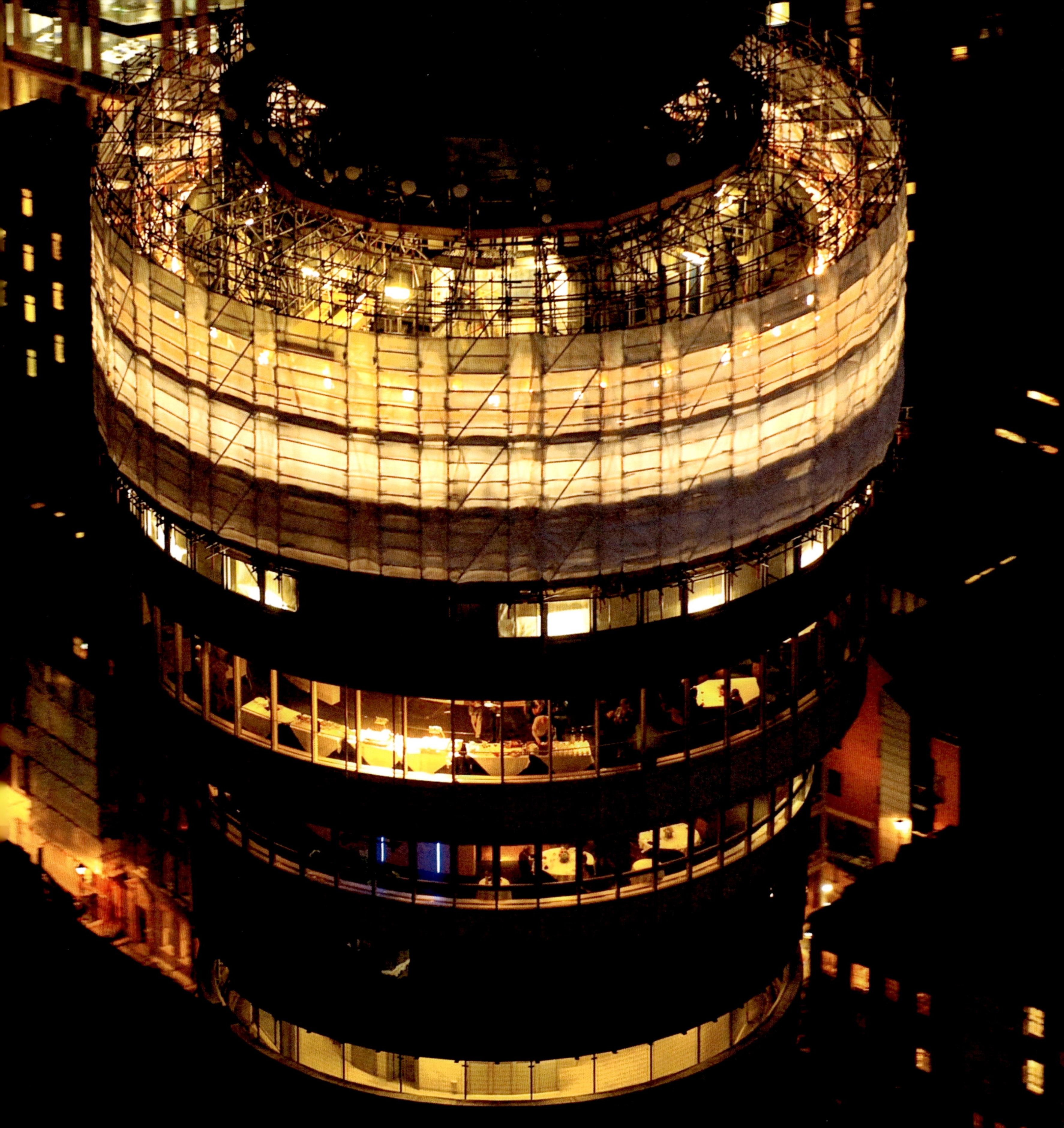

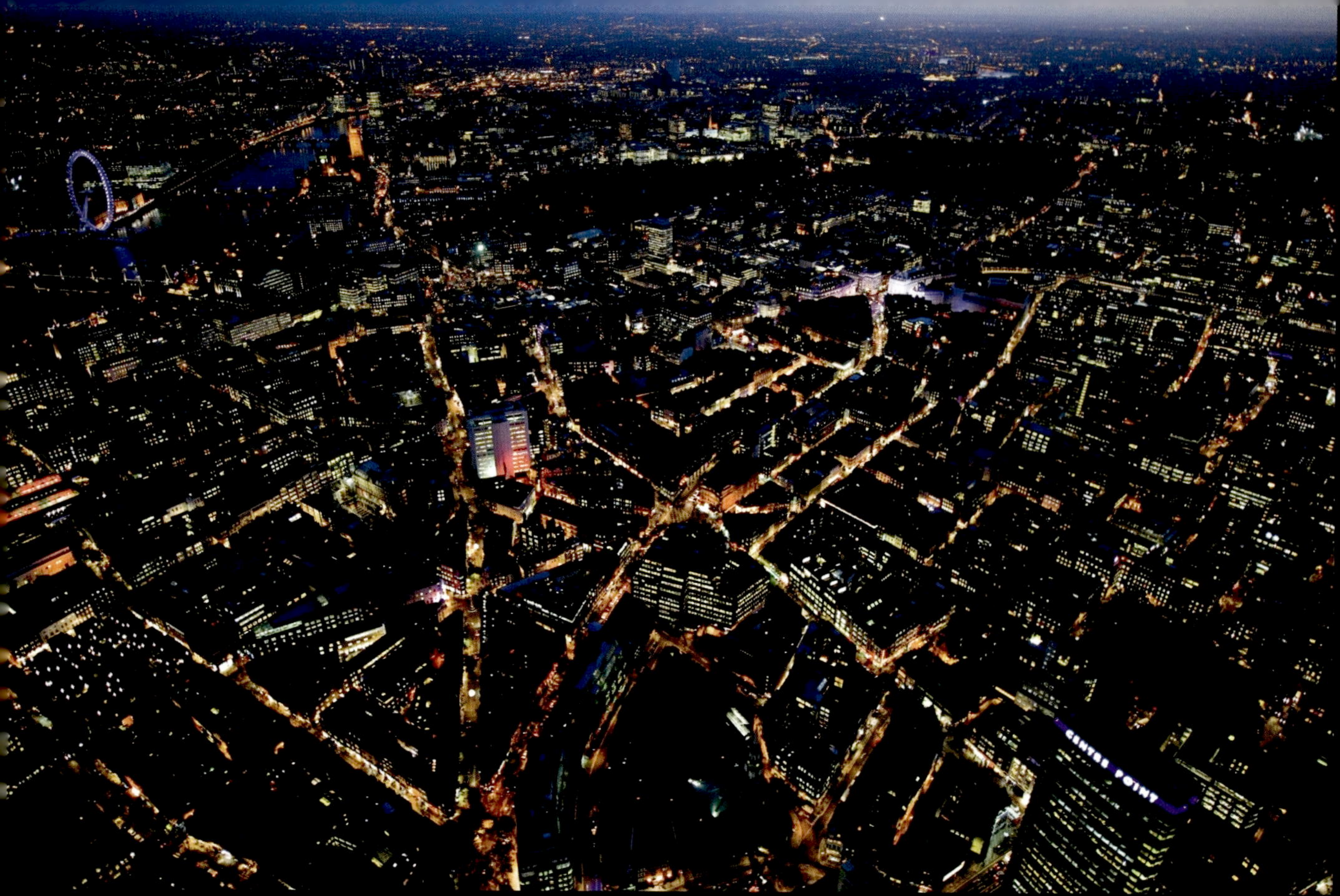

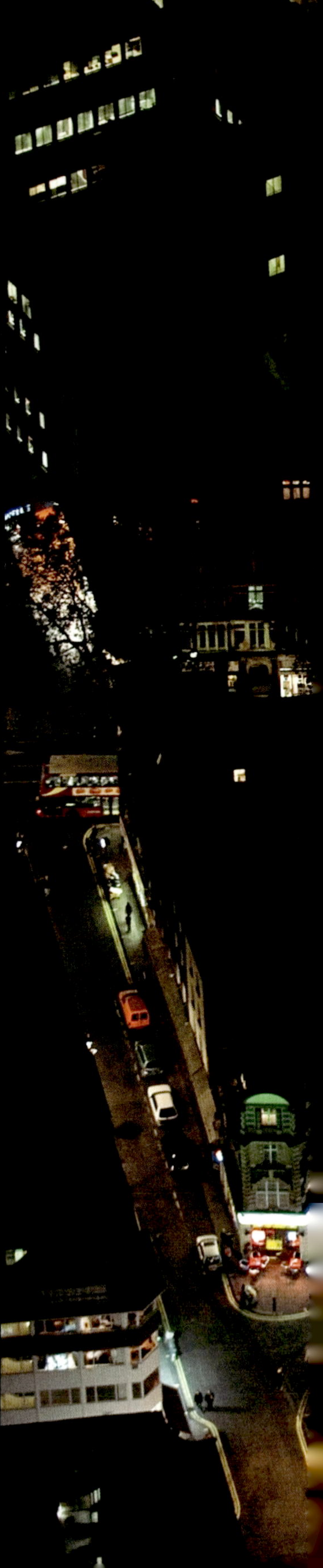

●●●
Soho and Theatreland are tricky places to navigate, and from above it is easy to see why. In the centre of the photograph above are the complicated junctions of Seven Dials and Cambridge Circus (also opposite). The street layouts here are much older than those of the more westerly parts of London. Once the old parish of St Giles, this area is now presided over by Centre Point, the top of which is just visible above.

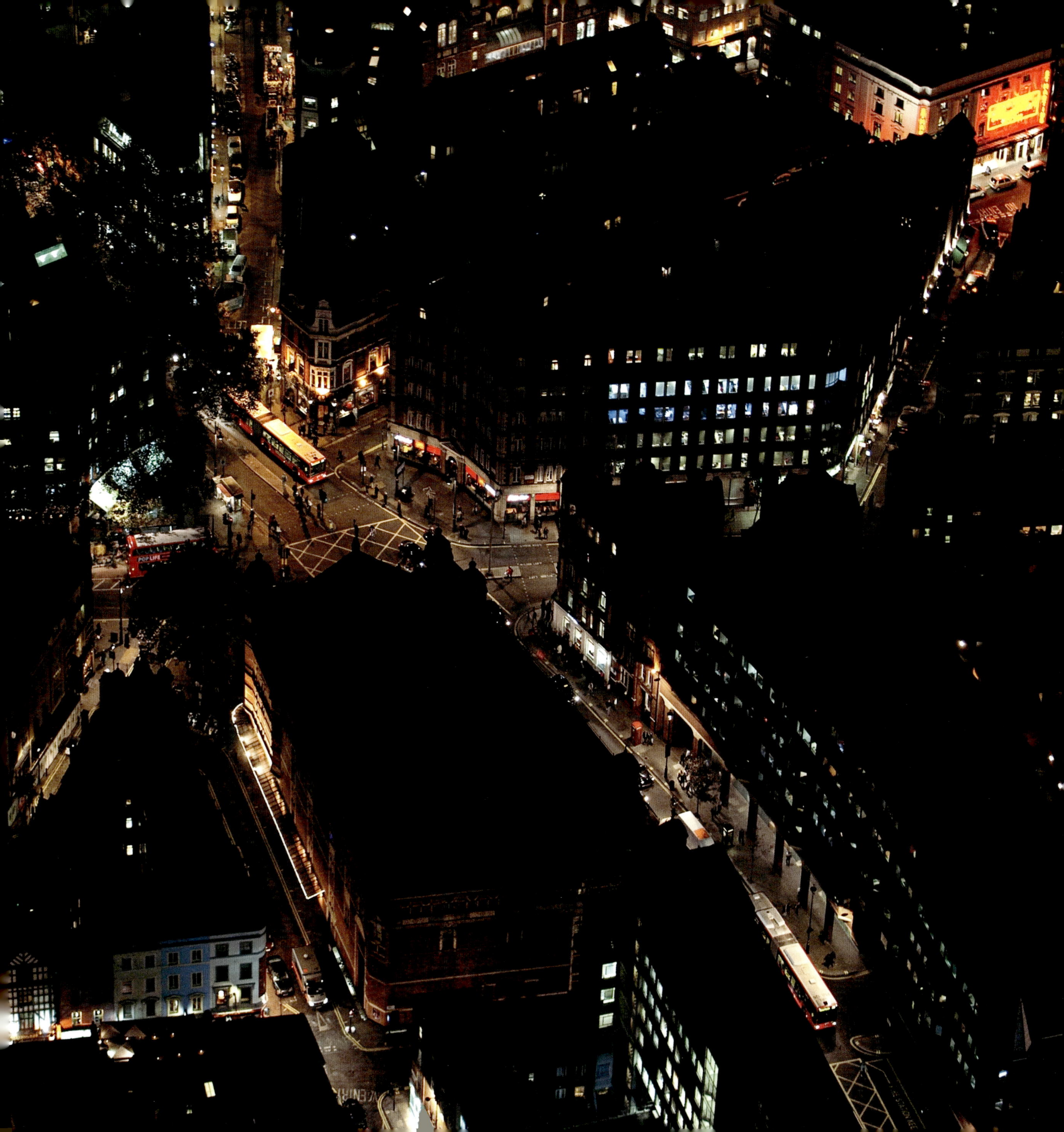

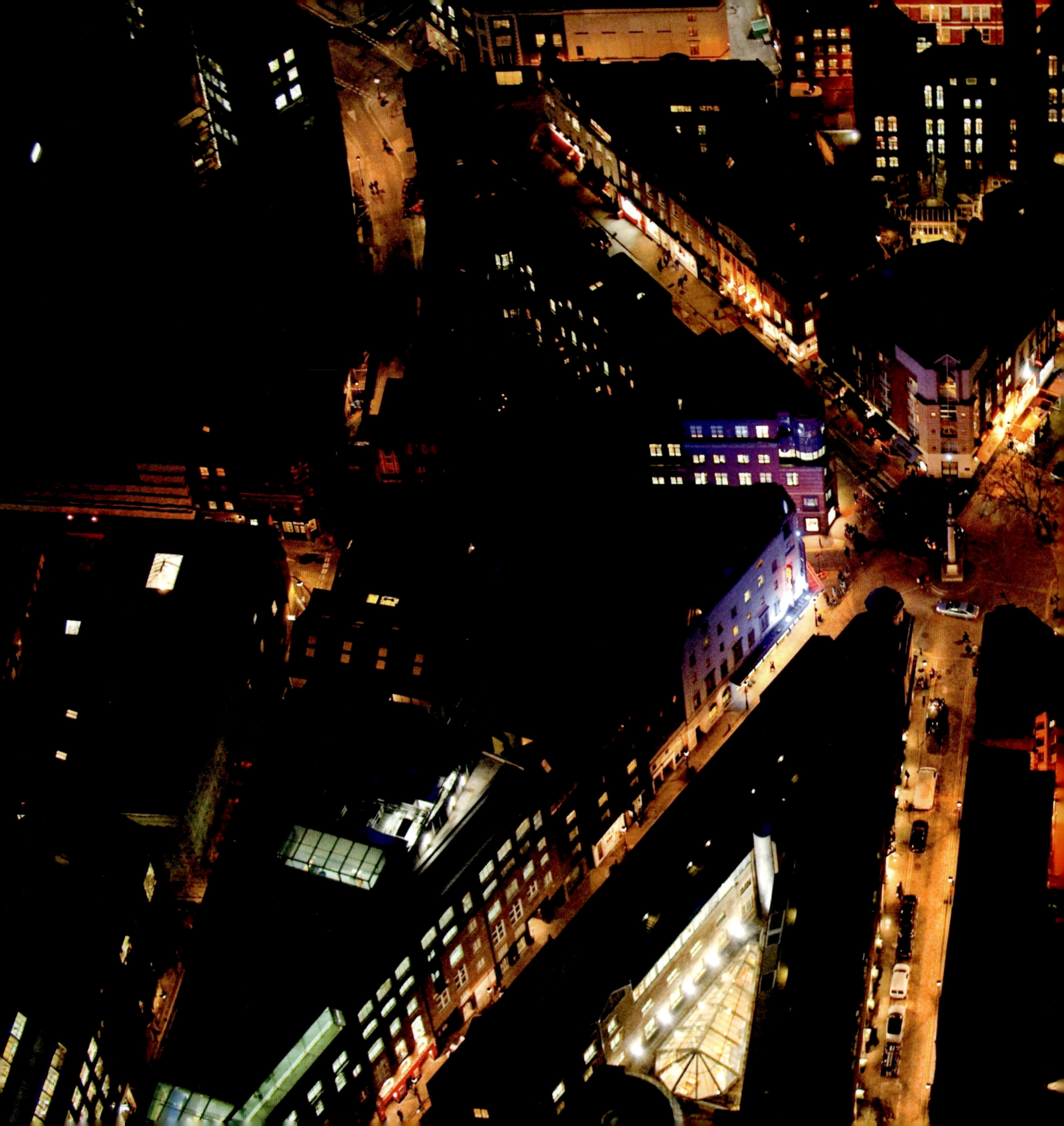

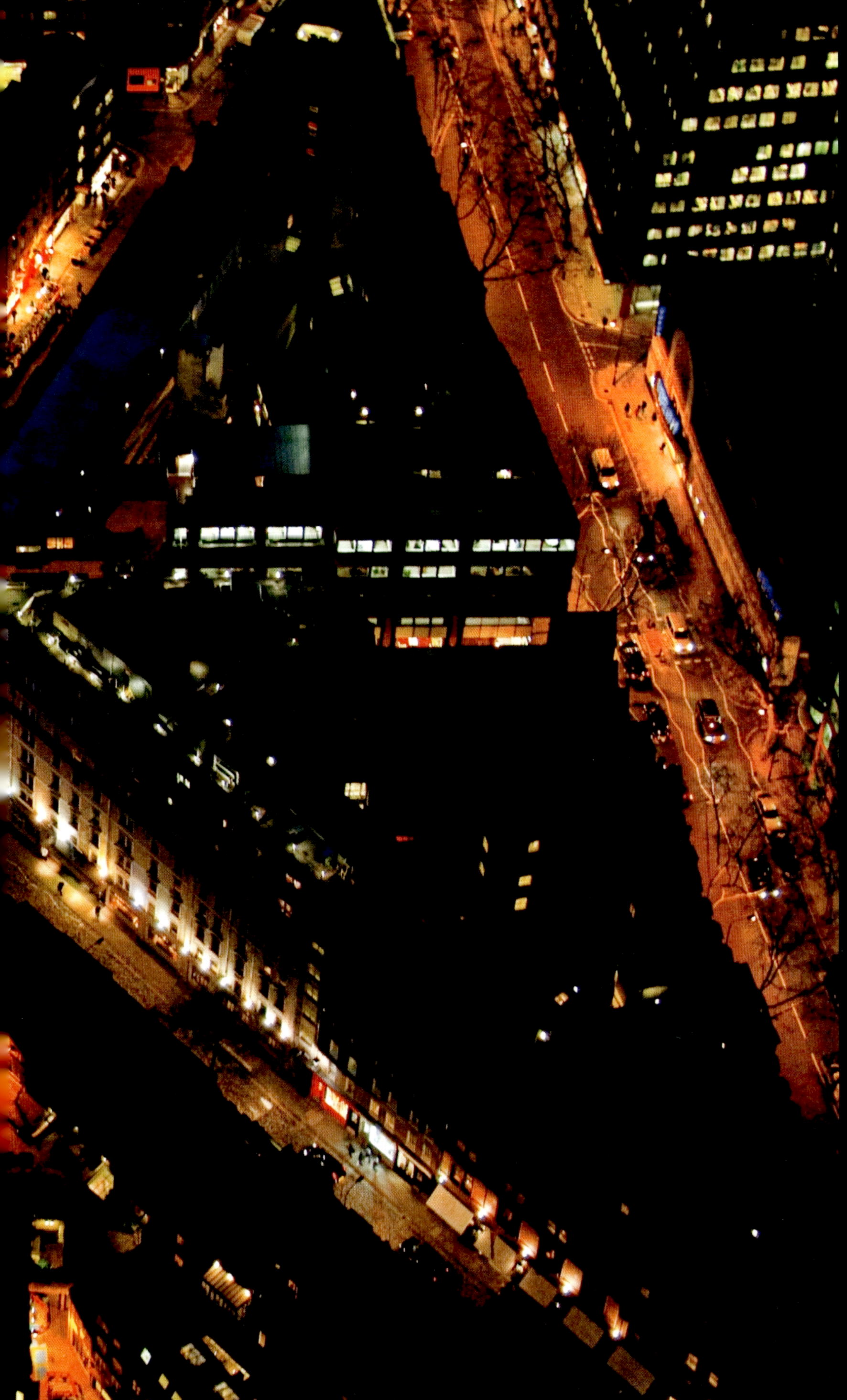

Seven Dials is at the centre of a thriving and quirky area, tucked behind the busy and touristy Charing Cross Road. Since the seventeenth century it has been home to practitioners of alternative medicine, occultists and astrologers, attracted by its central sundial and the meeting-point of the seven streets. It was at one time a notorious slum, with pubs on each corner, their cellars connecting below ground to allow patrons to escape if necessary. The district is now known for theatres and their suppliers, record shops, crafts, wholefoods and one-off fashion boutiques.

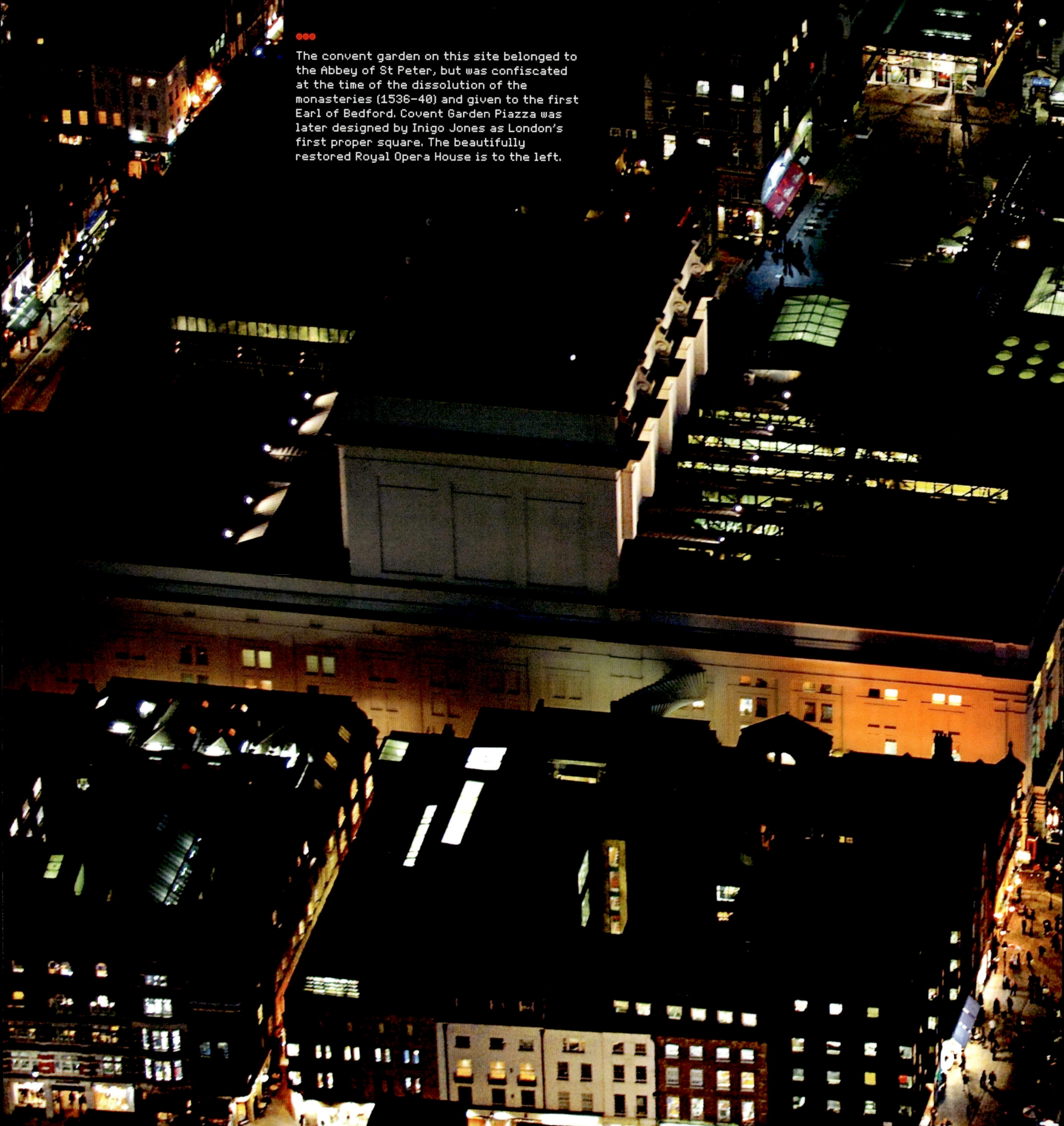

The convent garden on this site belonged to the Abbey of St Peter, but was confiscated at the time of the dissolution of the monasteries (1536-40) and given to the first Earl of Bedford. Covent Garden Piazza was later designed by Inigo Jones as London's first proper square. The beautifully restored Royal Opera House is to the left.

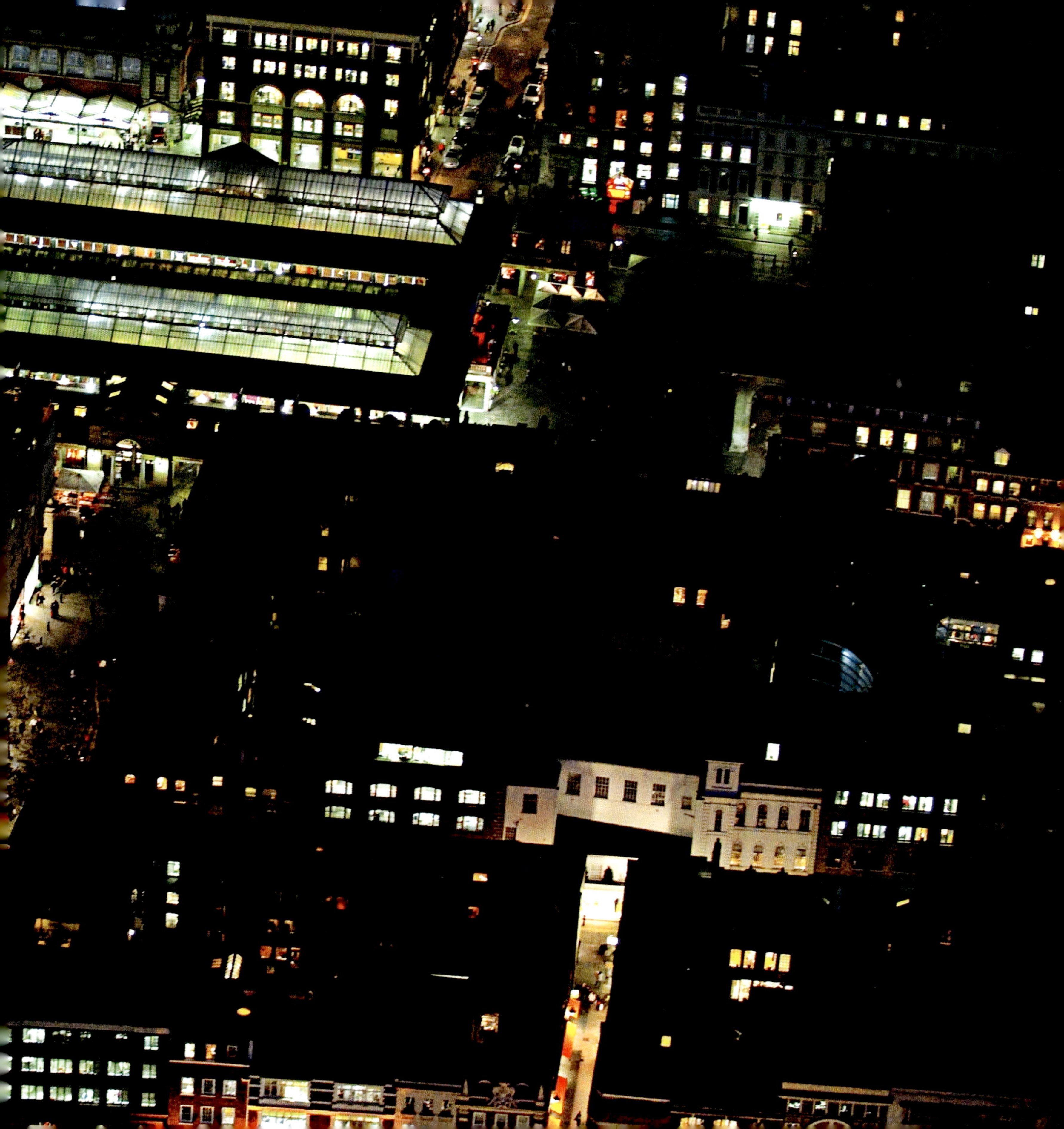

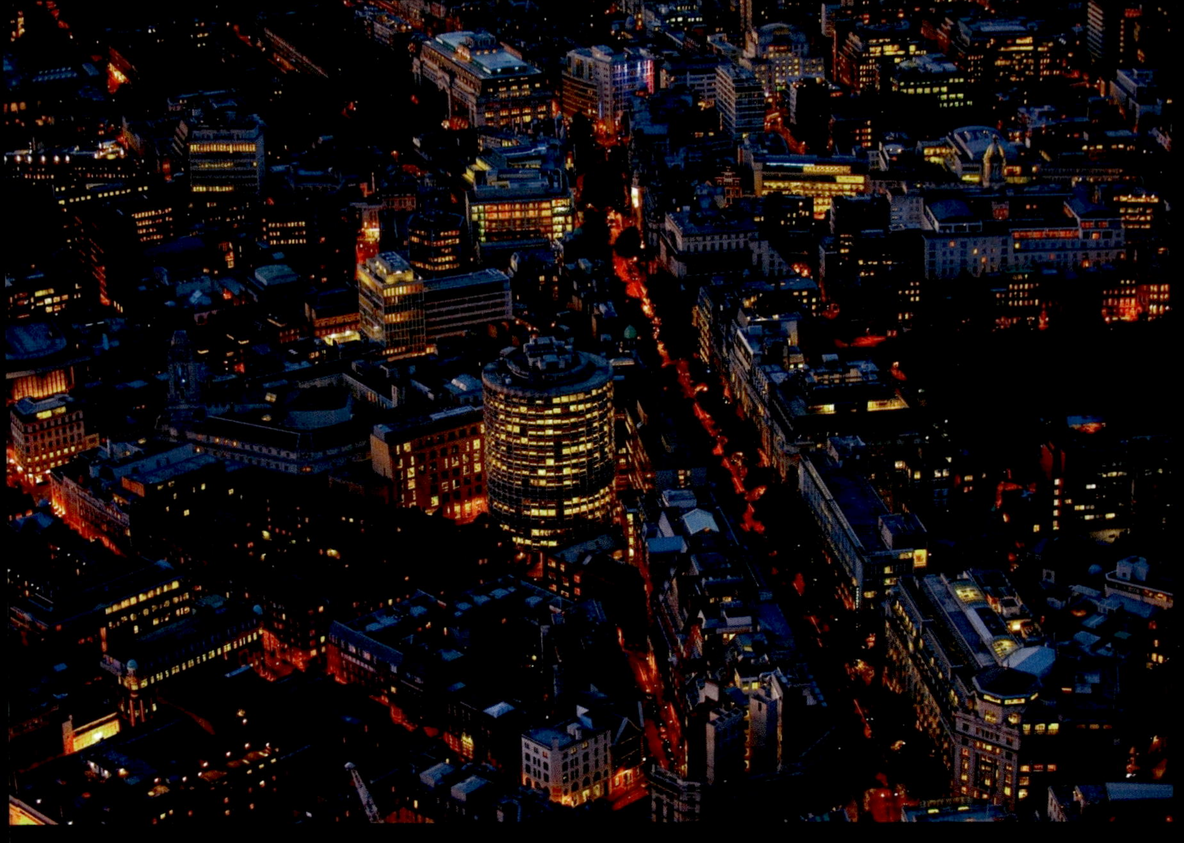

← The circular, futuristically named Space House was designed by Richard Seifert (architect of Centre Point). It is now known as One Kemble Street, and houses – ironically, some might say – the Commission for Architecture and the Built Environment, among others. The broad avenue of Kingsway was the last of the series of thoroughfares (Regent Street was the first) that sought to gentrify notorious slum areas in the nineteenth and early twentieth centuries.

↙ The Victoria Embankment was built partly to ease congestion on the Strand, and partly to help speed the river, decreasing the amount of deposited mud and reducing the risk of cholera. A great feat of engineering, it carries a road, a sewer and an underground railway. The building on the left with the brightest lights is the Art Deco Adelphi; to its right are Shell Mex House and the darkened façade of the mid-refurbishment Savoy Hotel. On the other side of Waterloo Bridge is the long, floodlit frontage of Somerset House (also opposite).

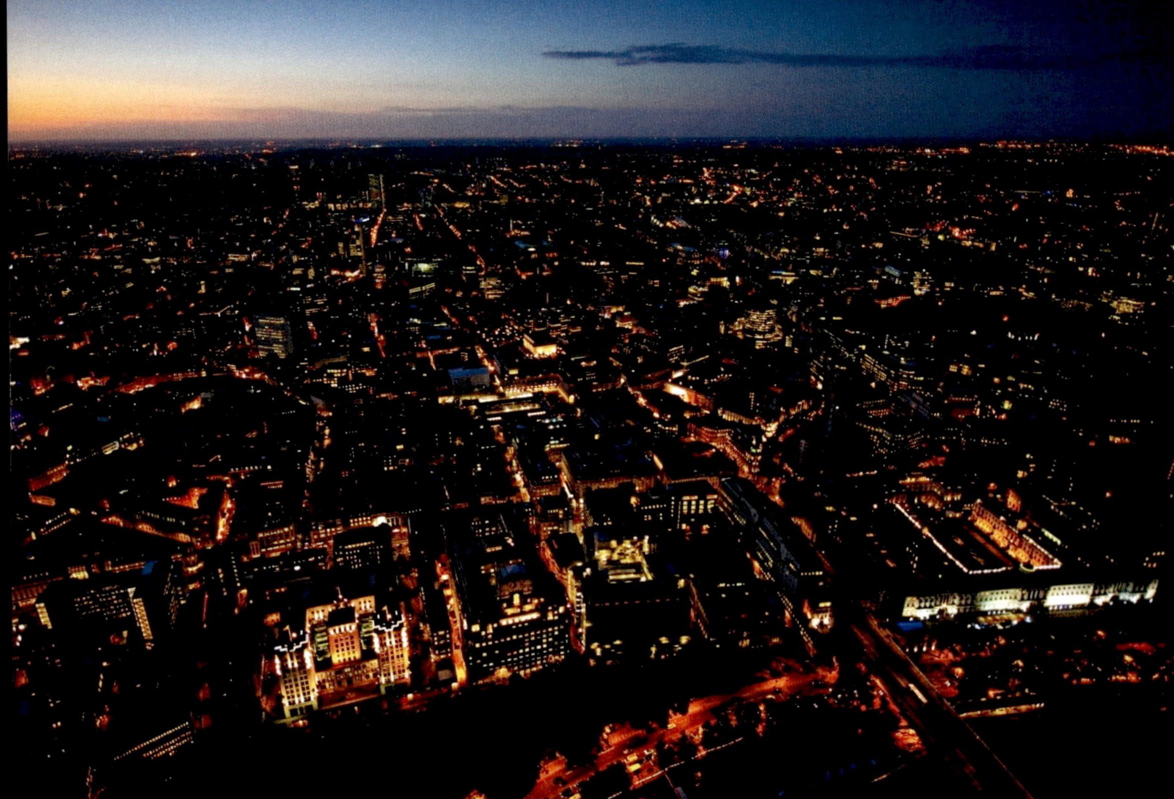

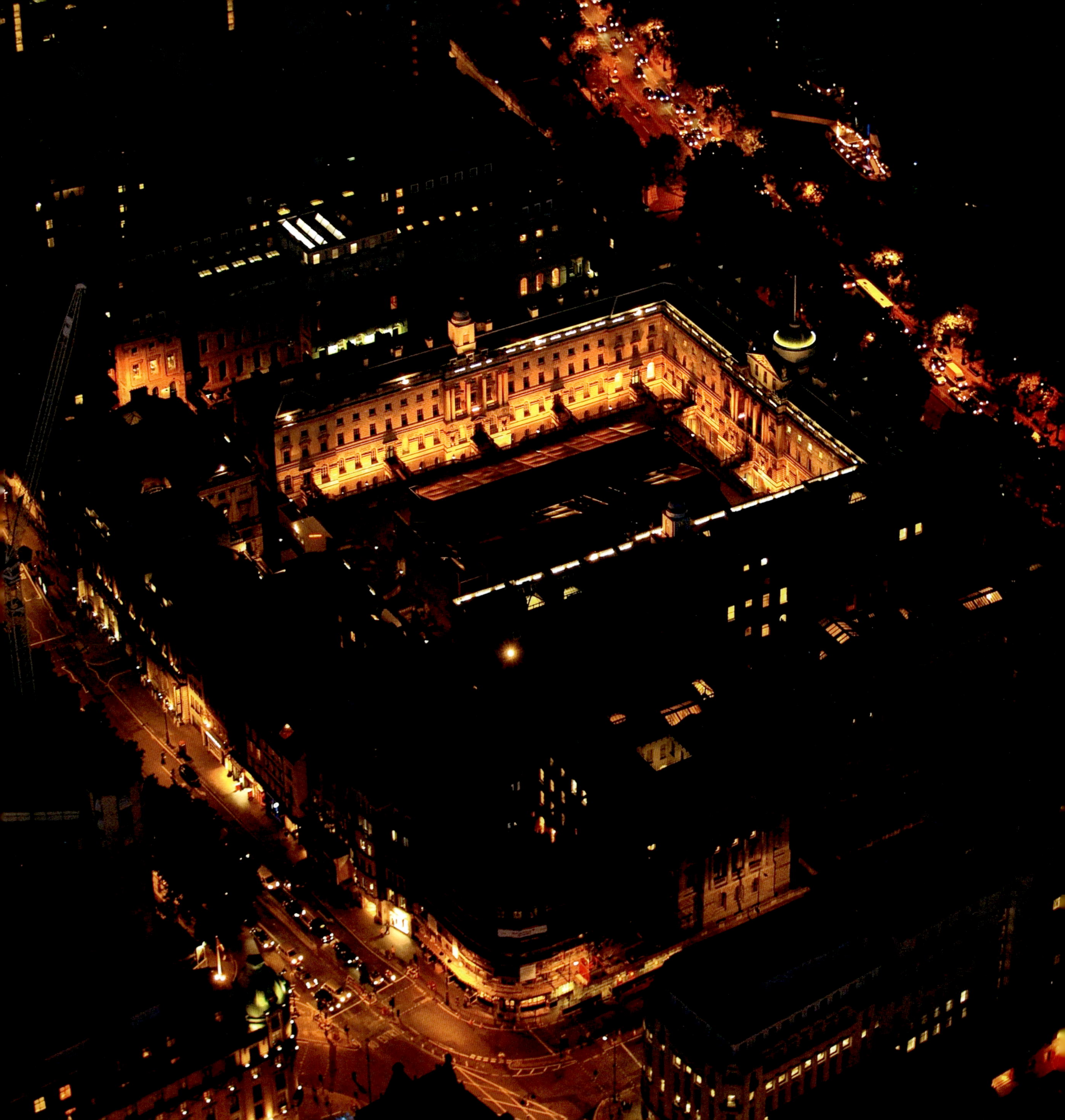

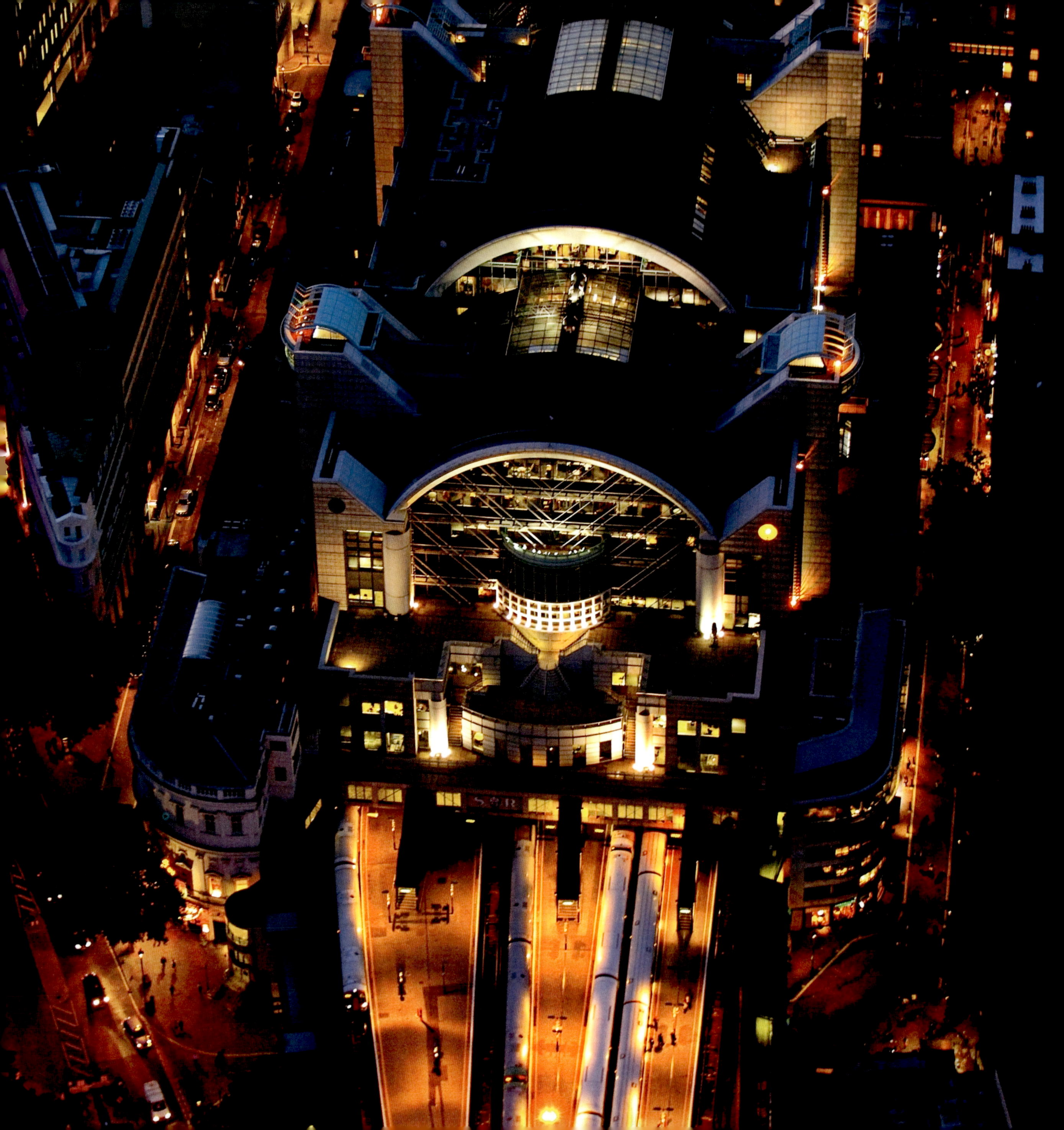

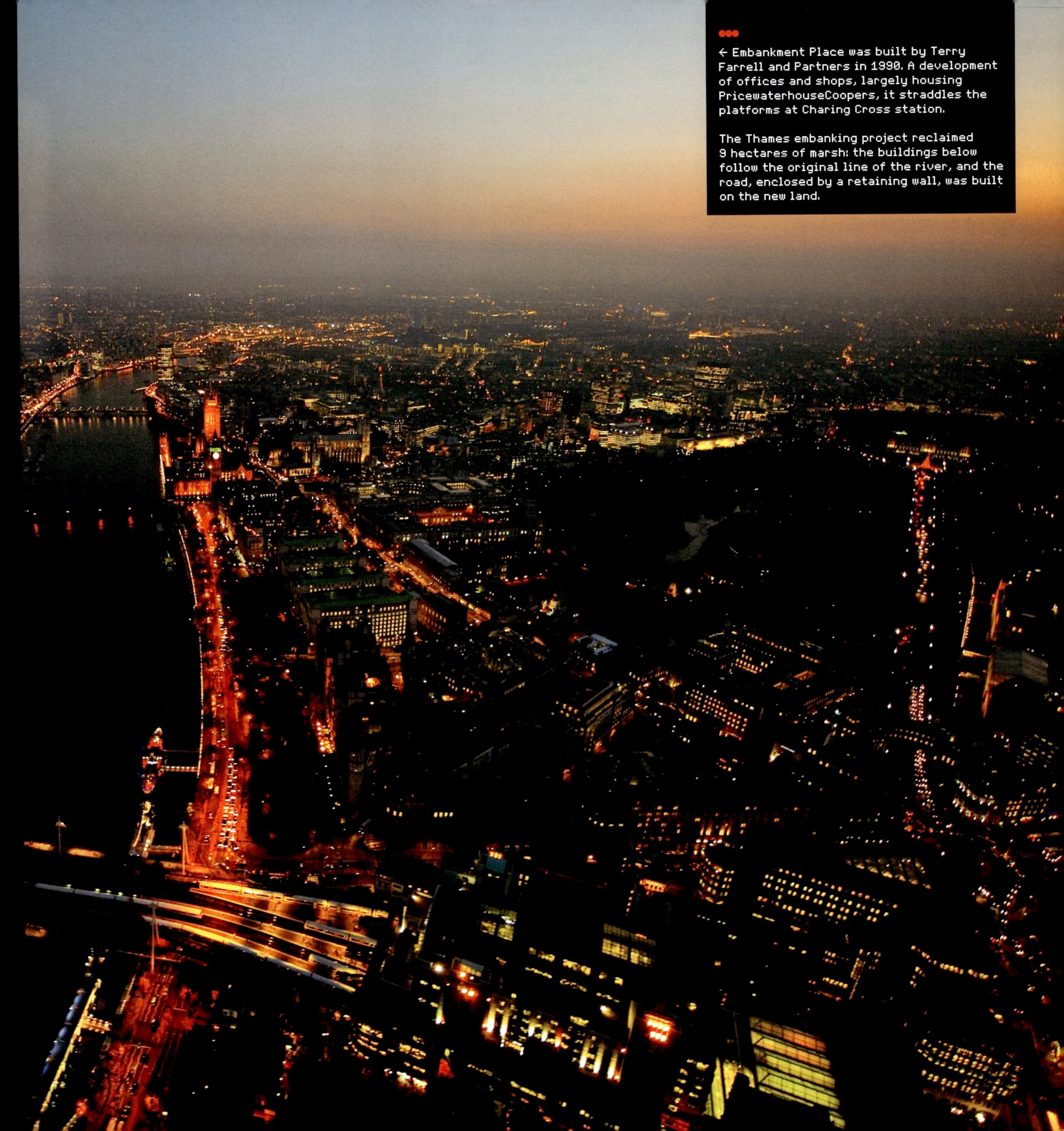

← Embankment Place was built by Terry Farrell and Partners in 1990. A development of offices and shops, largely housing PricewaterhouseCoopers, it straddles the platforms at Charing Cross station.

The Thames embanking project reclaimed 9 hectares of marsh: the buildings below follow the original line of the river, and the road, enclosed by a retaining wall, was built on the new land.

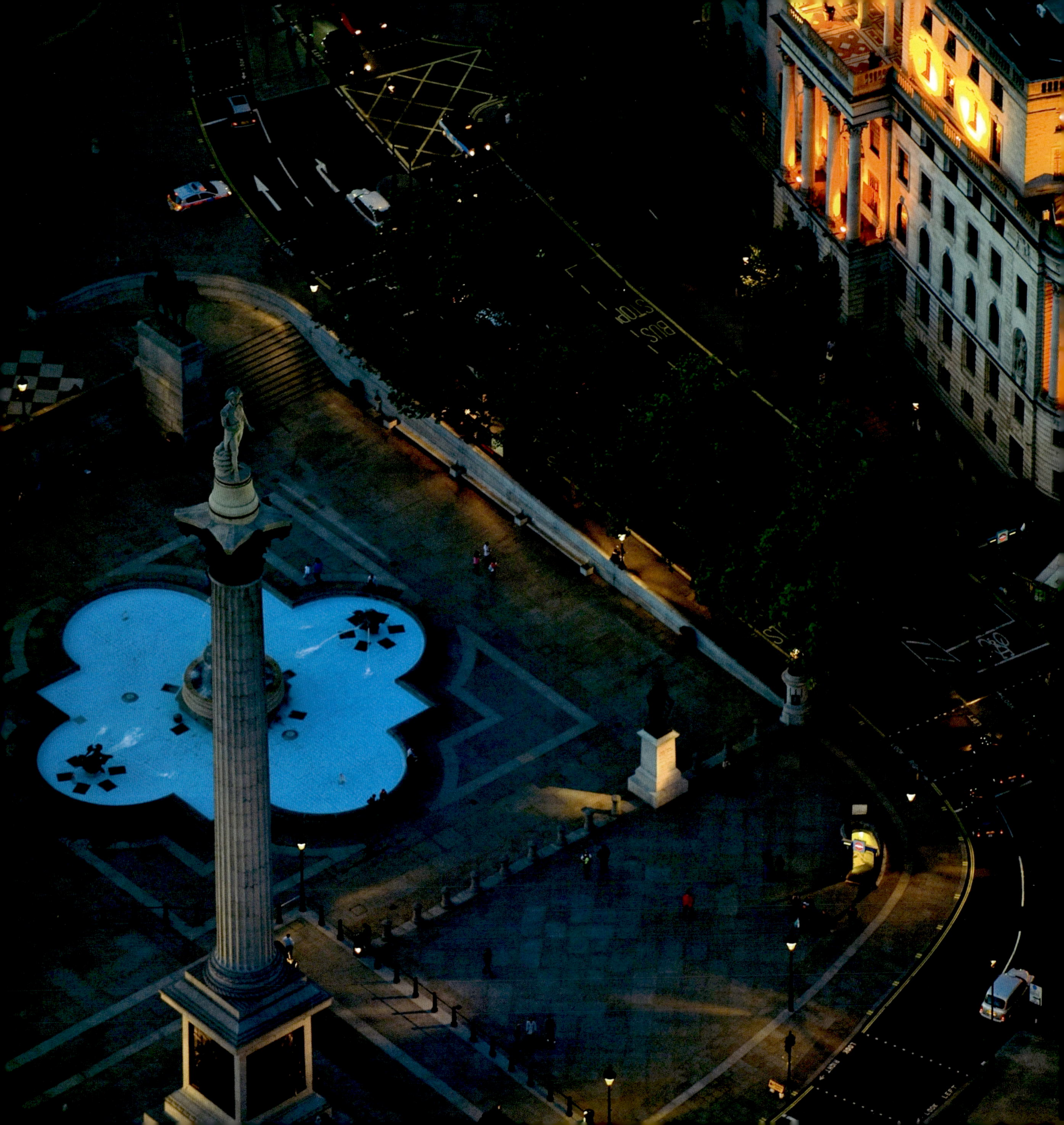

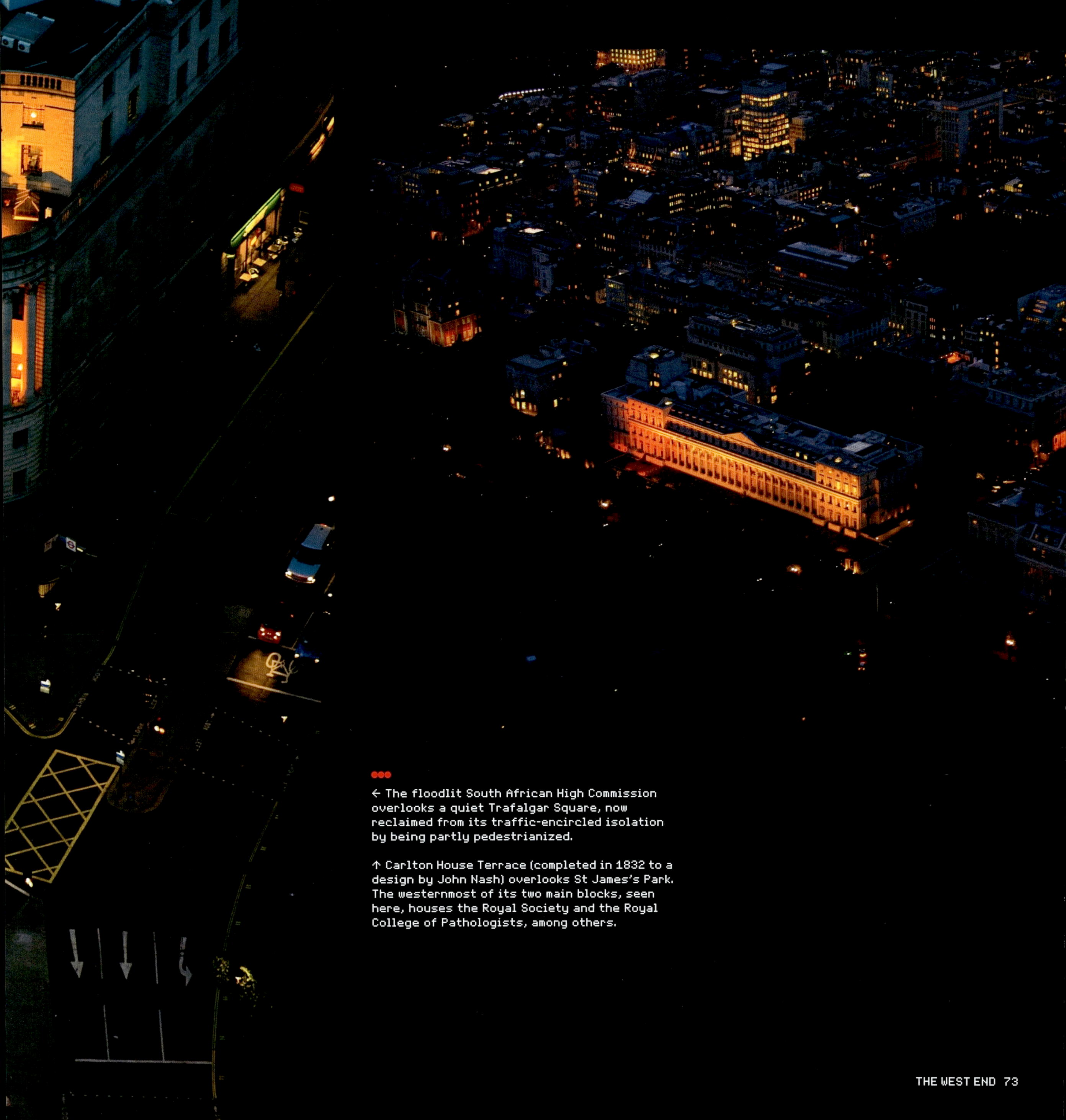

← The floodlit South African High Commission overlooks a quiet Trafalgar Square, now reclaimed from its traffic-encircled isolation by being partly pedestrianized.

↑ Carlton House Terrace (completed in 1832 to a design by John Nash) overlooks St James's Park. The westernmost of its two main blocks, seen here, houses the Royal Society and the Royal College of Pathologists, among others.

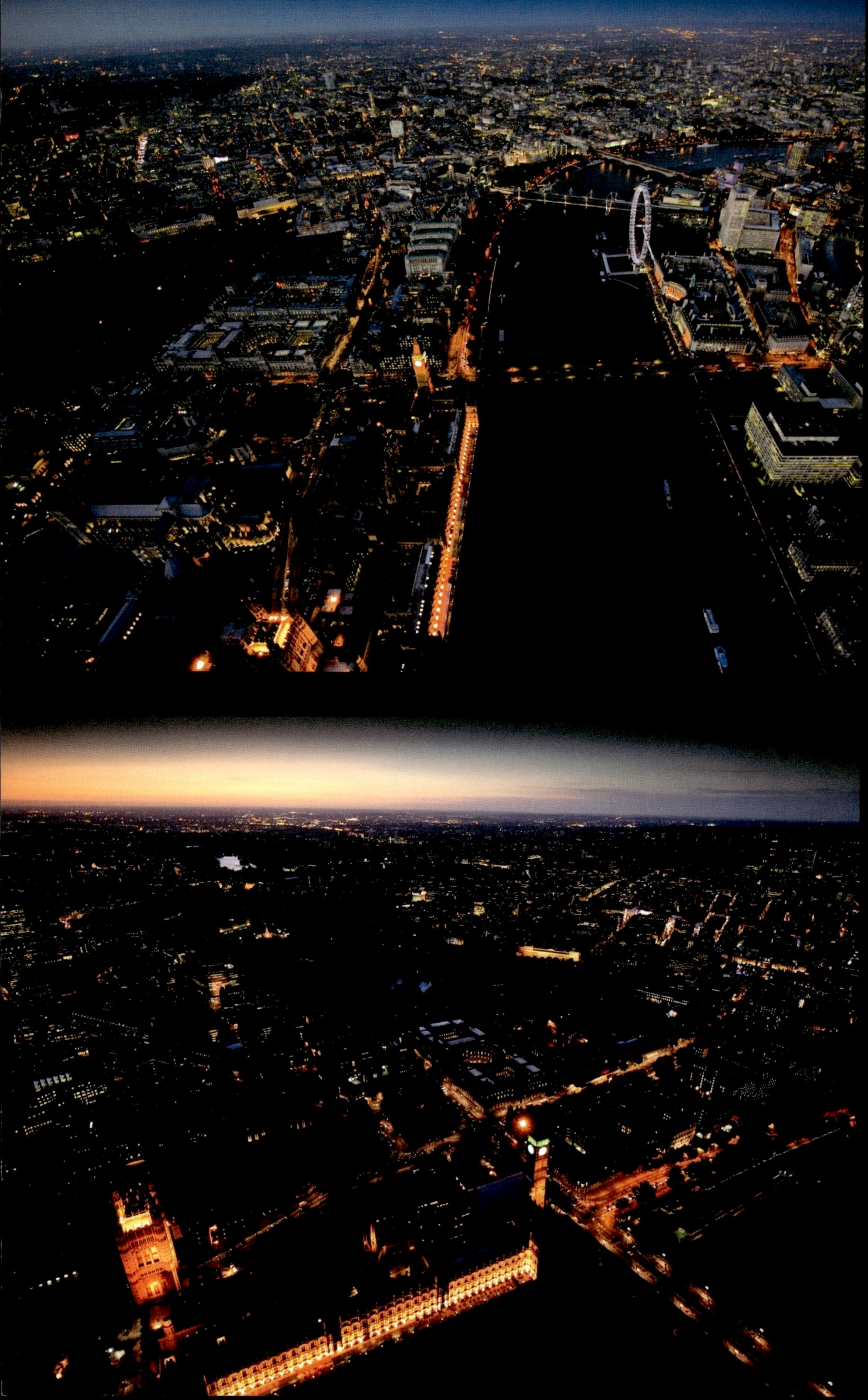

← ↖ Most Londoners think of the Thames as being an east-west dividing line. The sunset here, though (below left), shows that the river runs north-south, as it begins the 'M'-shaped bends that enclose the South Bank area. The view is of Whitehall, the Palace of Westminster and Westminster Abbey – the headquarters of both church and state.

→ Big Ben, which stands at the western end of Westminster Bridge, is possibly the world's most recognizable clock tower. It leans about 22 centimetres to the north-west, largely because of tunnelling work undertaken in the building of the Jubilee line extension.

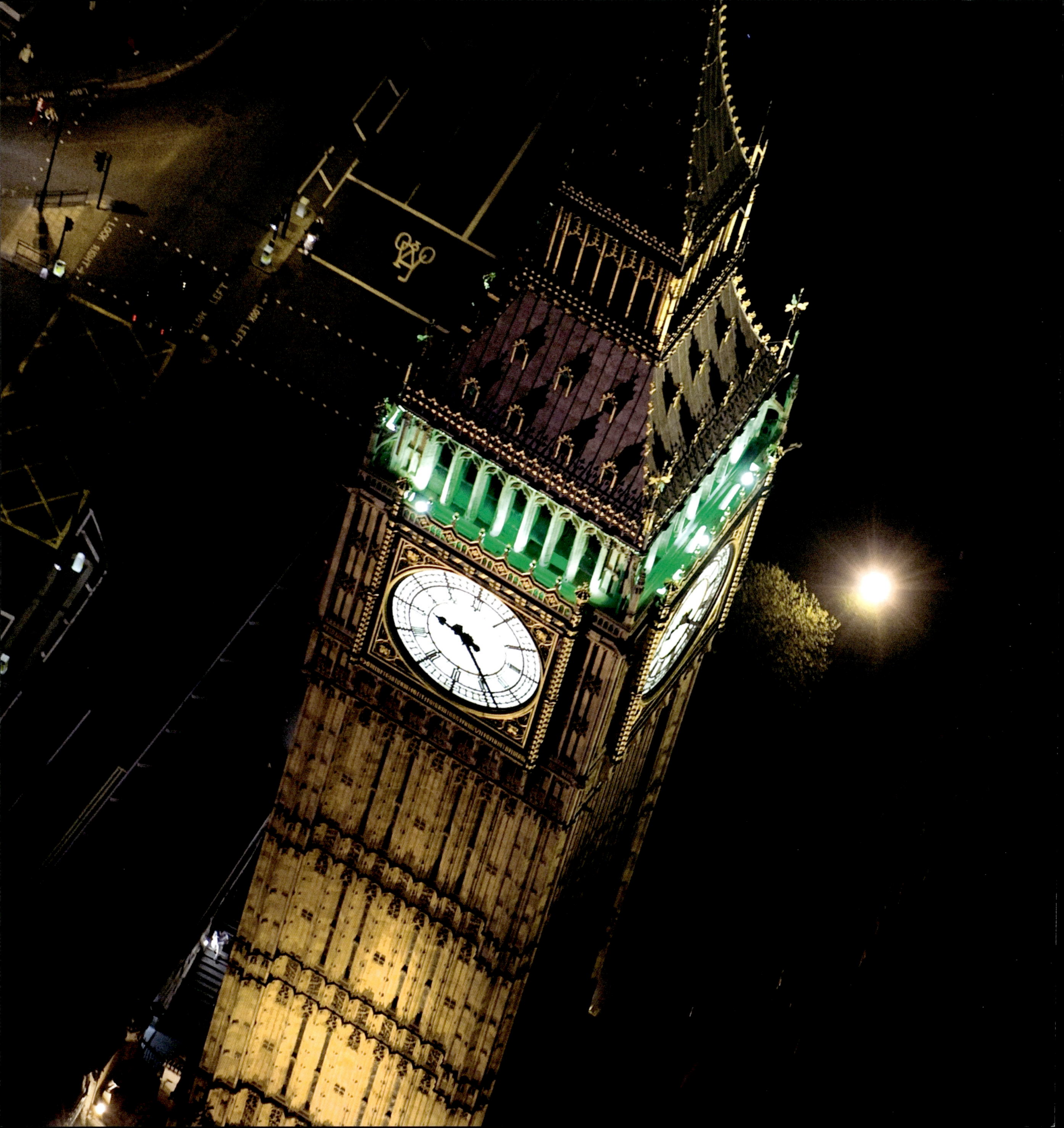

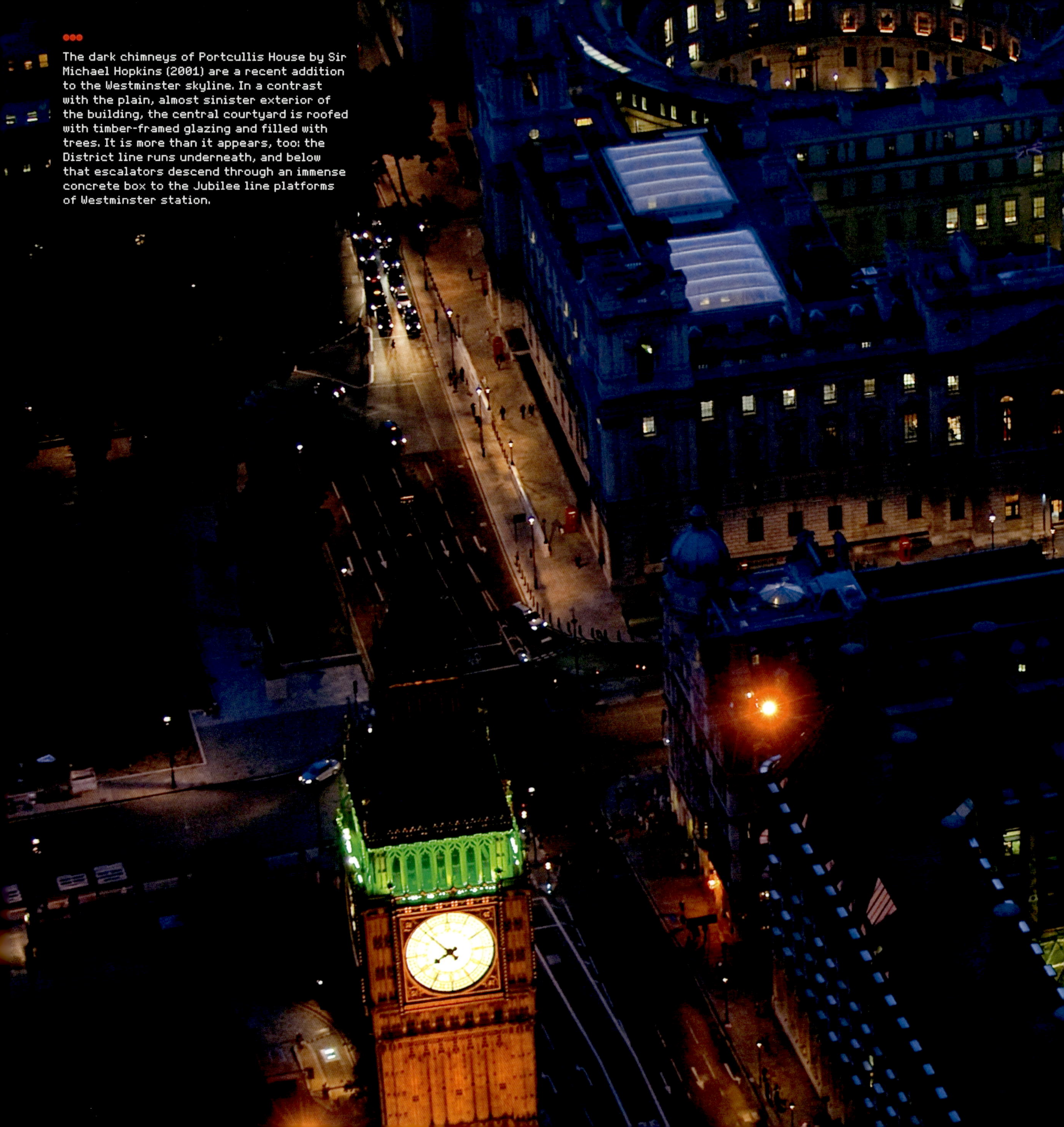

The dark chimneys of Portcullis House by Sir
Michael Hopkins (2001) are a recent addition
to the Westminster skyline. In a contrast
with the plain, almost sinister exterior of
the building, the central courtyard is roofed
with timber-framed glazing and filled with
trees. It is more than it appears, too: the
District line runs underneath, and below
that escalators descend through an immense
concrete box to the Jubilee line platforms
of Westminster station.

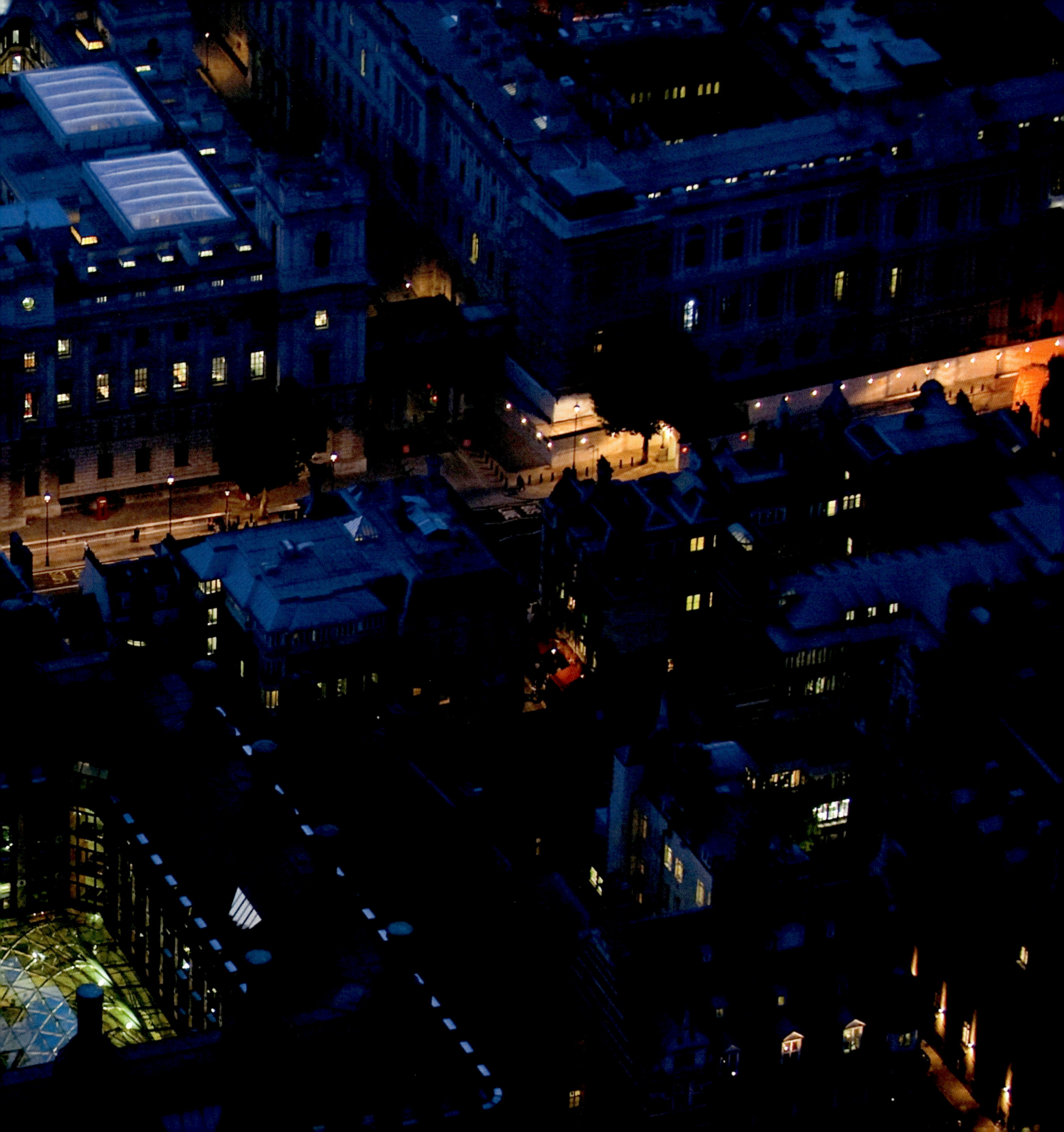

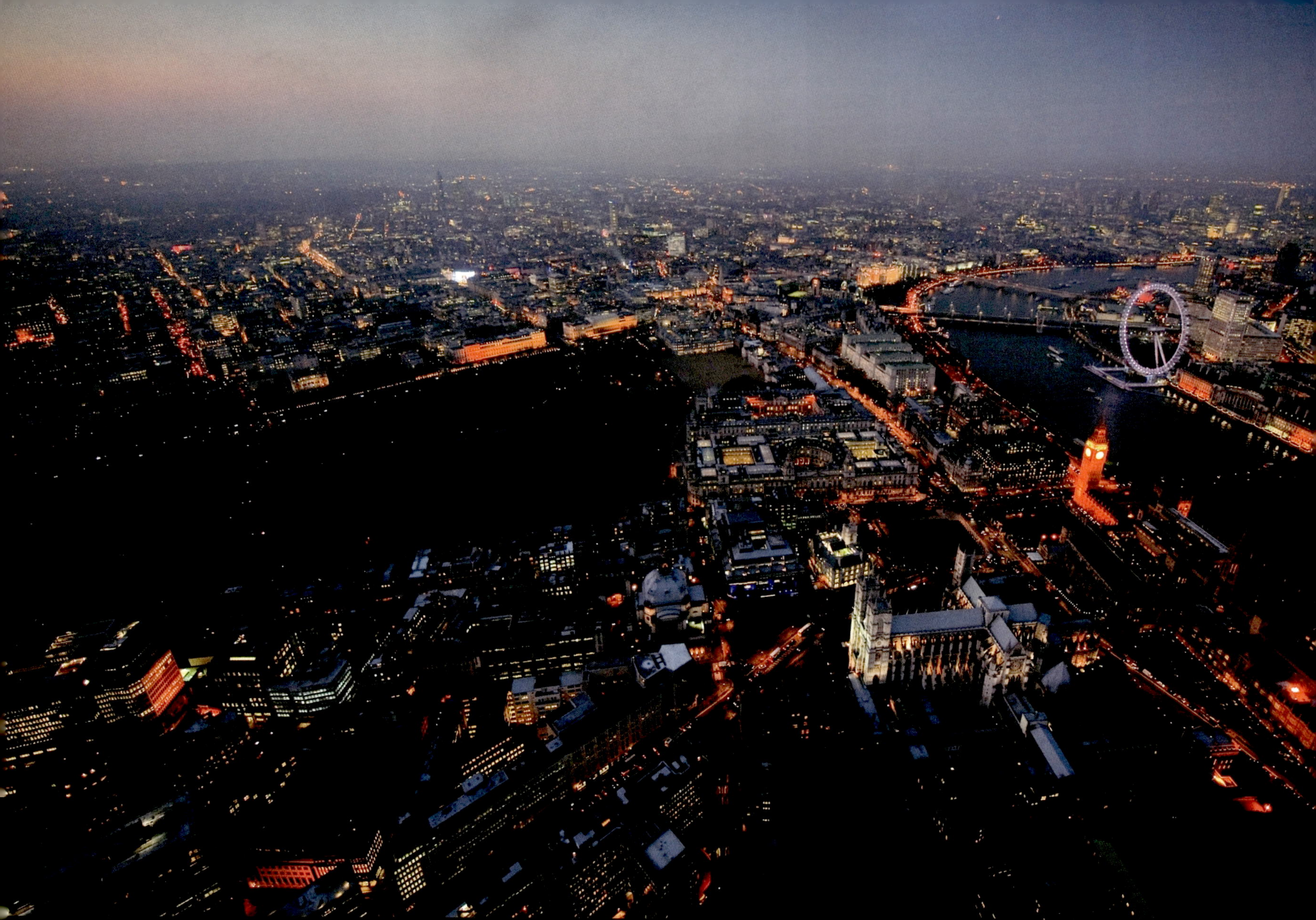

London was established as the royal capital of
England in 1065, when Edward the Confessor built
an abbey at Westminster. Much of the present
building dates from the mid-thirteenth century,
although the nave is later. The striking
neo-Gothic west towers, designed by Nicholas
Hawksmoor, were completed in 1745; one contains
the peal of ten bells. The building has long been
the site of coronations. It contains the tombs of
seventeen monarchs, as well as monuments to
other great Britons, from Purcell and Handel
to Cromwell and Darwin.

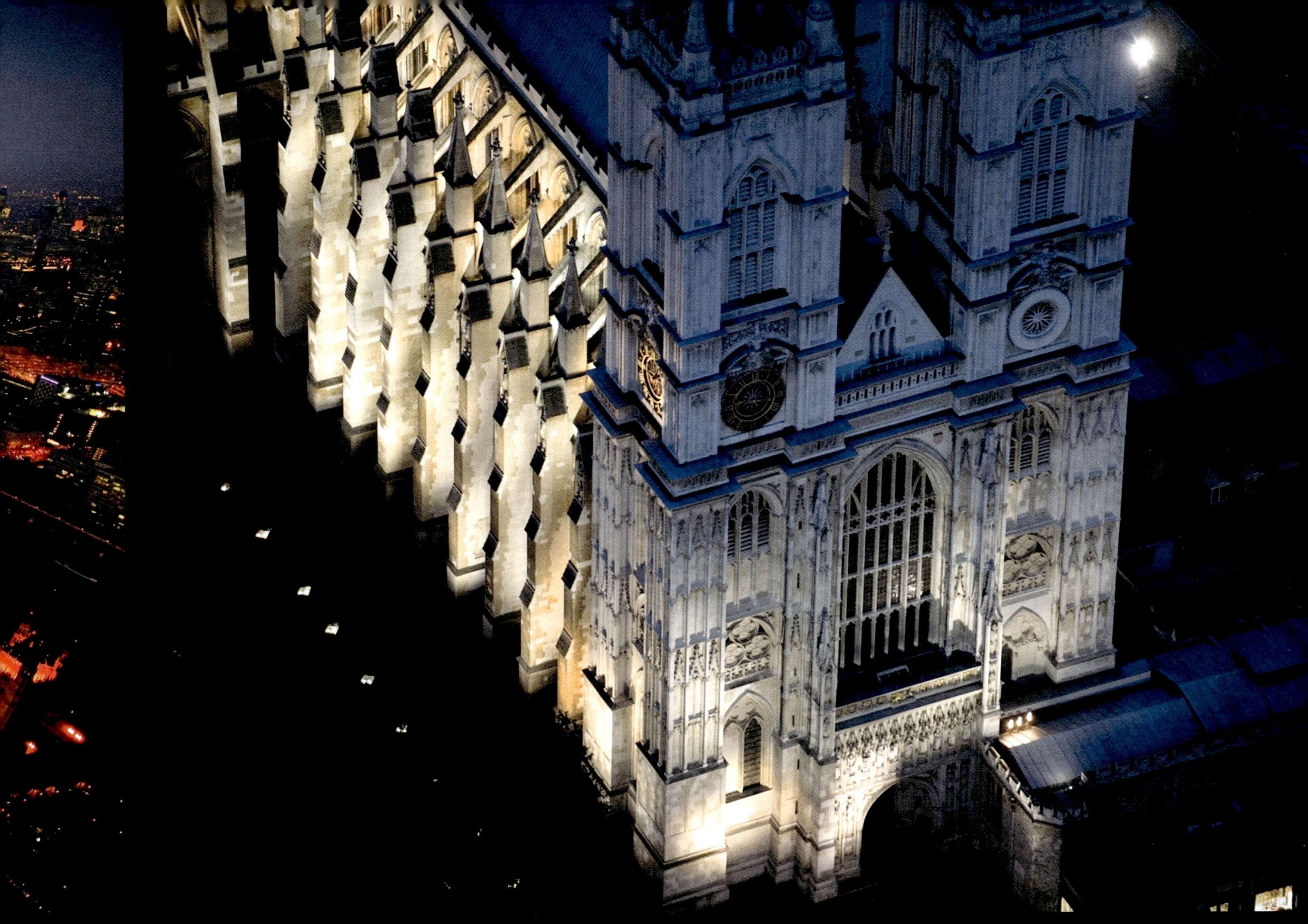

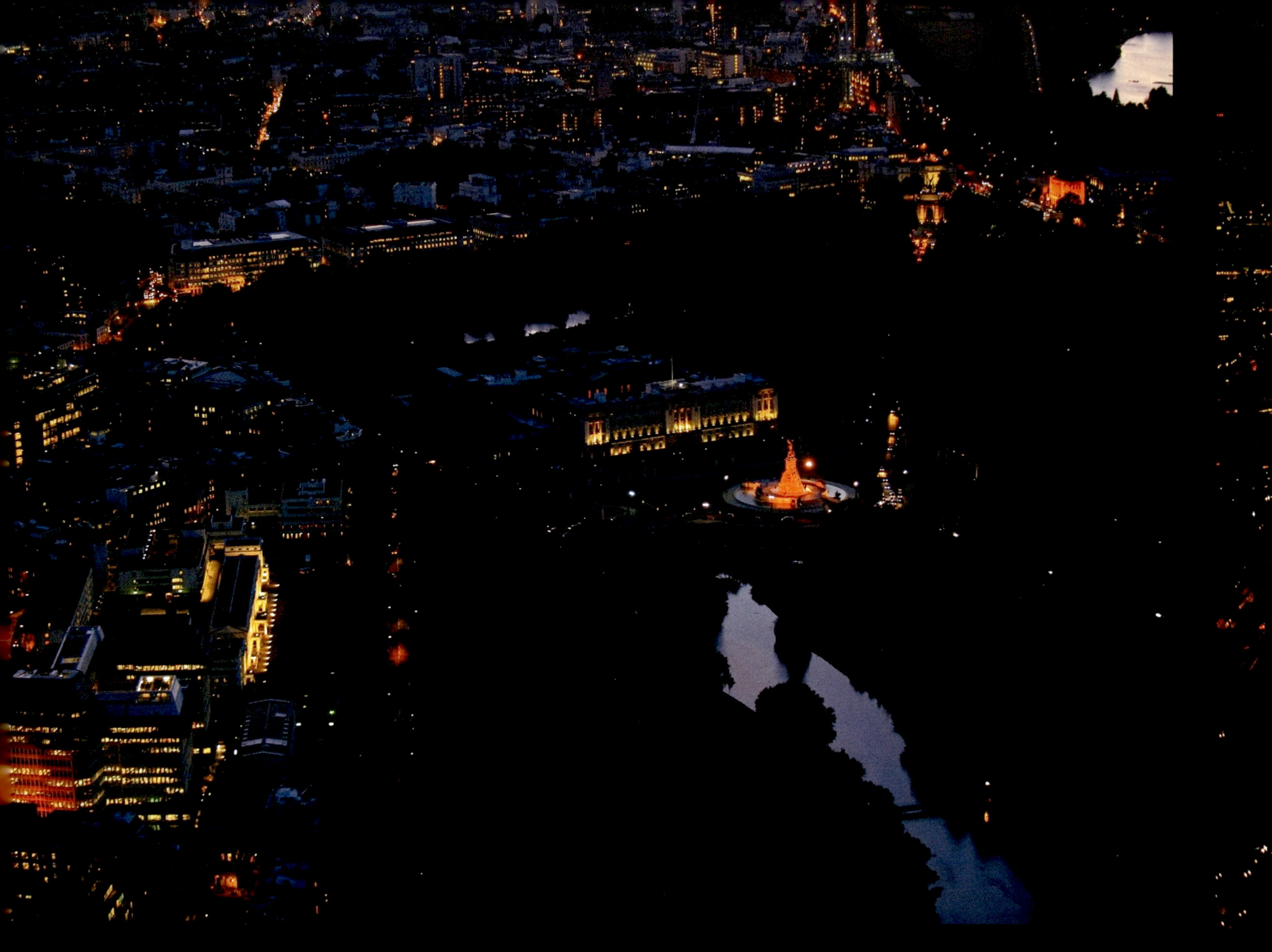

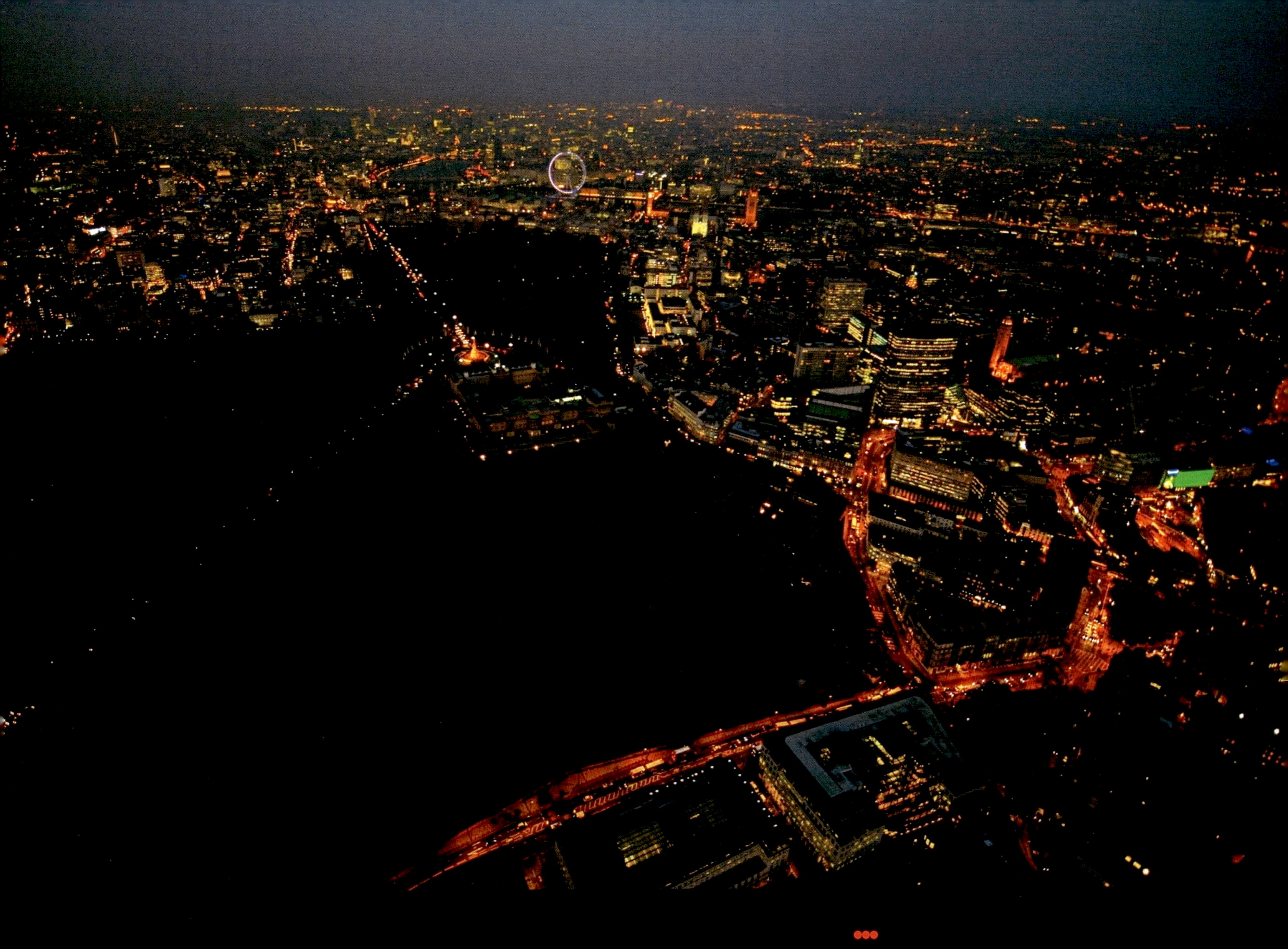

Constitution Hill is named after the morning walks taken there by royalty, rather than for any official document or statute. It leads diagonally between Green Park and Buckingham Palace Gardens towards Buckingham Palace, from where the Mall leads to the West End. The peace of the Queen's back garden is in stark contrast with the hubbub of the area around Victoria station (above, bottom right).

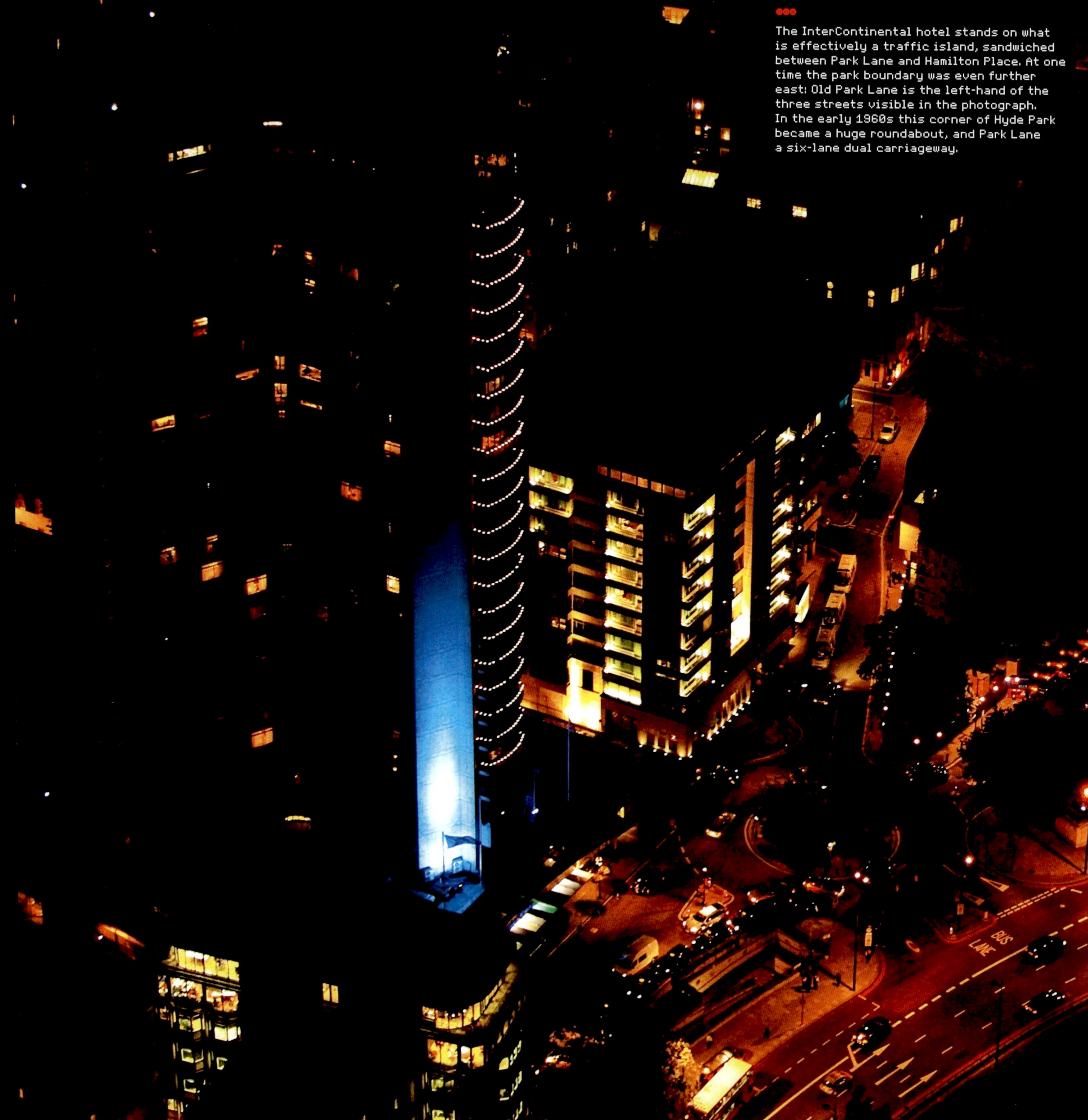

The InterContinental hotel stands on what
is effectively a traffic island, sandwiched
between Park Lane and Hamilton Place. At one
time the park boundary was even further
east: Old Park Lane is the left-hand of the
three streets visible in the photograph.
In the early 1960s this corner of Hyde Park
became a huge roundabout, and Park Lane
a six-lane dual carriageway.

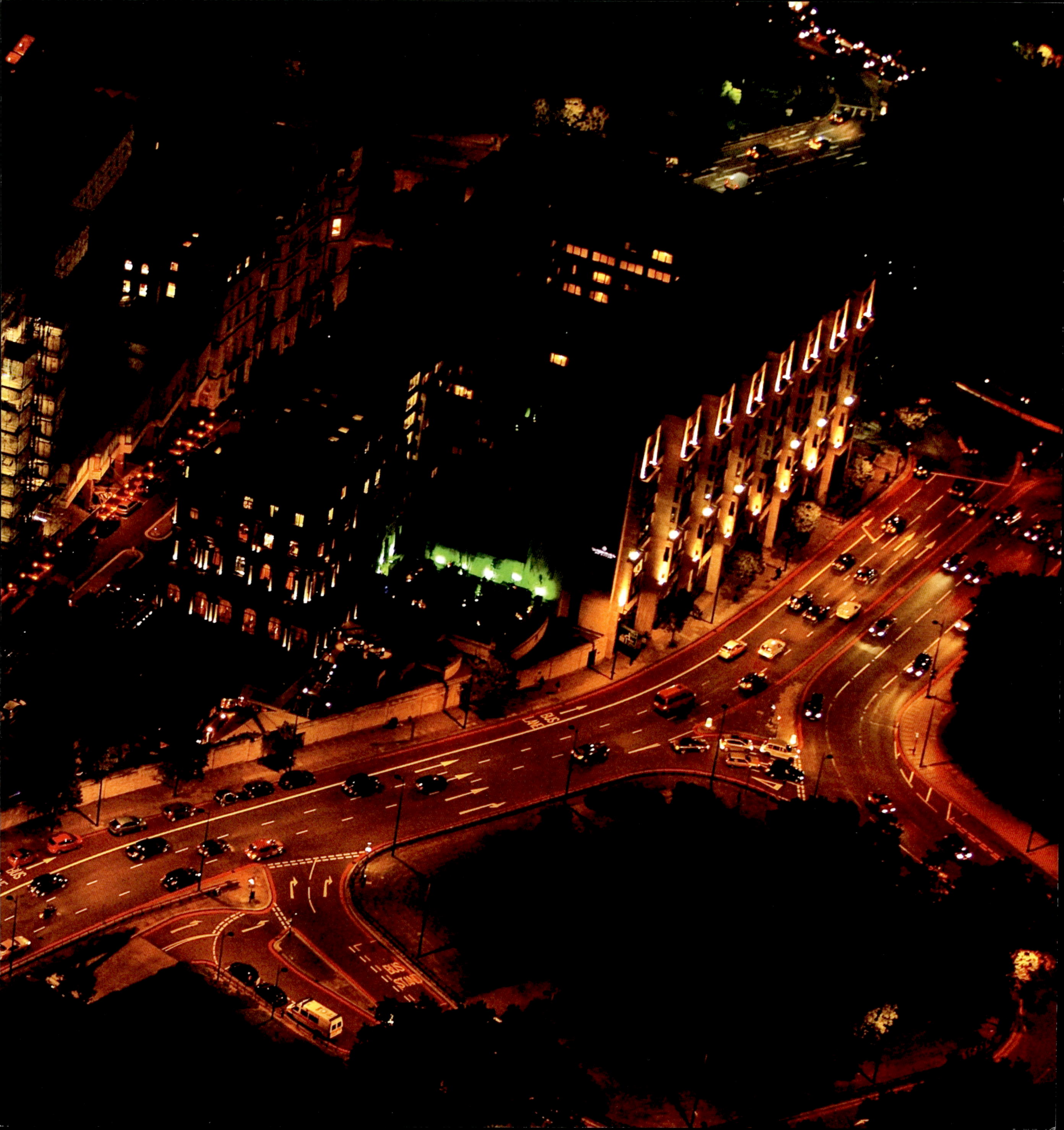

North London begins at Euston Road. The New Road, as it was originally titled, was
constructed in the 1750s as a bypass to London: in effect, the Georgian version
of the M25, running through what remained the semi-rural edge of the city. The coming
of the railways, with a major terminus at Euston, followed by others at King's Cross
and St Pancras, saw Euston Road firmly absorbed into central London. During the 1960s
planning transformed much of it into an urban motorway, with office development
extending to the north, most visibly with the construction of the bulky Euston Tower.

To the west, Regent's Park reflects the enlightened planning of an earlier age and
connects to Primrose Hill, with its excellent views across London. Beyond the big stations
lie miles of streets lined with late Georgian and Victorian terraces and villas. Prominent
landmarks include those temples of sport, Emirates Stadium and the spectacular new
Wembley, its arch visible across much of north London. Rail tracks and major roads snake
across the landscape. Further north, the ponderous mass of Alexandra Palace rises close
to Muswell Hill, and Hampstead Heath provides north London – which lacks the commons
of Clapham, Wandsworth and Tooting – with a vast green lung. Hampstead and Highgate,
safely elevated above the surrounding sprawl, retain much of their village character.

Along the arterial roads inter-war shopping parades have lost their appeal in
the face of competition from Brent Cross, a pioneering out-of-town shopping centre,
and the retail parks that have proliferated on the North Circular. The far suburbs fade
seamlessly into what is left of rural Hertfordshire. Driving along the M25, you pass
through an extraordinary range of terrains: landscaped parks, golf courses, industrial
tat and genteel villadom. The new face of London is out here, on the edge.

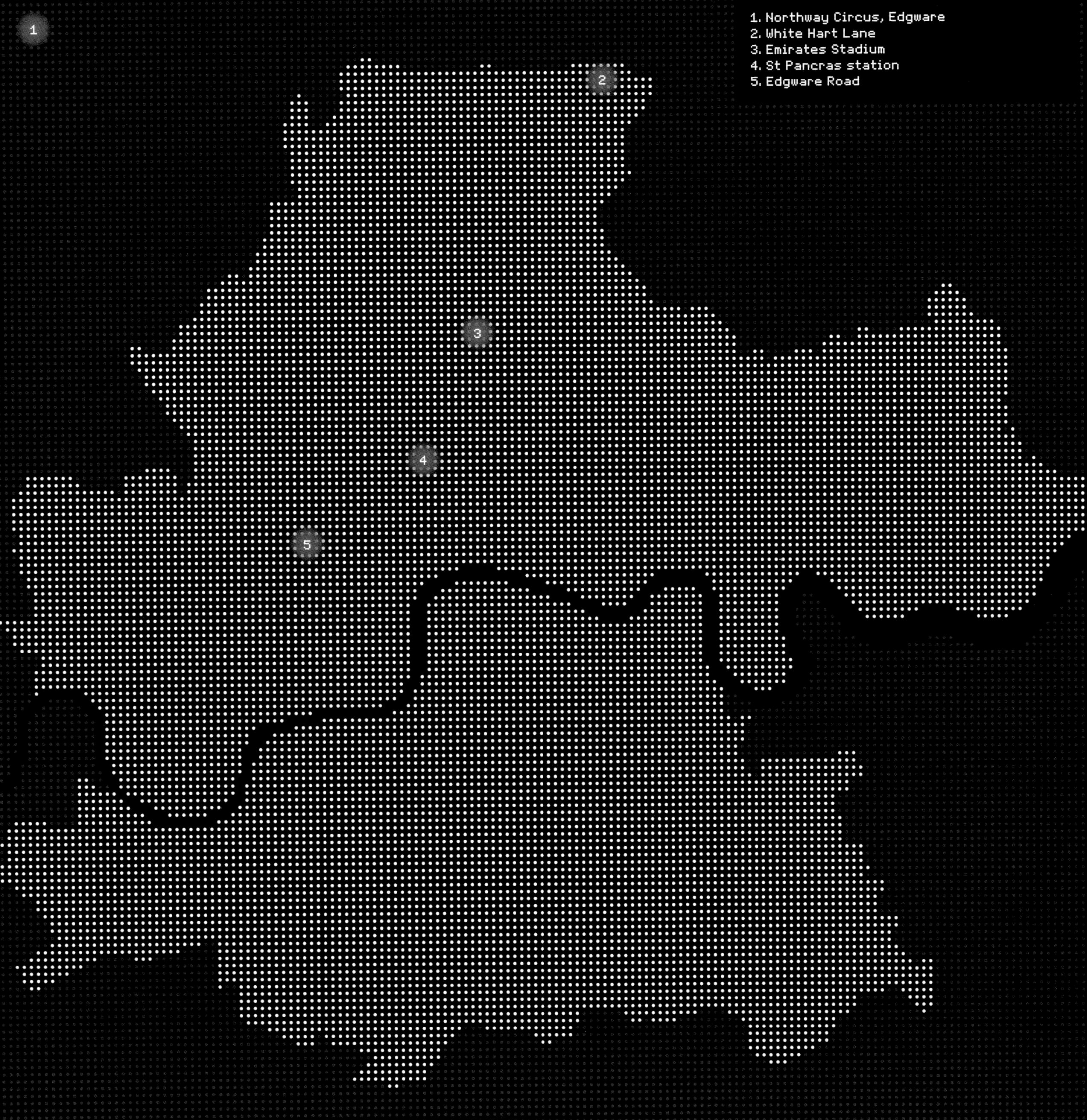

1. Northway Circus, Edgware
2. White Hart Lane
3. Emirates Stadium
4. St Pancras station
5. Edgware Road

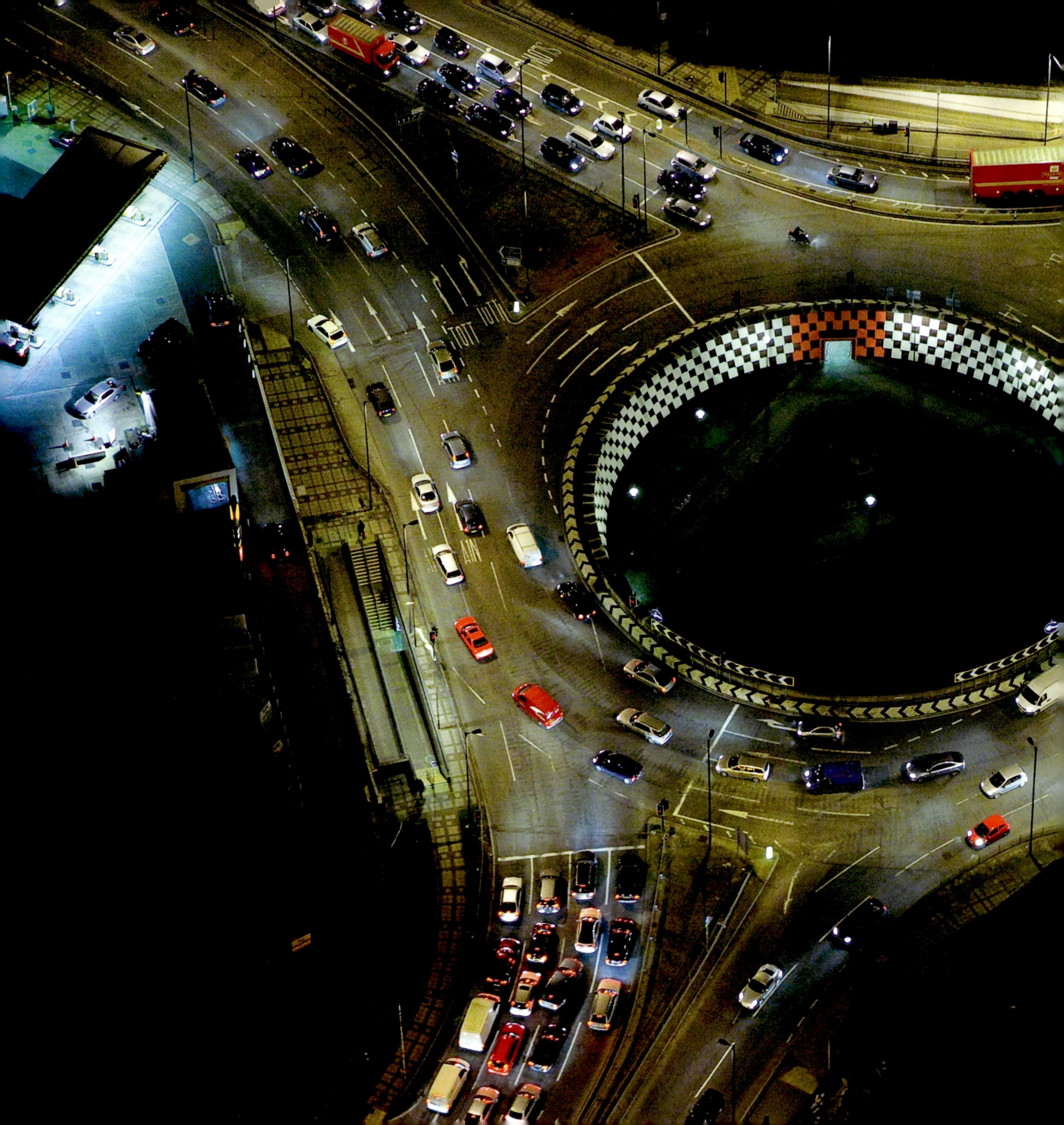

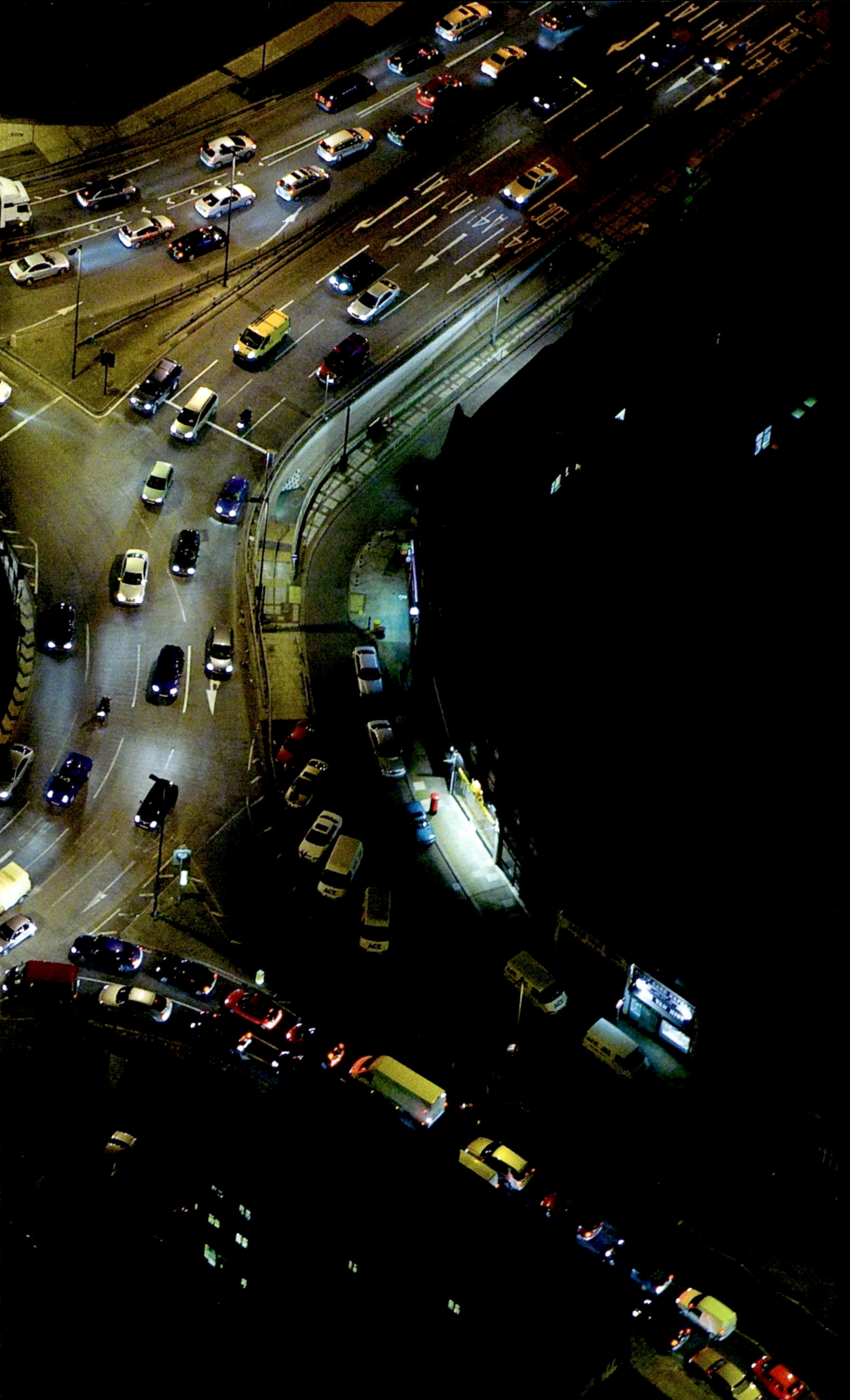

Northway Circus in Edgware, better known as 'Apex Corner', links the A1 and the A41. Traffic for the north leaves at the top left-hand corner of the image; the North Circular goes east at the top right-hand corner. Despite the proximity of the M1 (just 50 metres to the west), there is no access to the motorway from here. Jaunty tiling attempts to ameliorate the pedestrian's experience in the bleak underpasses.

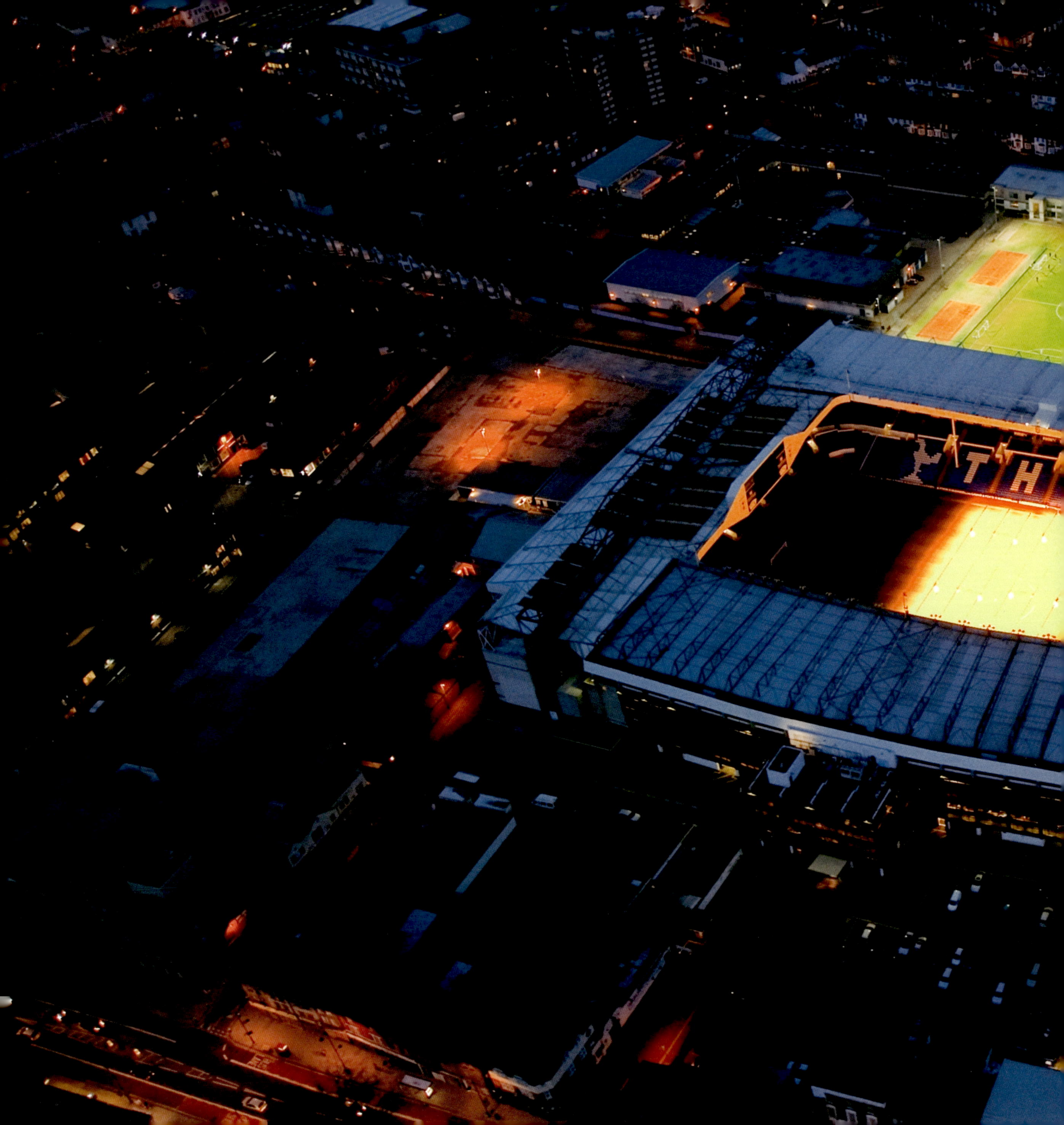
YTH

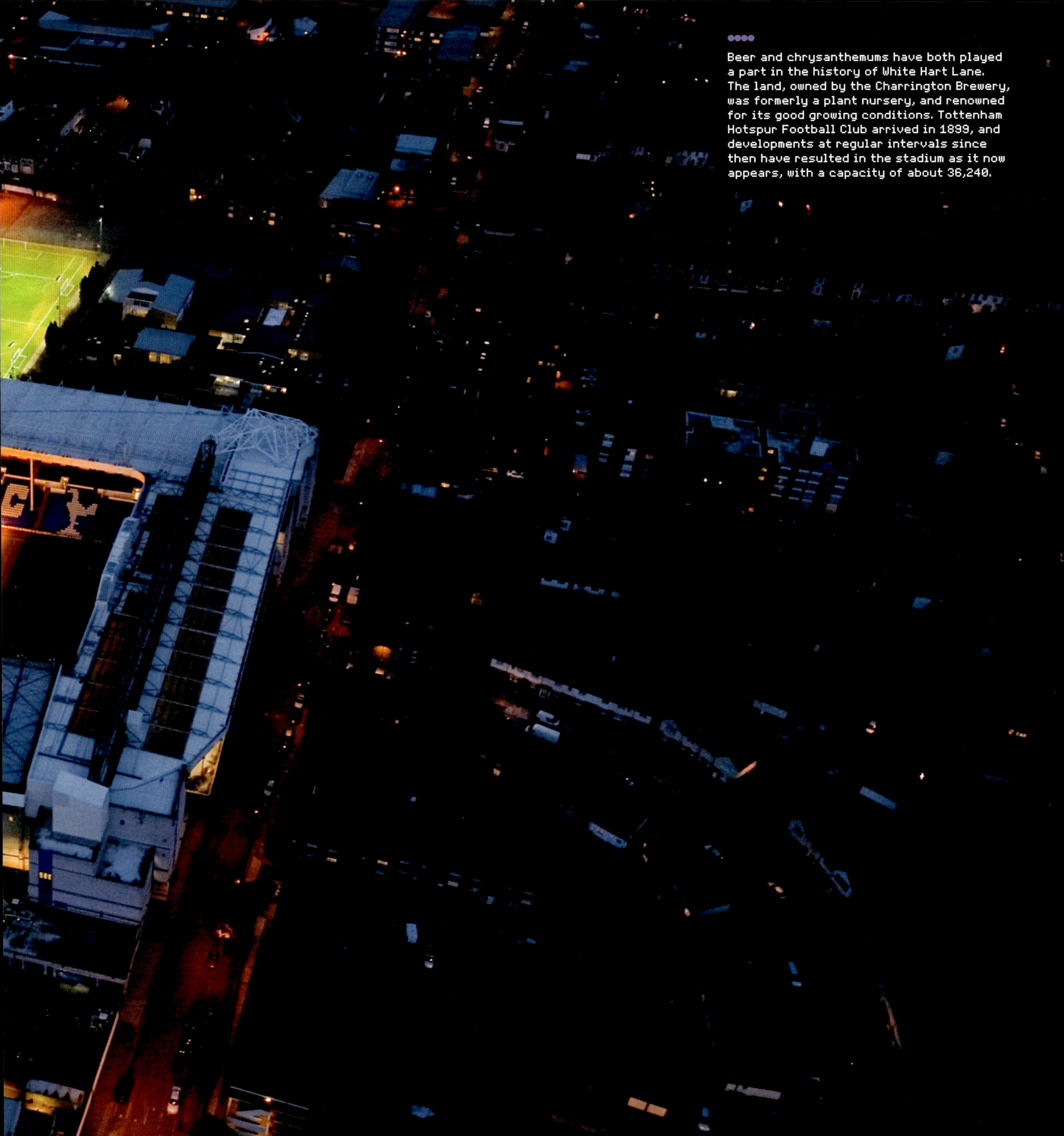

●●●●
Beer and chrysanthemums have both played
a part in the history of White Hart Lane.
The land, owned by the Charrington Brewery,
was formerly a plant nursery, and renowned
for its good growing conditions. Tottenham
Hotspur Football Club arrived in 1899, and
developments at regular intervals since
then have resulted in the stadium as it now
appears, with a capacity of about 36,240.

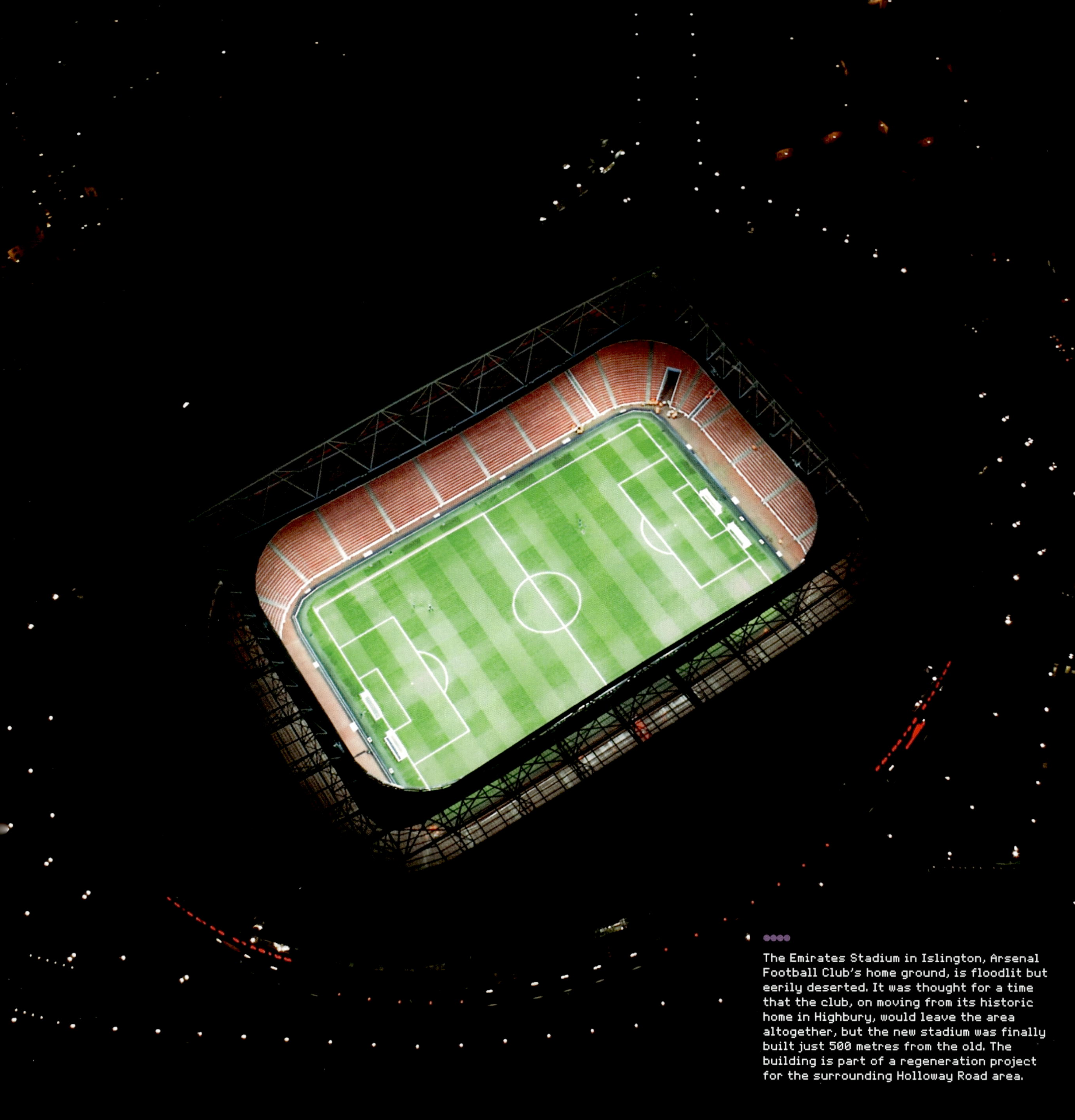

The Emirates Stadium in Islington, Arsenal
Football Club's home ground, is floodlit but
eerily deserted. It was thought for a time
that the club, on moving from its historic
home in Highbury, would leave the area
altogether, but the new stadium was finally
built just 500 metres from the old. The
building is part of a regeneration project
for the surrounding Holloway Road area.

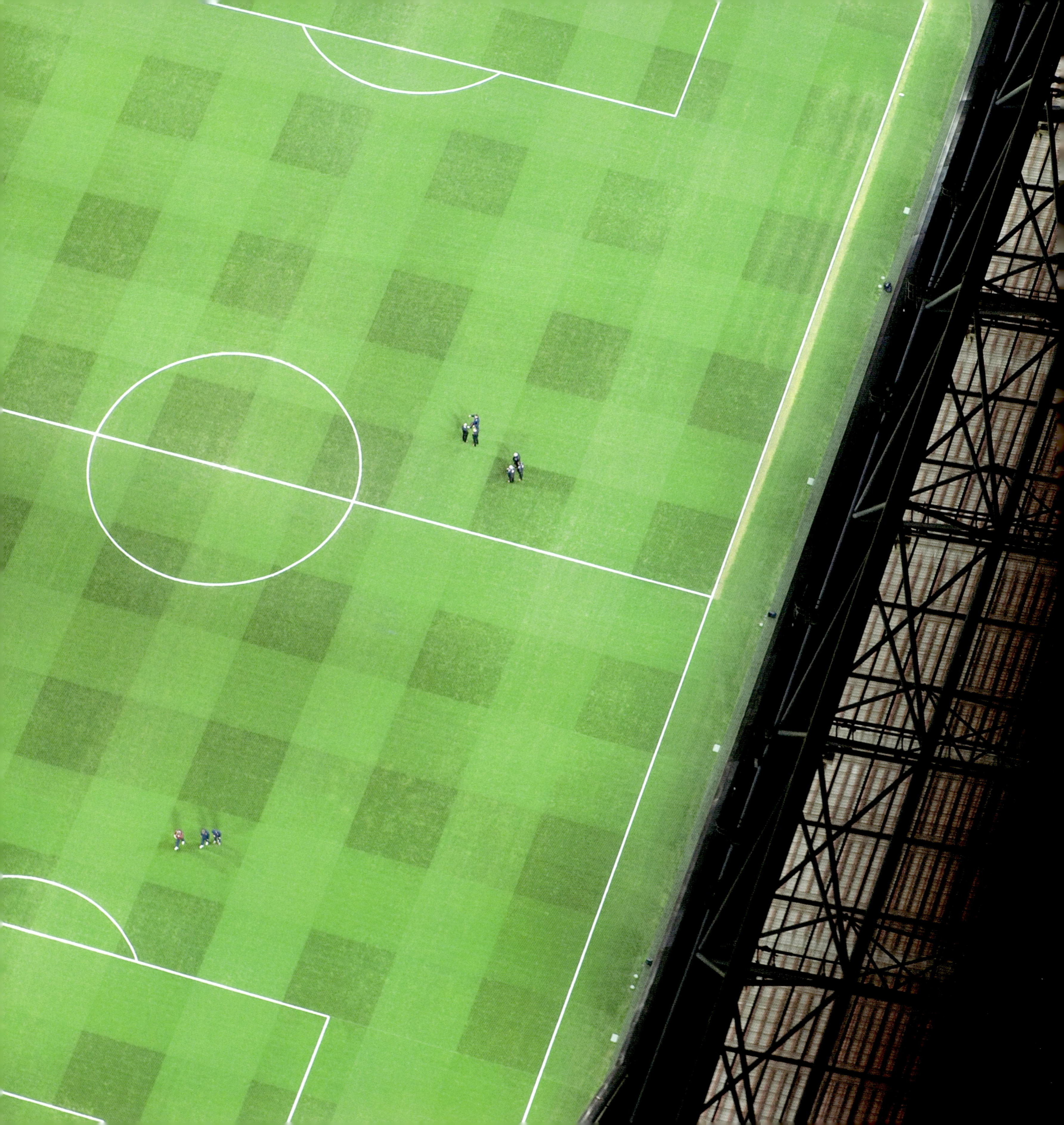

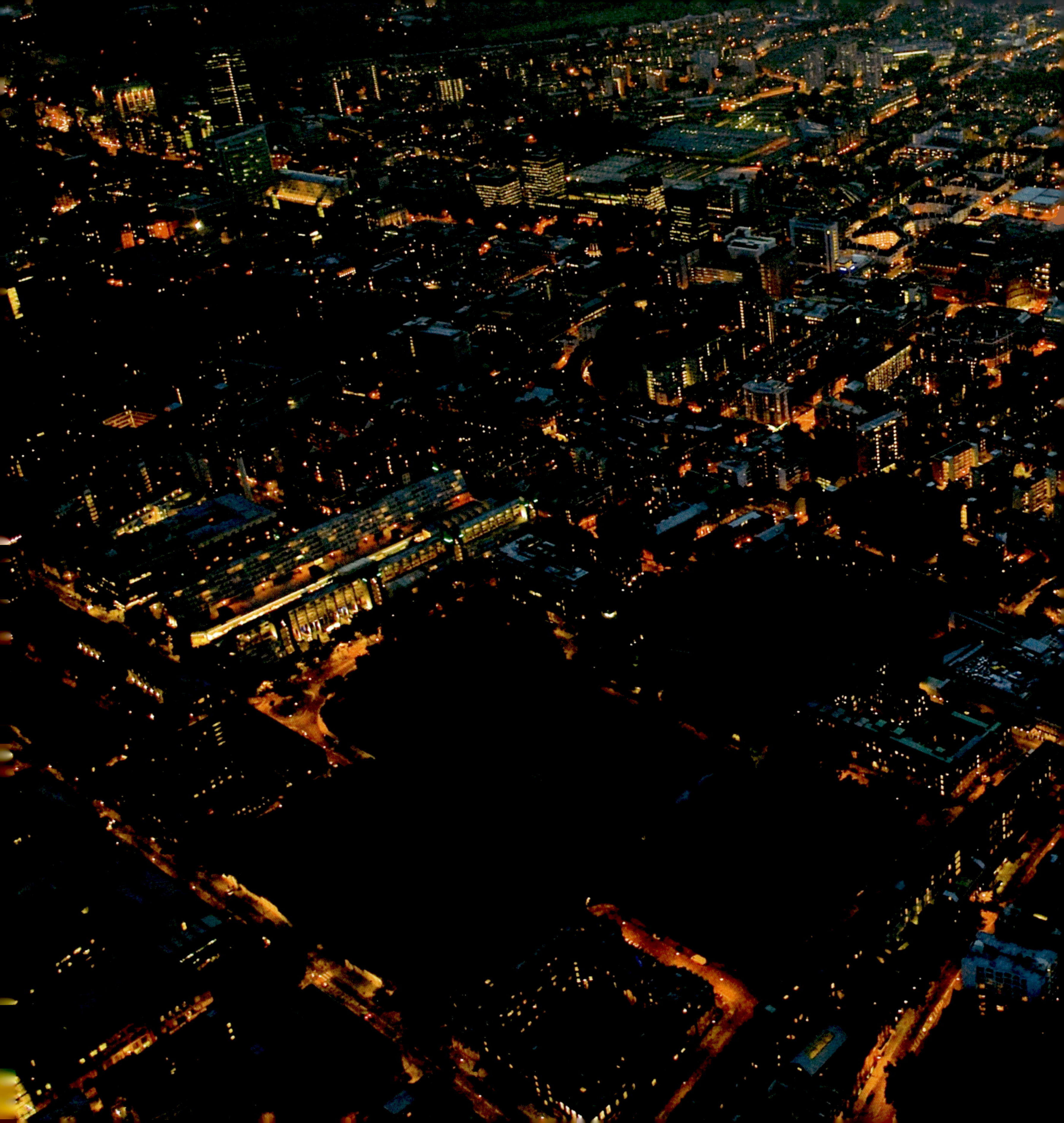

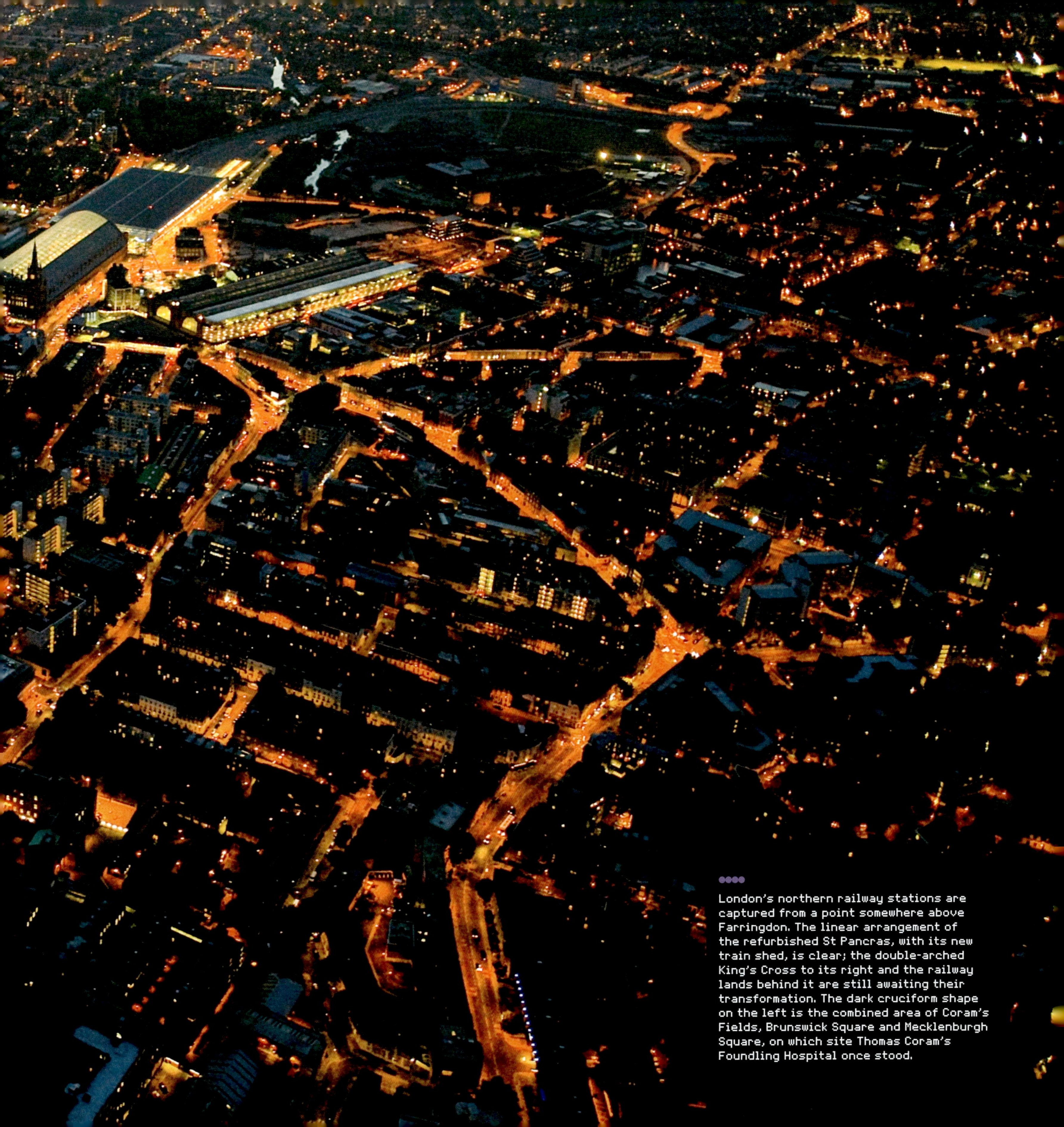

London's northern railway stations are captured from a point somewhere above Farringdon. The linear arrangement of the refurbished St Pancras, with its new train shed, is clear; the double-arched King's Cross to its right and the railway lands behind it are still awaiting their transformation. The dark cruciform shape on the left is the combined area of Coram's Fields, Brunswick Square and Mecklenburgh Square, on which site Thomas Coram's Foundling Hospital once stood.

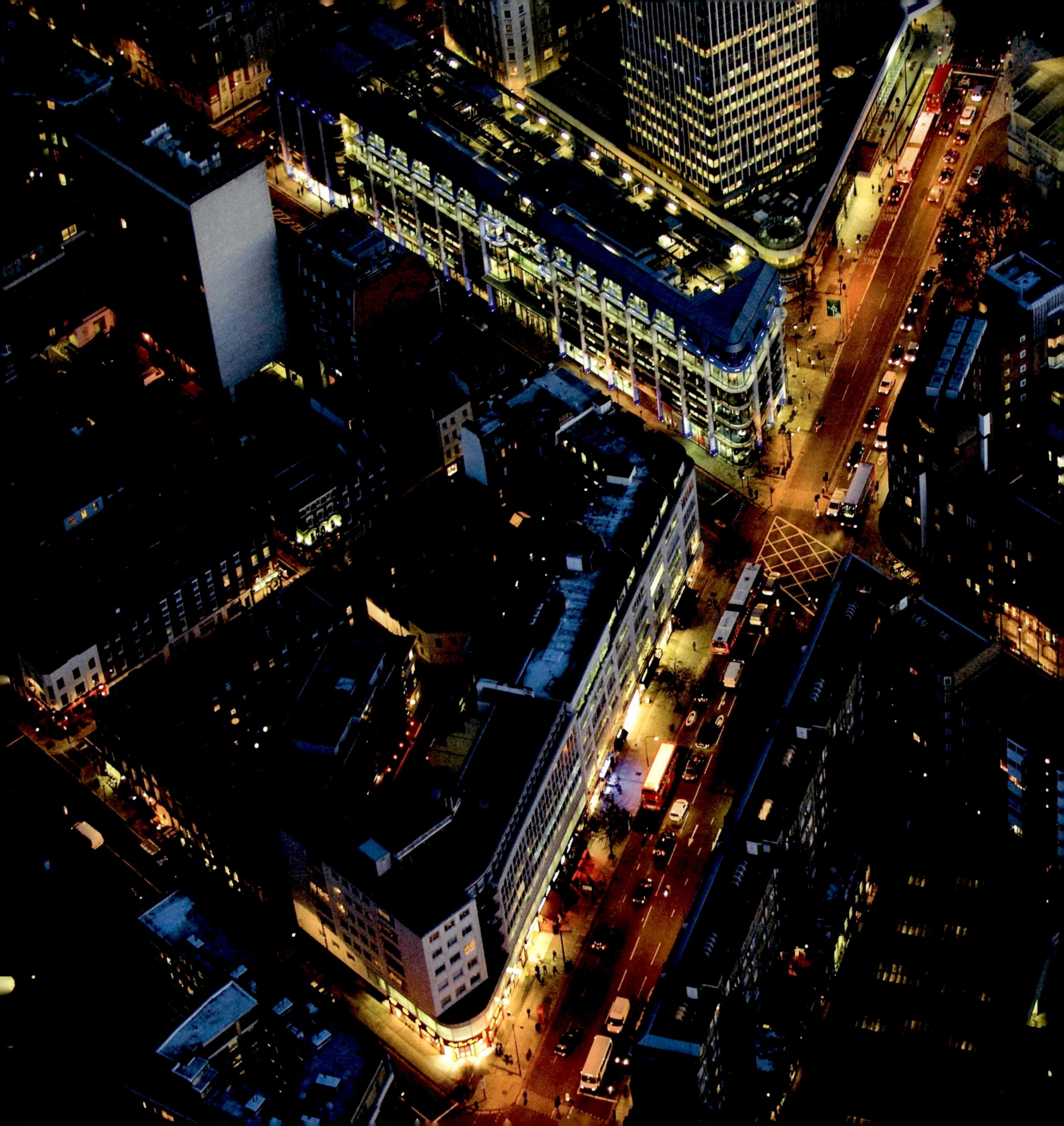

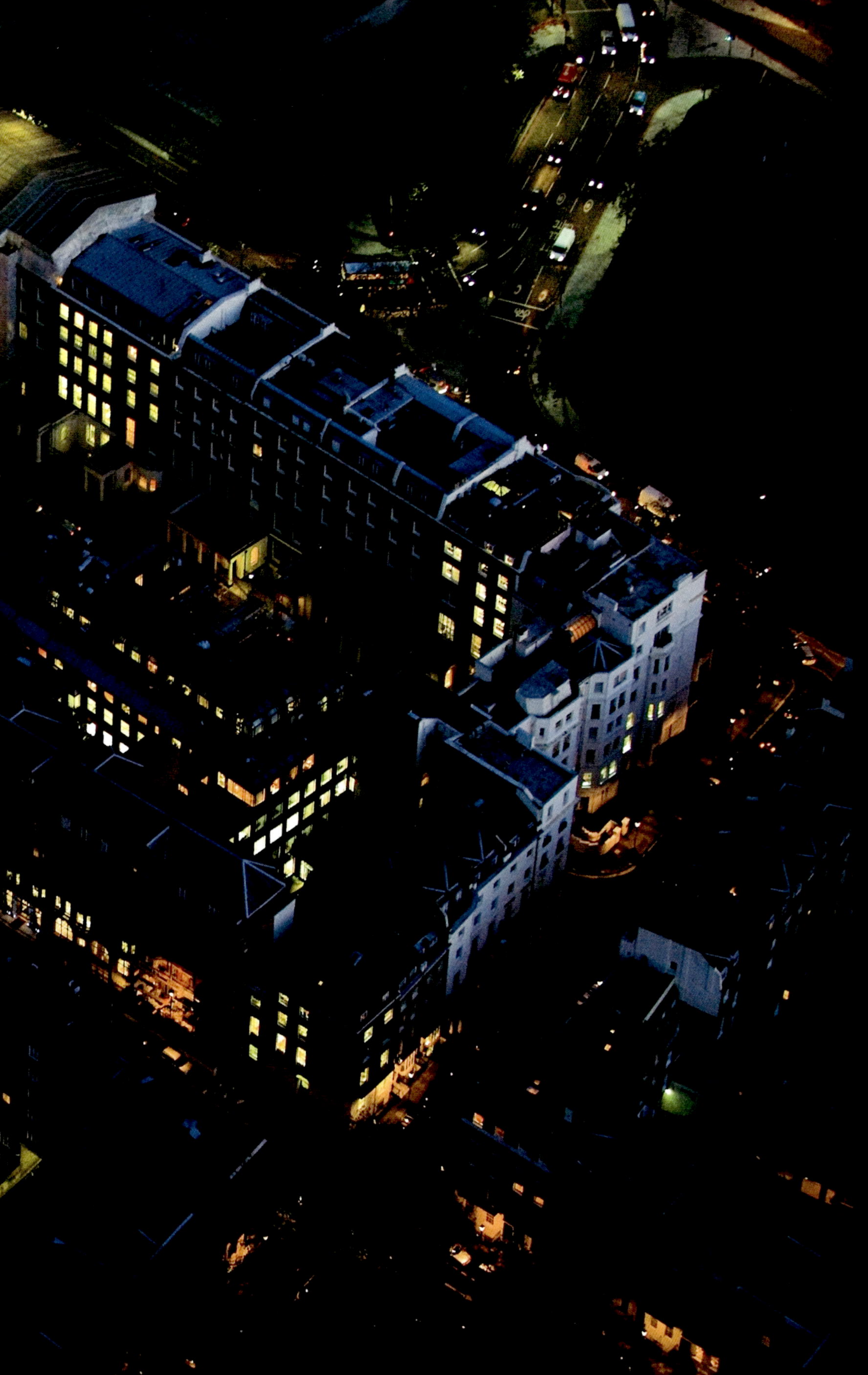

The southern end of Edgware Road was once the site of London's first permanent gallows. During the eighteenth century the gallows, at Tyburn, near the present location of Marble Arch, was the main place of execution for Londoners condemned to death. The area is now busy with traffic and shoppers. The blue-lit building at the crossroads is York House, the headquarters of property developer British Land; it was completed in 2007 by EPR Architects and also contains shops and flats.

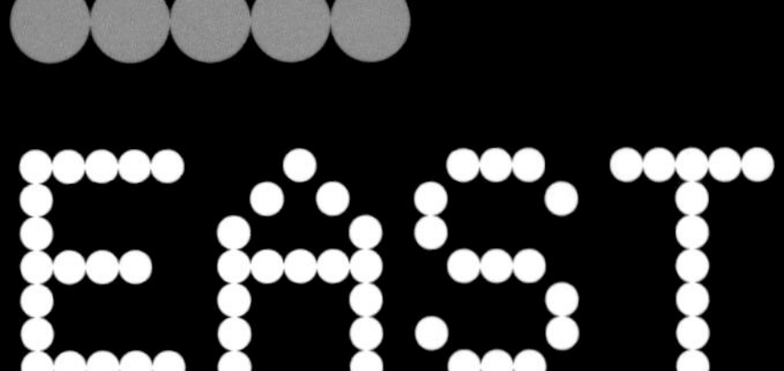

The East End once began at Bishopsgate. Just opposite Liverpool Street station, Spitalfields wholesale market formed a down-to-earth preface to the rundown, if historic, streets beyond, with Hawksmoor's monumental Christ Church presiding over the dereliction. Today Spitalfields is regenerated – even fashionable – and the market is long gone, replaced by offices of highly paid lawyers, and shops, restaurants and bars aimed at affluent City professionals. Hoxton has been colonized by artists and art dealers, and Hackney is now a smart address. New office developments, along with the excellent Whitechapel Art Gallery, are changing the face of Aldgate, another traditional City gateway. The City has moved eastwards, while the future of the East End has been increasingly uncertain. For two centuries it was the larder and workshop of London, with the docks (nearly 21 square kilometres in total area), extending from the Pool of London to the Royals, employing up to 100,000 men and supporting a range of industries from match manufacture to food processing. The total closure of the docks from the late 1960s onwards was traumatic, but regeneration followed, initially producing offices for bankers at Canary Wharf and flats for the wealthy lining much of the riverside westwards.

Now east London is undergoing another wave of renewal, with the redevelopment of former railway land at Stratford – in many respects the 'capital of the East End' – as the site of the 2012 Olympic Games and the vast Stratford City project of offices, shops and housing. A new station is served by Eurostar. New transport links have driven regeneration throughout east London: the new London Overground can be seen snaking across Shoreditch and Hoxton to link New Cross with Highbury & Islington; and London City Airport, along with a campus for the University of East London and the ExCel conference centre, has transformed the Royal Docks. There is a new confidence in the air, and a feeling that at last the renewal of the East End is benefiting everyone who lives there.

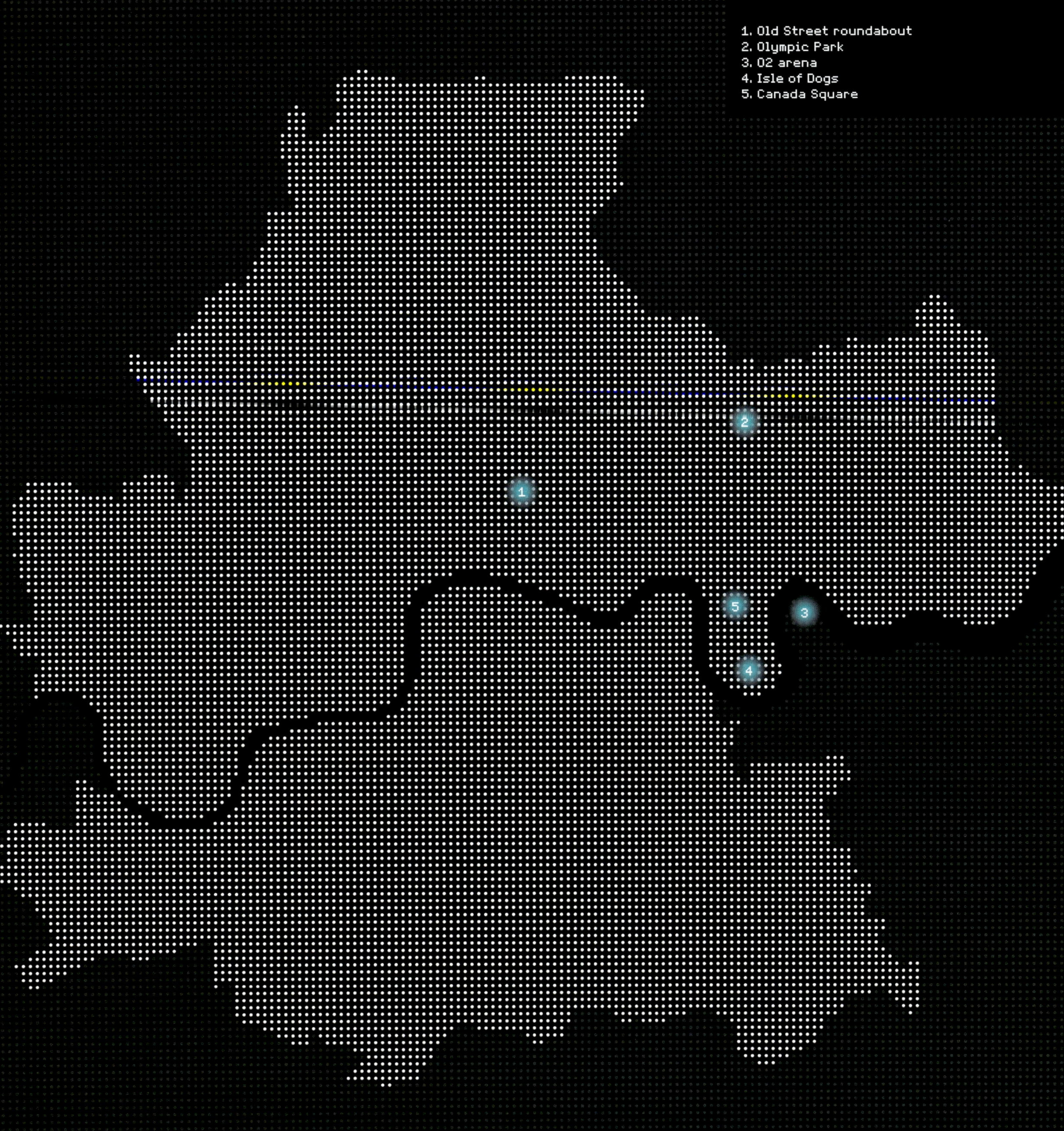

1. Old Street roundabout
2. Olympic Park
3. O2 arena
4. Isle of Dogs
5. Canada Square

Old Street roundabout, surely one of London's
most soulless places, is nevertheless the
meeting-point for several important old roads.
Here we look east towards Hackney and the dark
expanse of Victoria Park. City Road leads right
and left; Old Street leads away, and from it
forks Great Eastern Street, which becomes
Commercial Street, a crucial link between the
wharves and warehouses of Wapping and the
coachroads to the north of England.

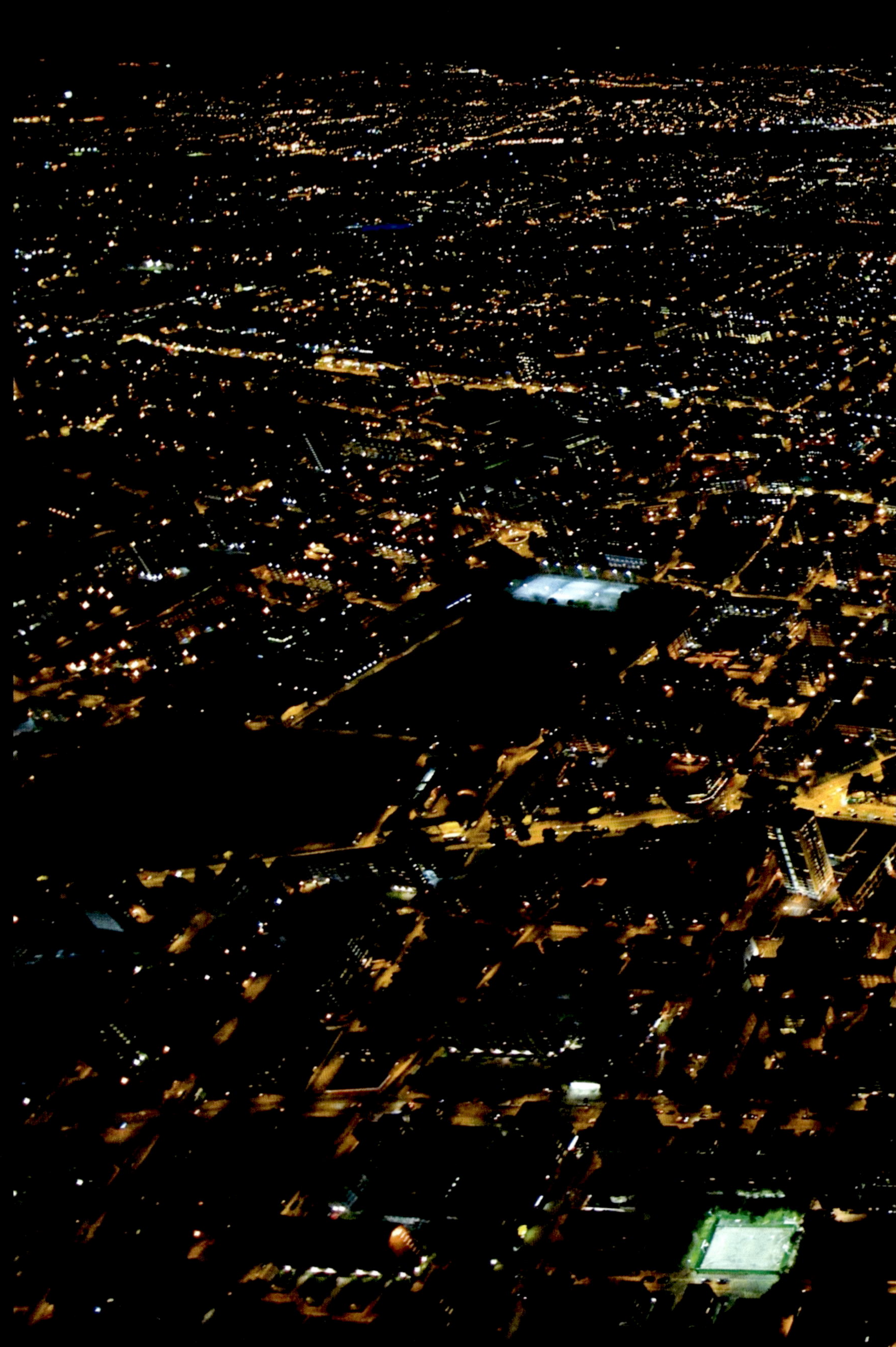

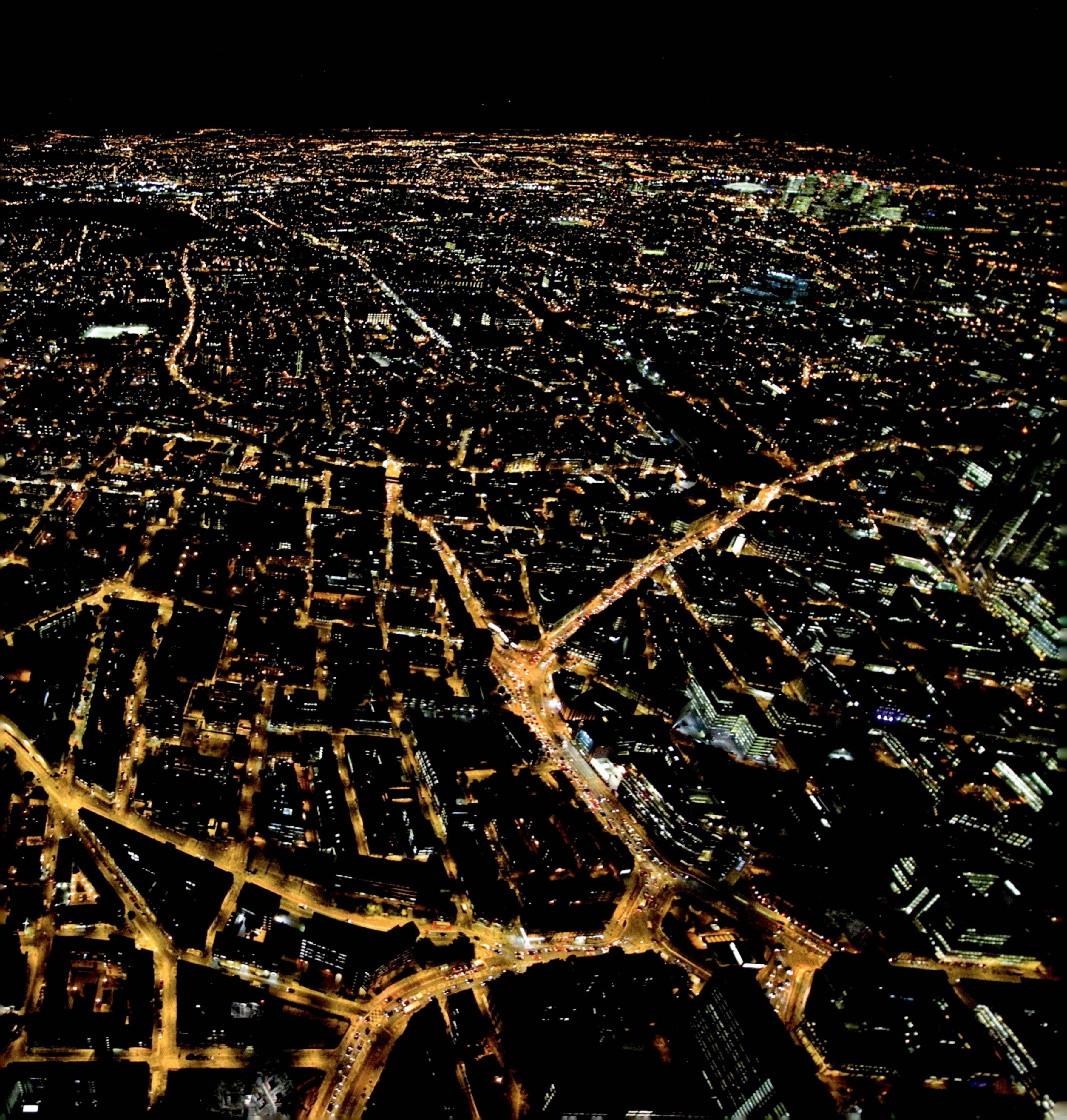

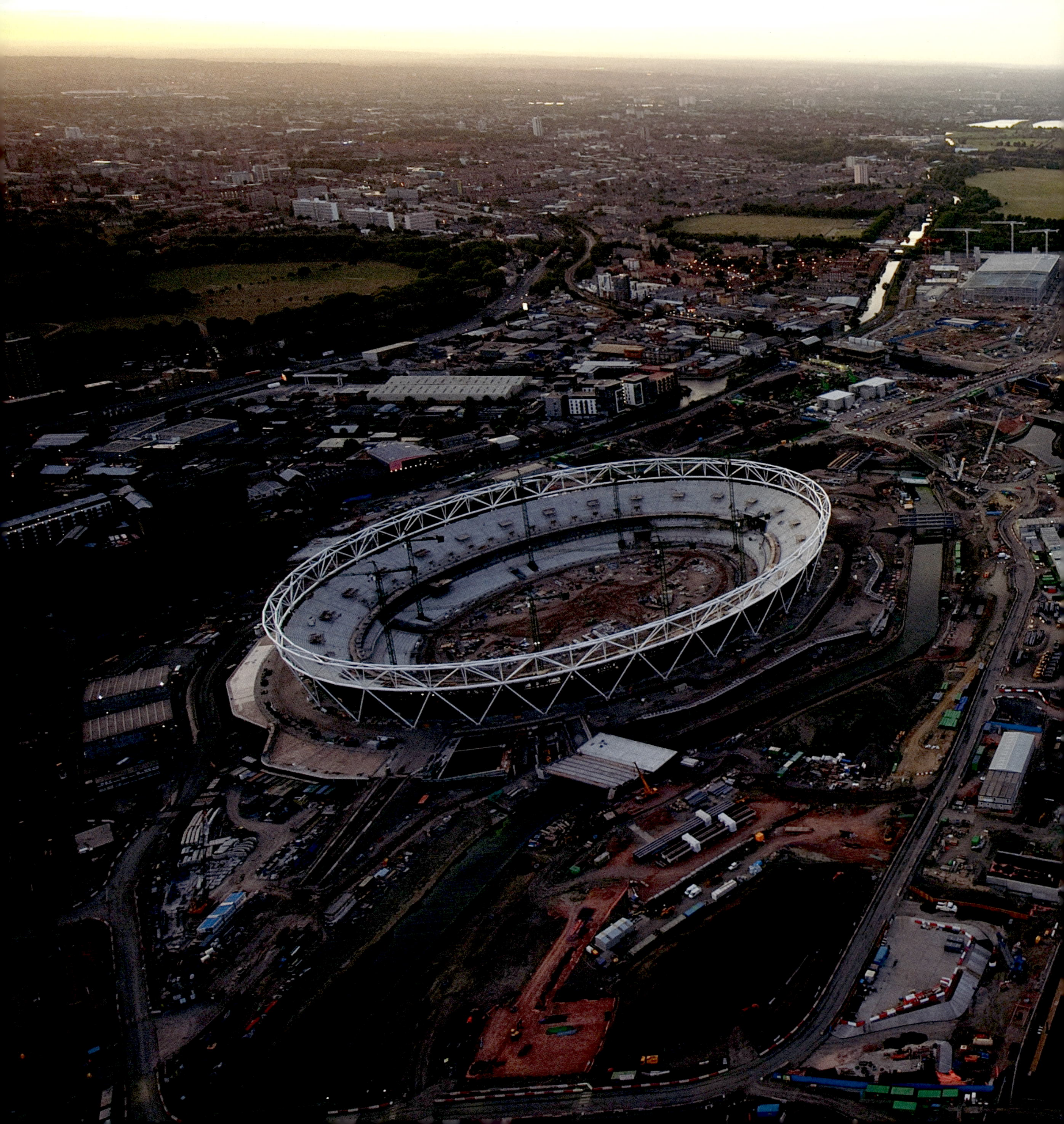

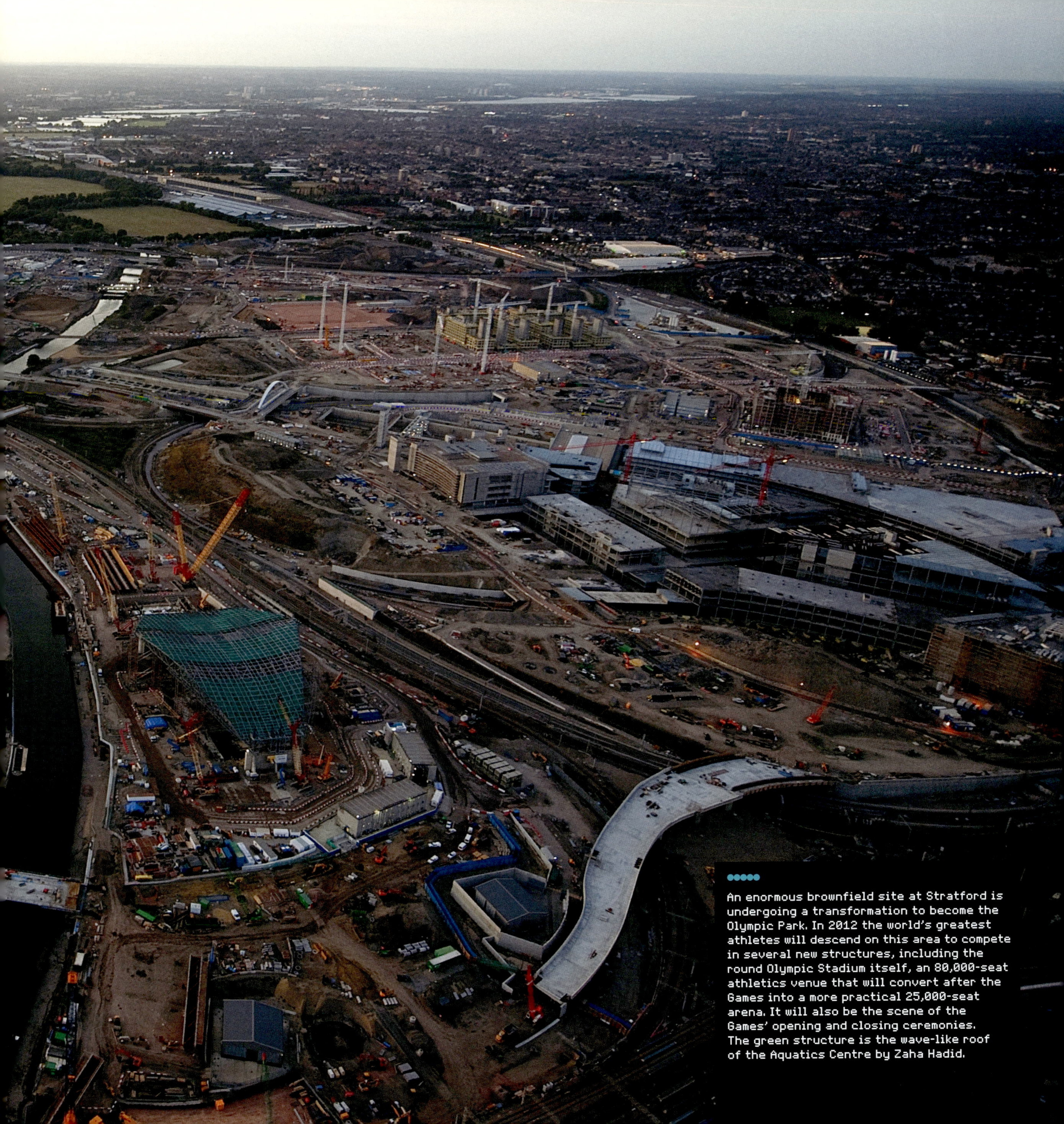

An enormous brownfield site at Stratford is
undergoing a transformation to become the
Olympic Park. In 2012 the world's greatest
athletes will descend on this area to compete
in several new structures, including the
round Olympic Stadium itself, an 80,000-seat
athletics venue that will convert after the
Games into a more practical 25,000-seat
arena. It will also be the scene of the
Games' opening and closing ceremonies.
The green structure is the wave-like roof
of the Aquatics Centre by Zaha Hadid.

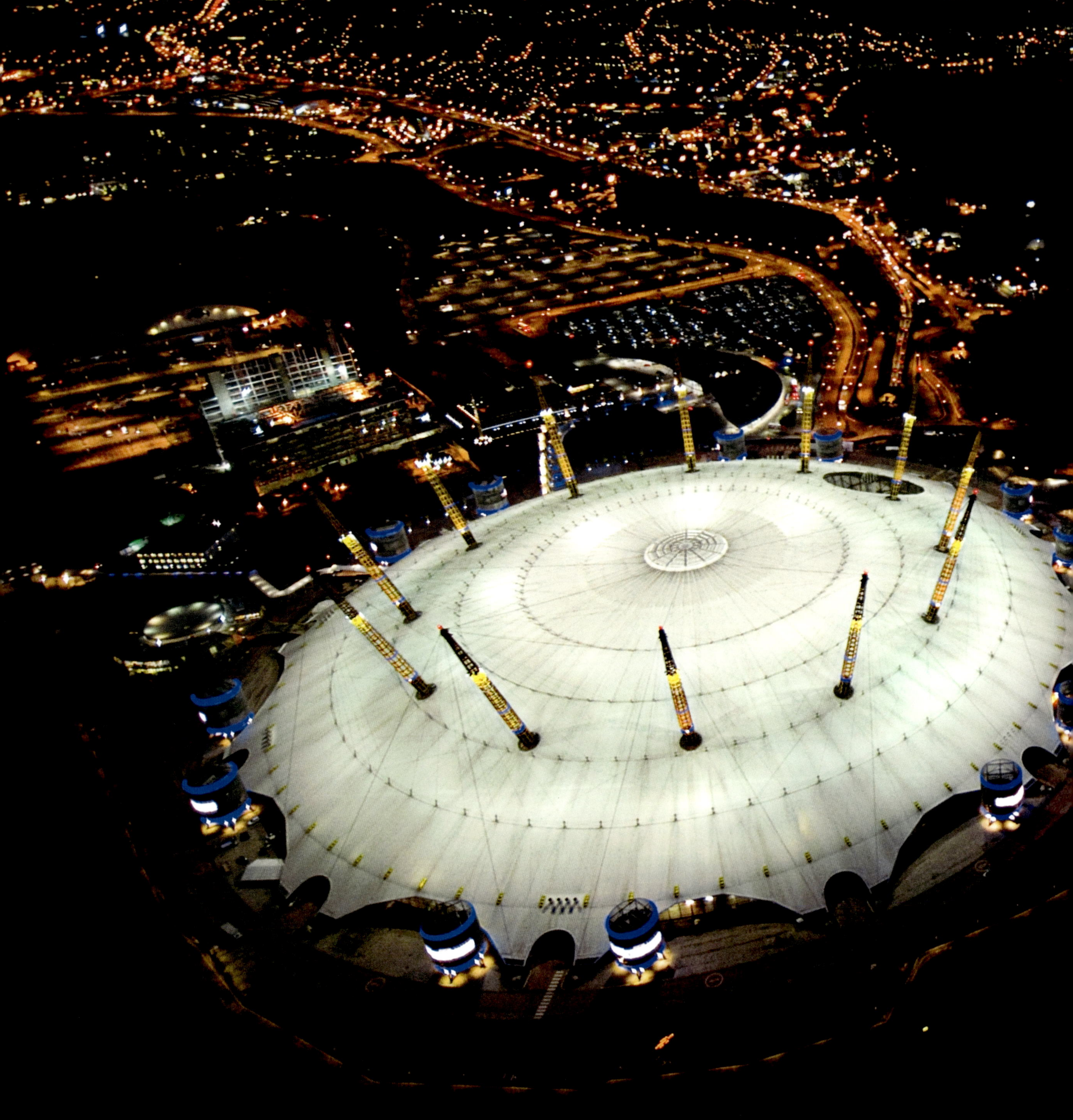

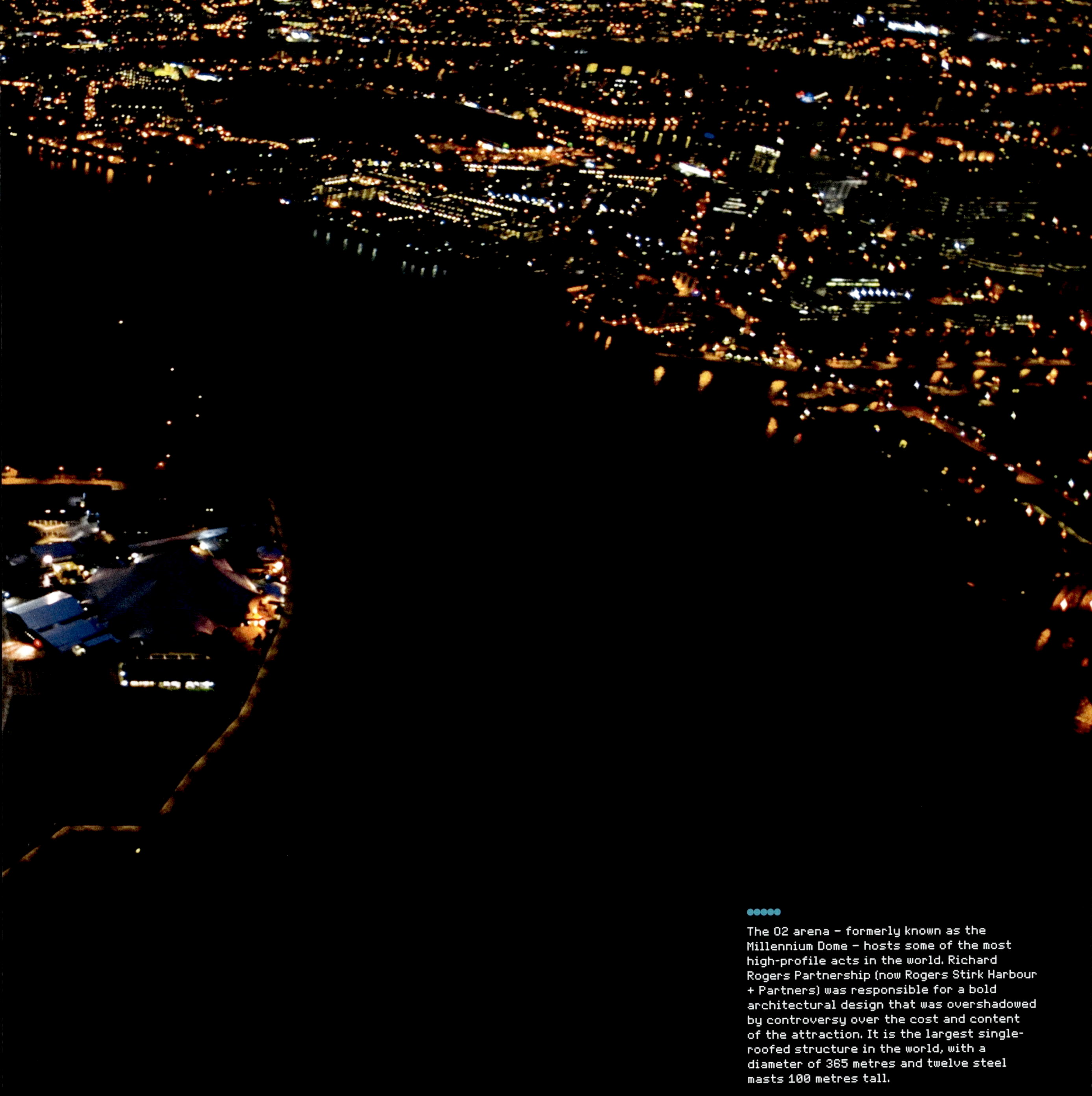

●●●●●
The O2 arena – formerly known as the
Millennium Dome – hosts some of the most
high-profile acts in the world. Richard
Rogers Partnership (now Rogers Stirk Harbour
+ Partners) was responsible for a bold
architectural design that was overshadowed
by controversy over the cost and content
of the attraction. It is the largest single-
roofed structure in the world, with a
diameter of 365 metres and twelve steel
masts 100 metres tall.

The Isle of Dogs, enclosed by a sweeping curve of the Thames, was not an island until 1805, when a canal was cut across the north side of the peninsula to save ships a round trip of nearly 5 kilometres. West India Docks, now underneath the cluster of towers, had been constructed shortly before that, with 1.2 kilometres of warehouses to store goods brought from, among other places, the Canary Islands. The docks closed in 1980.

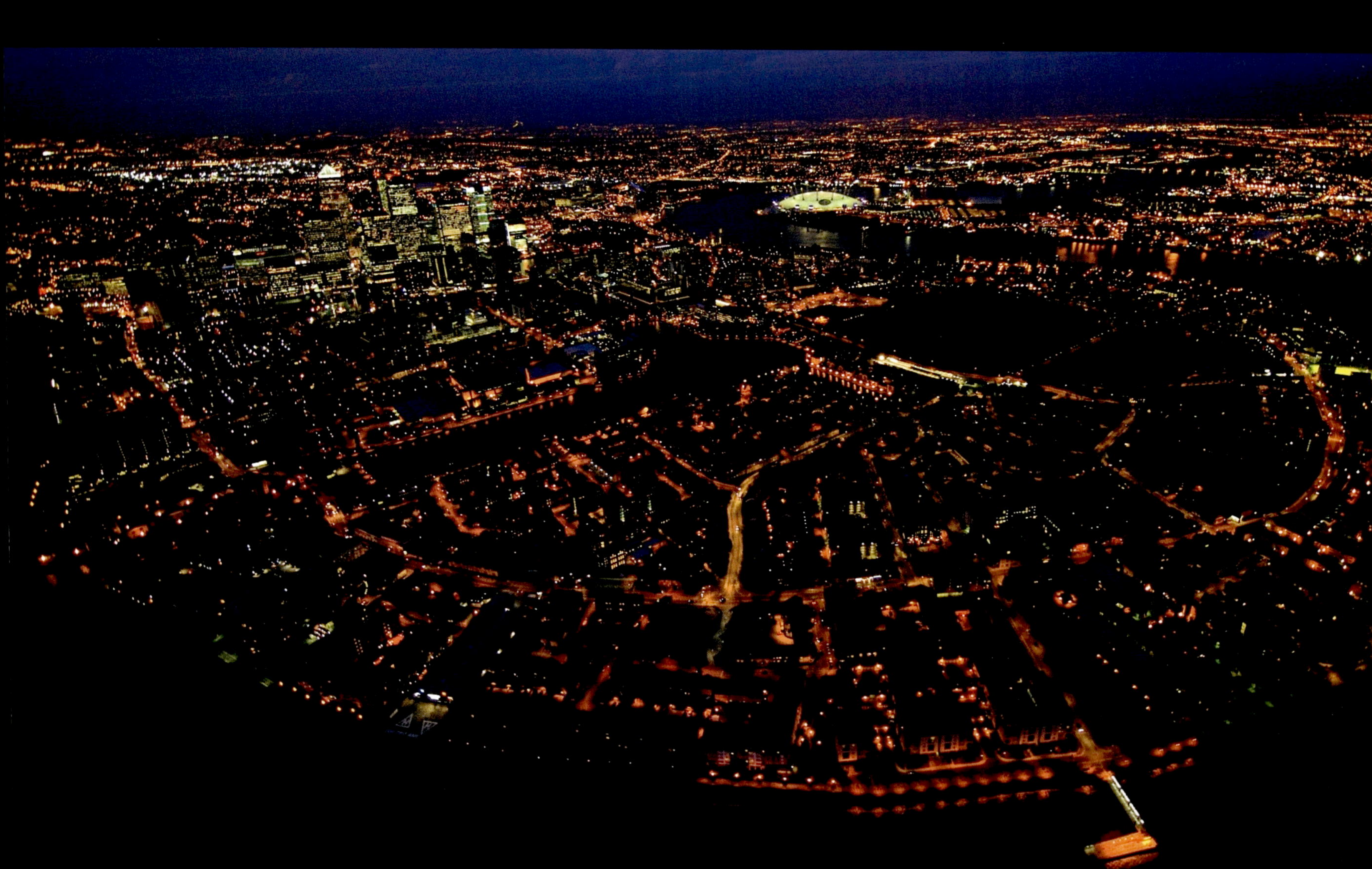

The public park of Island Gardens, at the
southern tip of the Isle of Dogs, was laid out
in 1895, and has fine views across the river to
Greenwich. The Greenwich Foot Tunnel comes out
here via a long, winding staircase underneath a
dome. The southern tip of Millwall Park and Island
Gardens DLR station are visible at the left-hand
side of the photograph.

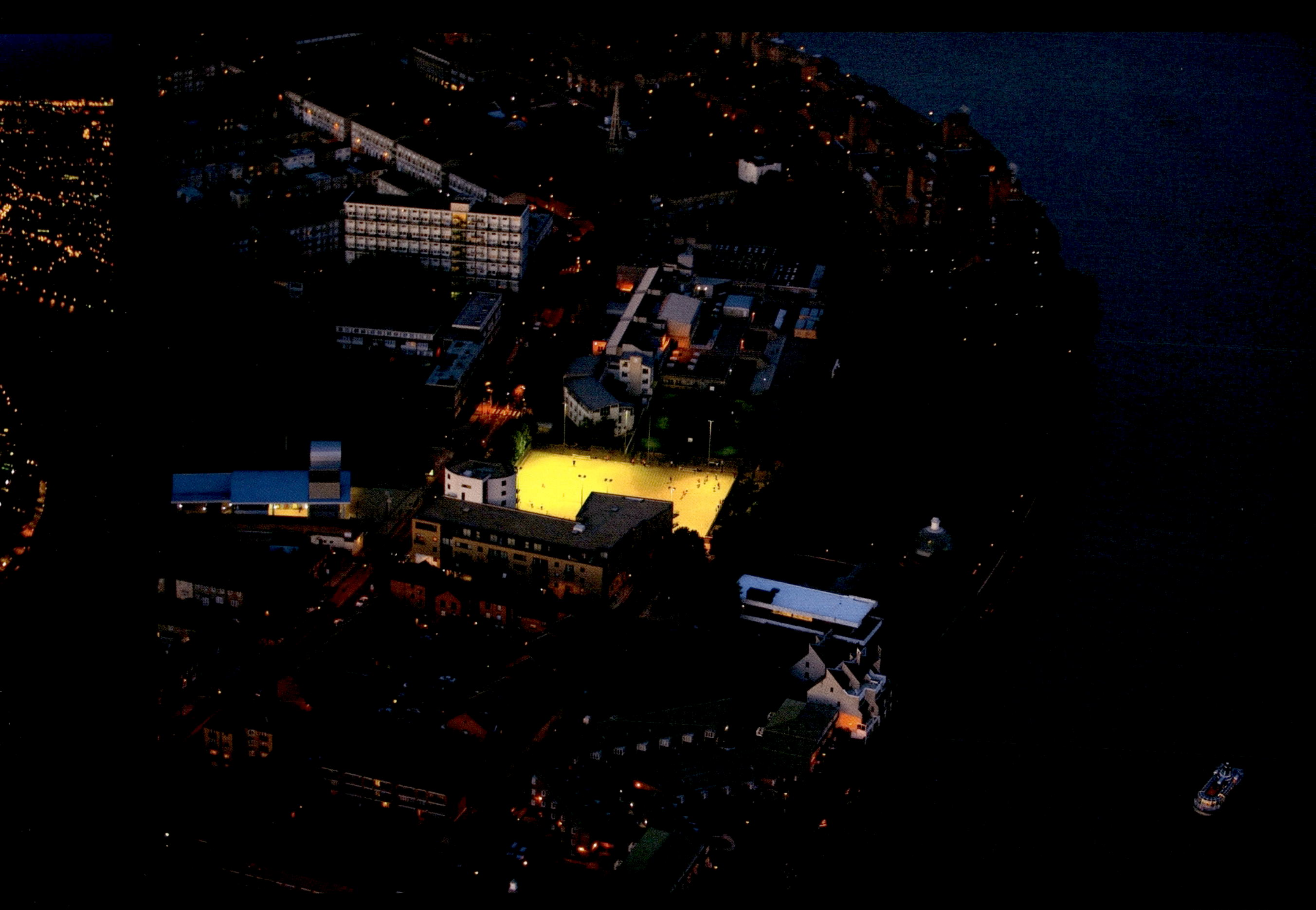

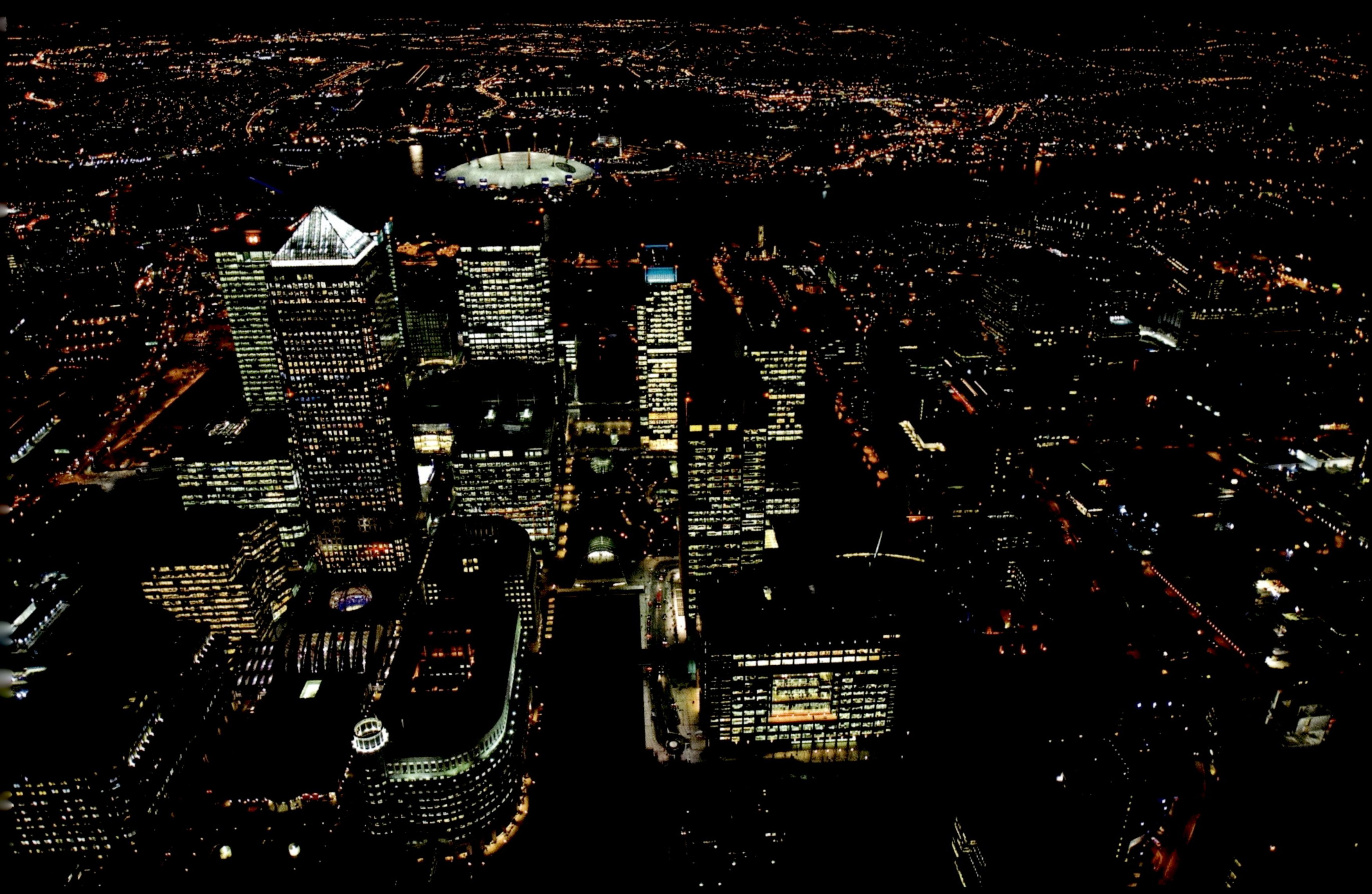

West India Docks were opened in 1802, part
of a process that would make London the
biggest port in the world by the late nineteenth
century. The docks were designed by William
Jessop, the engineer of the Grand Union Canal.
The three parallel basins were later colonized
by two waves of office construction, in the
1980s and the 1990s.

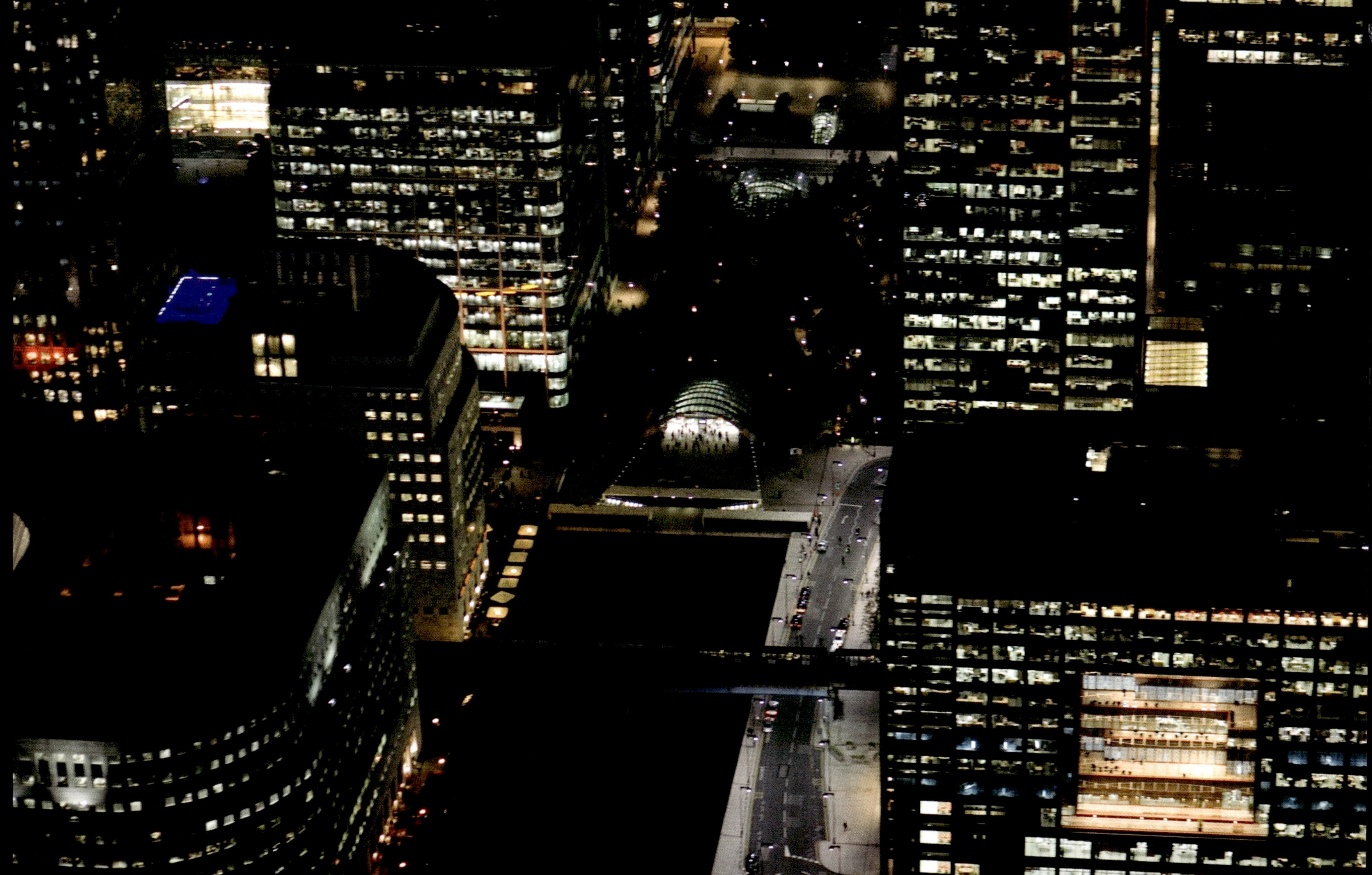

Crucial to the development of Canada Square
was supporting infrastructure. The Jubilee
line extension, completed in 2000, served
Foster + Partners' new station of Canary
Wharf, constructed in a filled-in arm of the
dock. Despite having little presence above
ground – just three glazed canopies set in
landscaped gardens – it is as long internally
as One Canada Square is tall, and handles
up to 70,000 passengers a day.

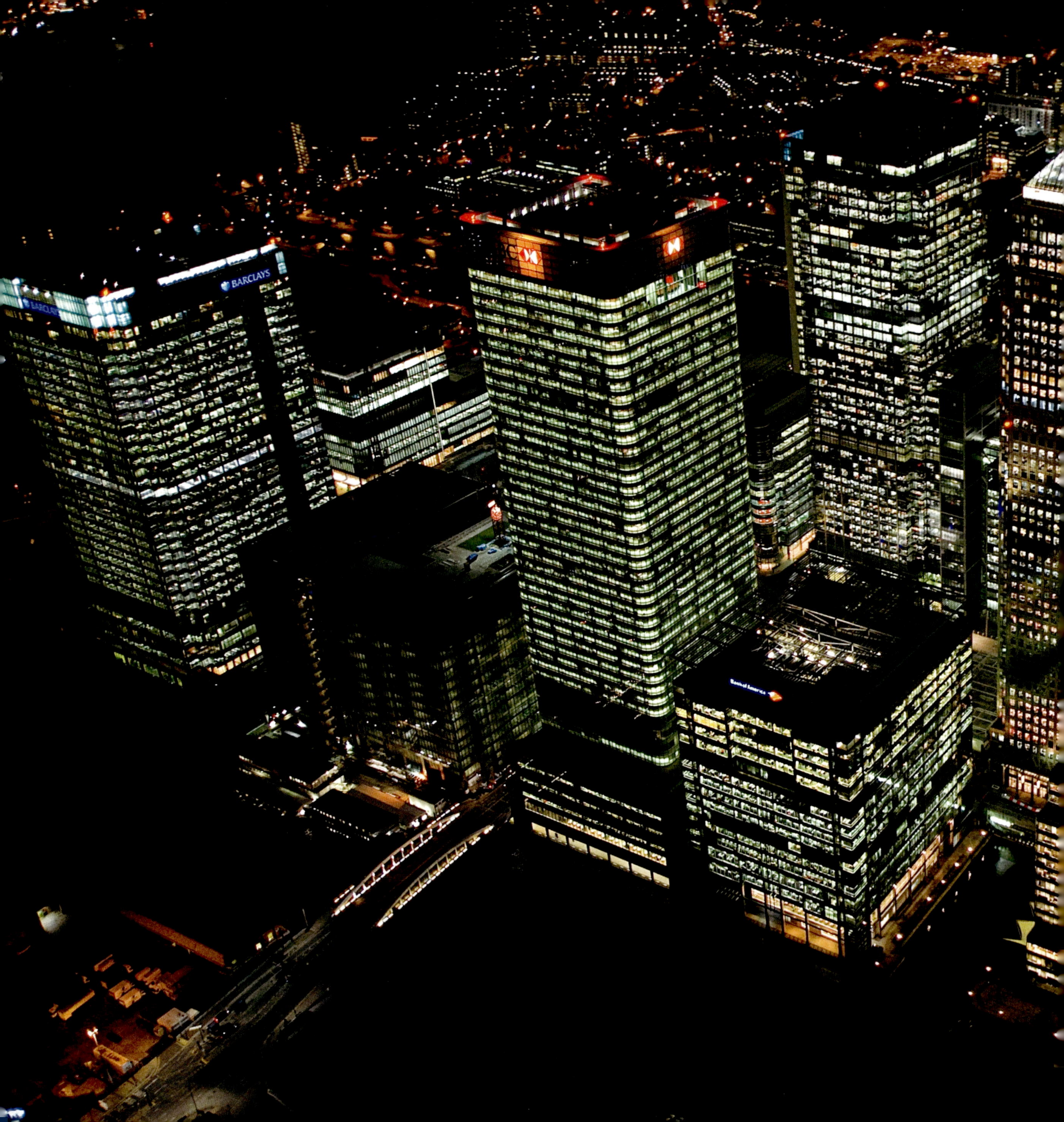

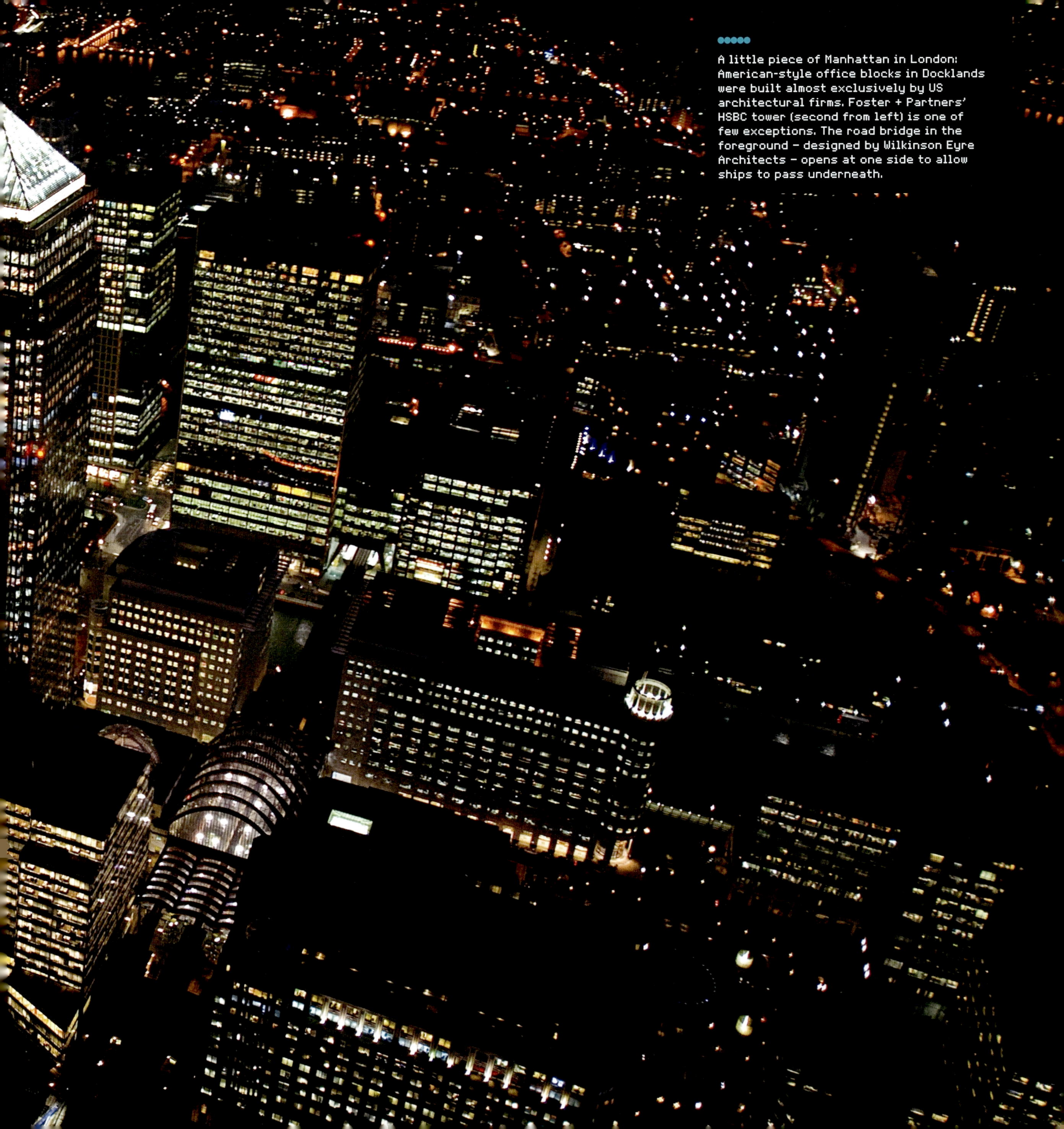

A little piece of Manhattan in London:
American-style office blocks in Docklands
were built almost exclusively by US
architectural firms. Foster + Partners'
HSBC tower (second from left) is one of
few exceptions. The road bridge in the
foreground – designed by Wilkinson Eyre
Architects – opens at one side to allow
ships to pass underneath.

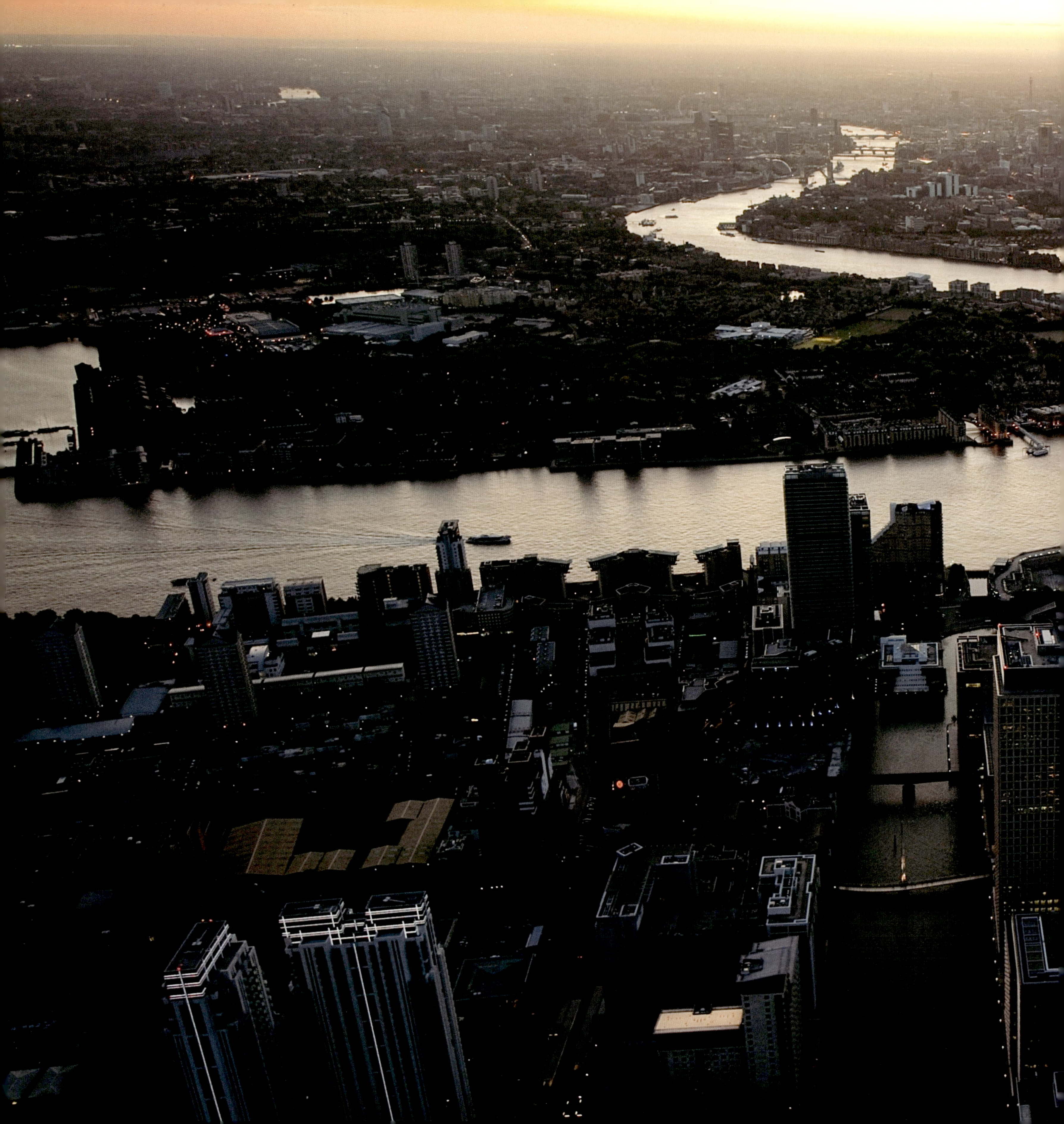

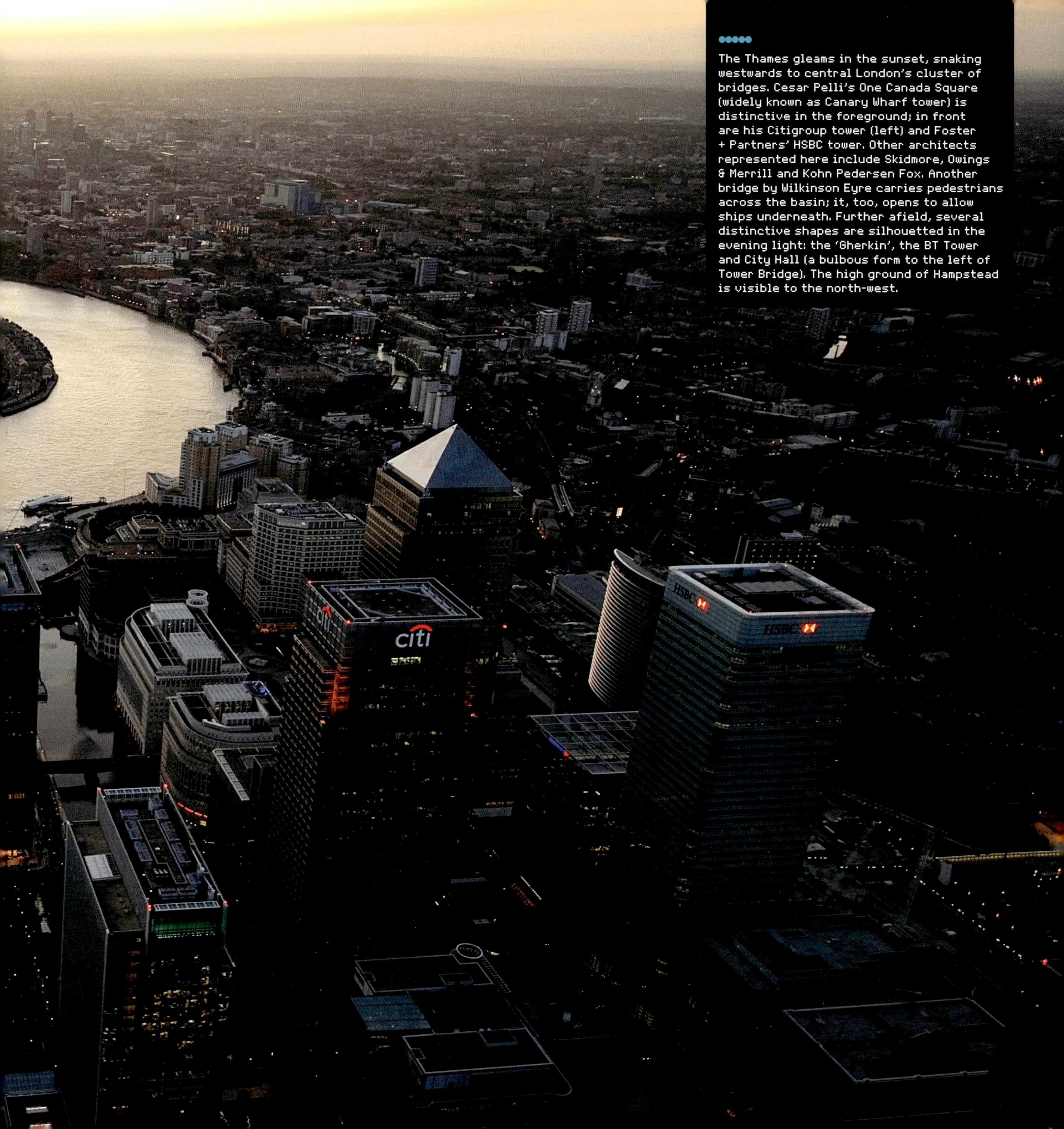

The Thames gleams in the sunset, snaking westwards to central London's cluster of bridges. Cesar Pelli's One Canada Square (widely known as Canary Wharf tower) is distinctive in the foreground; in front are his Citigroup tower (left) and Foster + Partners' HSBC tower. Other architects represented here include Skidmore, Owings & Merrill and Kohn Pedersen Fox. Another bridge by Wilkinson Eyre carries pedestrians across the basin; it, too, opens to allow ships underneath. Further afield, several distinctive shapes are silhouetted in the evening light: the 'Gherkin', the BT Tower and City Hall (a bulbous form to the left of Tower Bridge). The high ground of Hampstead is visible to the north-west.

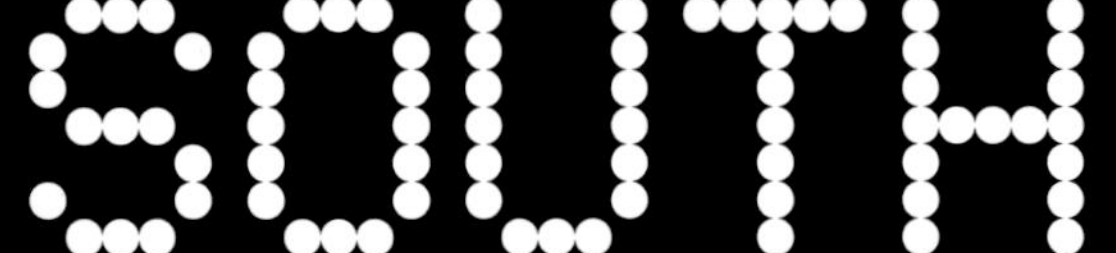

SOUTH

'South of the river' is a foreign country for north Londoners, but the real London for those who live there. The river is a very visible boundary, and the Borough, the heart of ancient Southwark, was traditionally the City's back yard, where undesirable activities (prostitution, the theatre, polluting industries) were concentrated. Today, however, the boundary is less clearly defined. Encouraged by the opening of the Jubilee line extension and the Thameslink rail service (now run by First Capital Connect), developers have realized that the south side of the Thames is a good location for offices; the success of More London (with London's City Hall) has opened the way for other projects, none more spectacular than Renzo Piano's 'Shard', under construction and set to become London's tallest building. Yards away, Southwark Cathedral is one of the most significant medieval buildings left in London. Close by are Borough Market and Bankside, with the reconstructed Globe Theatre, and, beyond Southwark Bridge, Tate Modern, housed in the former Bankside Power Station and linked to the City by a new bridge briefly famous for its 'wobble'.

The cultural belt of the South Bank continues past the National Theatre and the Southbank arts centre, with the London Eye providing less challenging entertainment. All this is impressive, but the massive project to reconstruct the Elephant and Castle, once 'the Piccadilly Circus of south London', has been slow to take off (although it is now happening). Beyond the densely packed streets of Walworth and Bermondsey, south London is a place of open skies and green spaces, parks and commons and spacious suburban gardens. London's greatest Victorian monument, the Crystal Palace (which gave its name to the surrounding area), has long vanished, but one of the greatest monuments of the inter-war era, Battersea Power Station, still stands, at the centre of a huge expanse of derelict land. It would have made a spectacular new home for the Science Museum, but still awaits a viable commercial development package to ensure its survival. It is hard to imagine London without it.

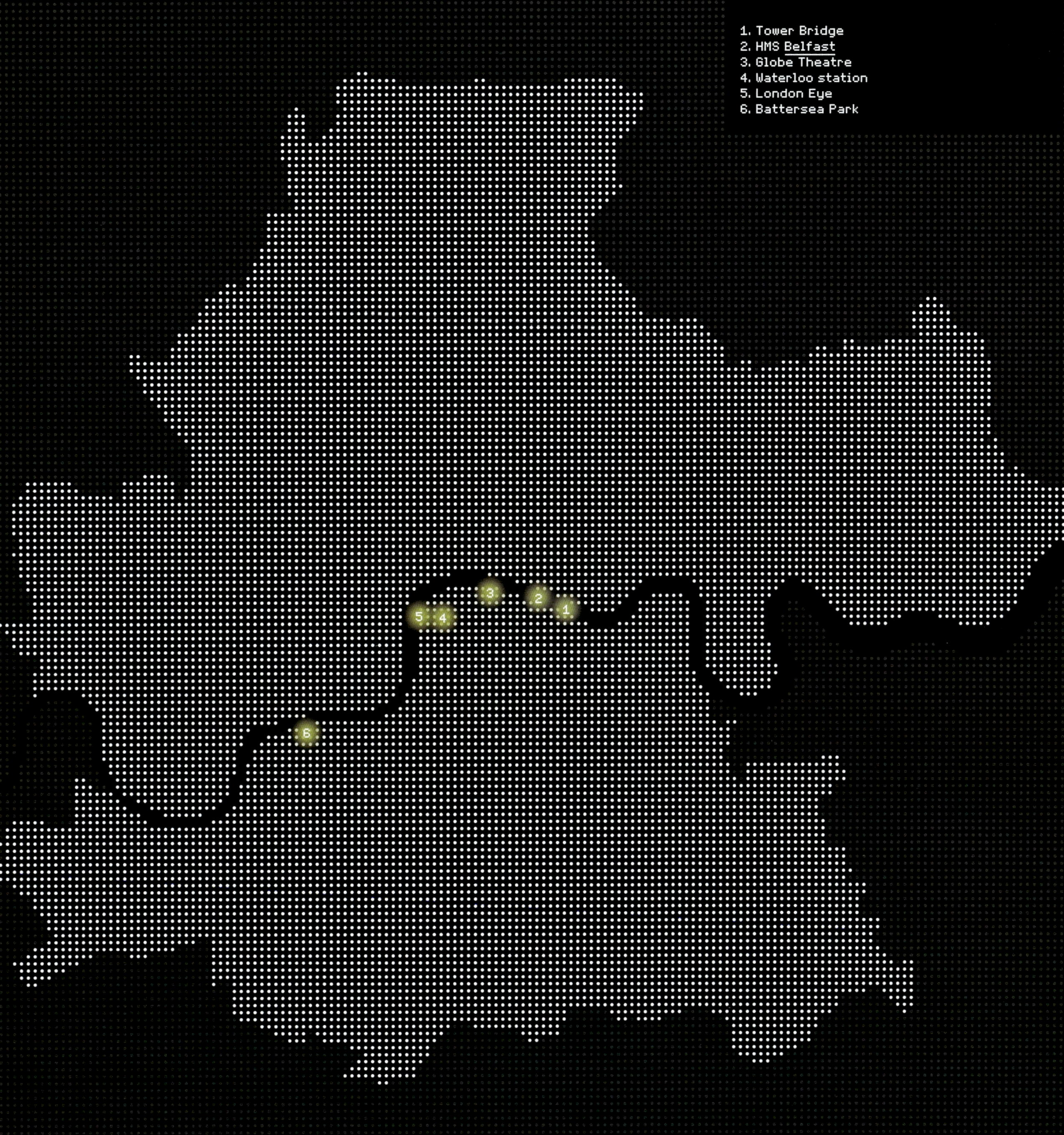

1. Tower Bridge
2. HMS Belfast
3. Globe Theatre
4. Waterloo station
5. London Eye
6. Battersea Park

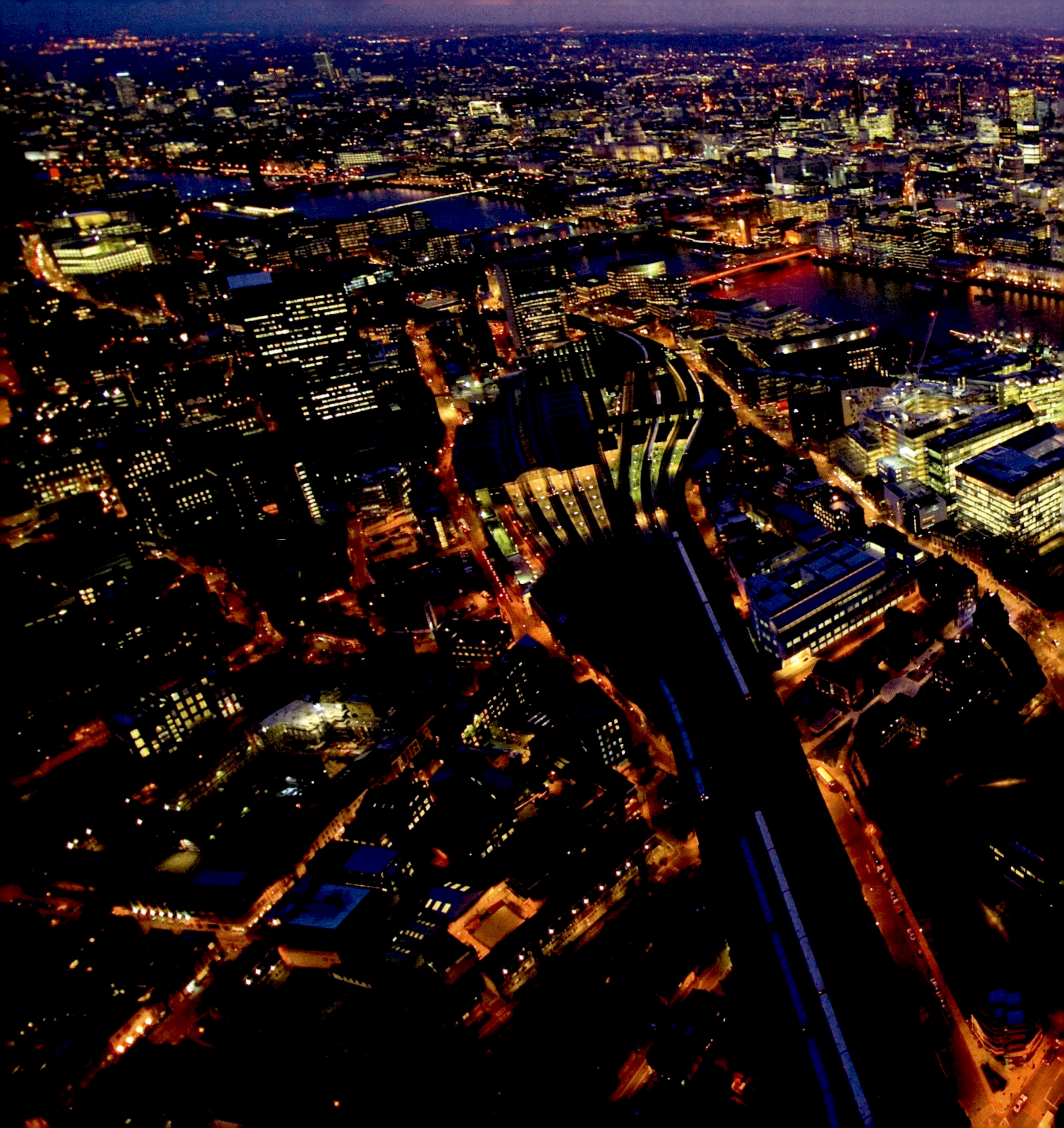

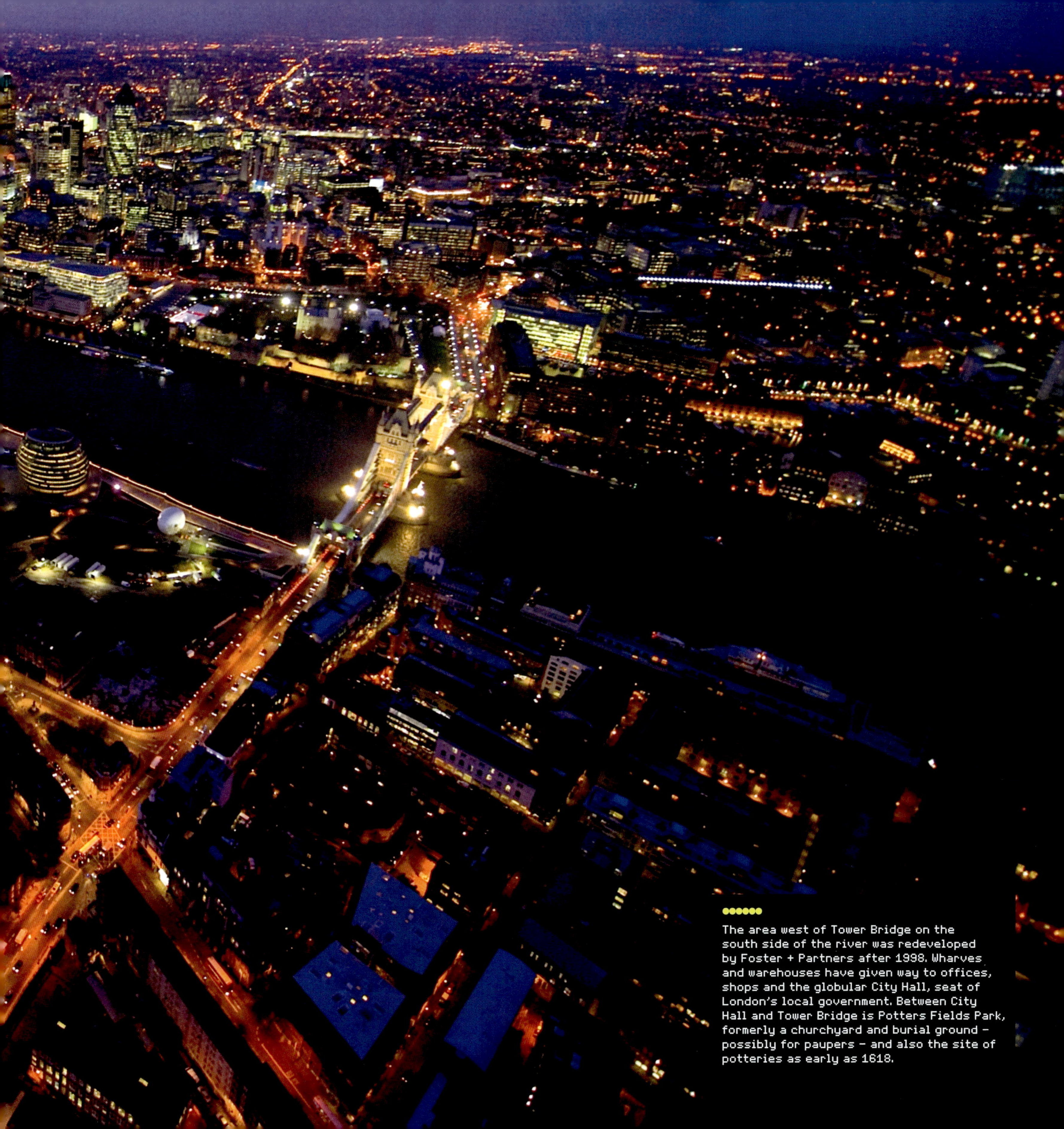

The area west of Tower Bridge on the
south side of the river was redeveloped
by Foster + Partners after 1998. Wharves
and warehouses have given way to offices,
shops and the globular City Hall, seat of
London's local government. Between City
Hall and Tower Bridge is Potters Fields Park,
formerly a churchyard and burial ground –
possibly for paupers – and also the site of
potteries as early as 1618.

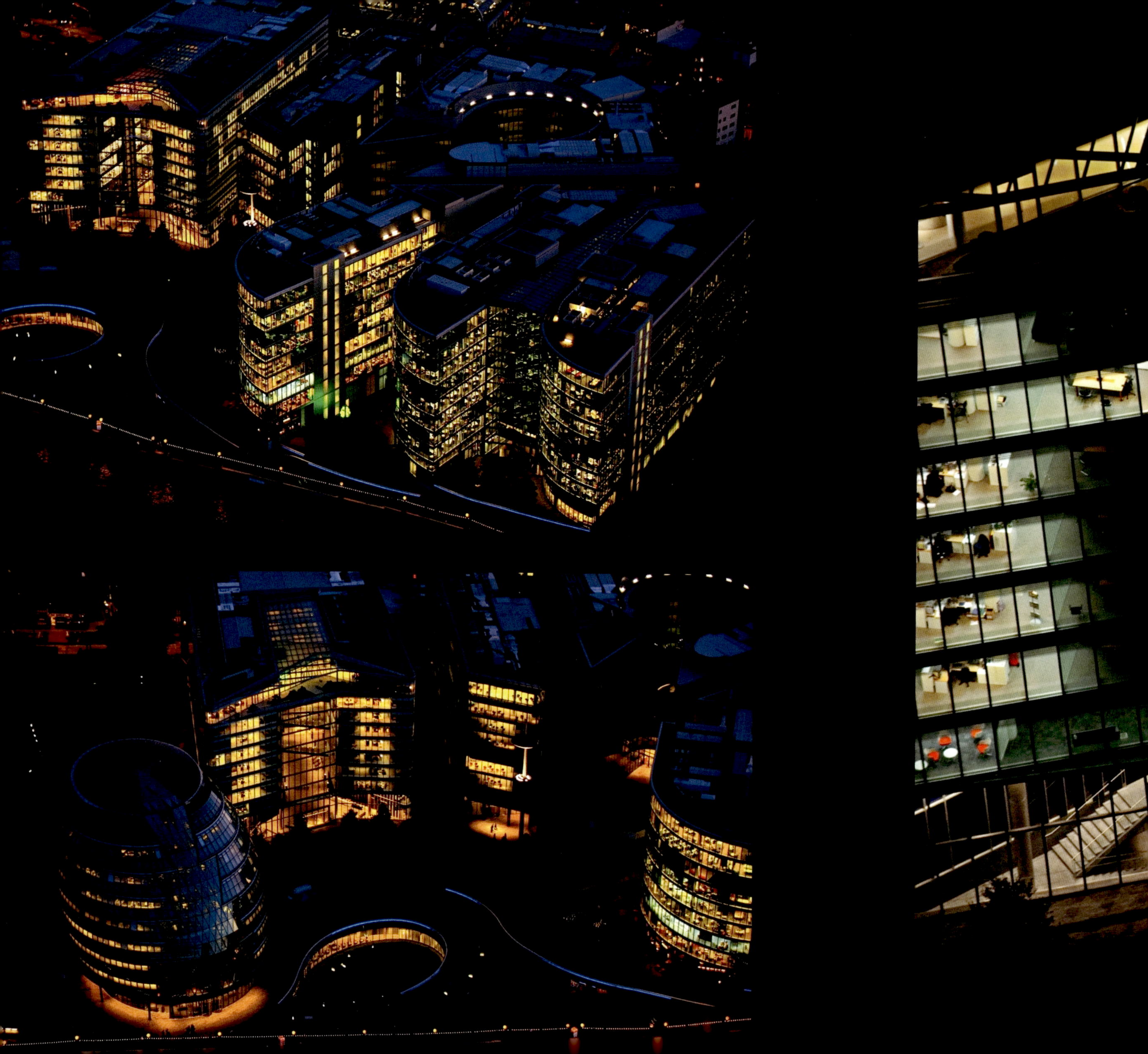

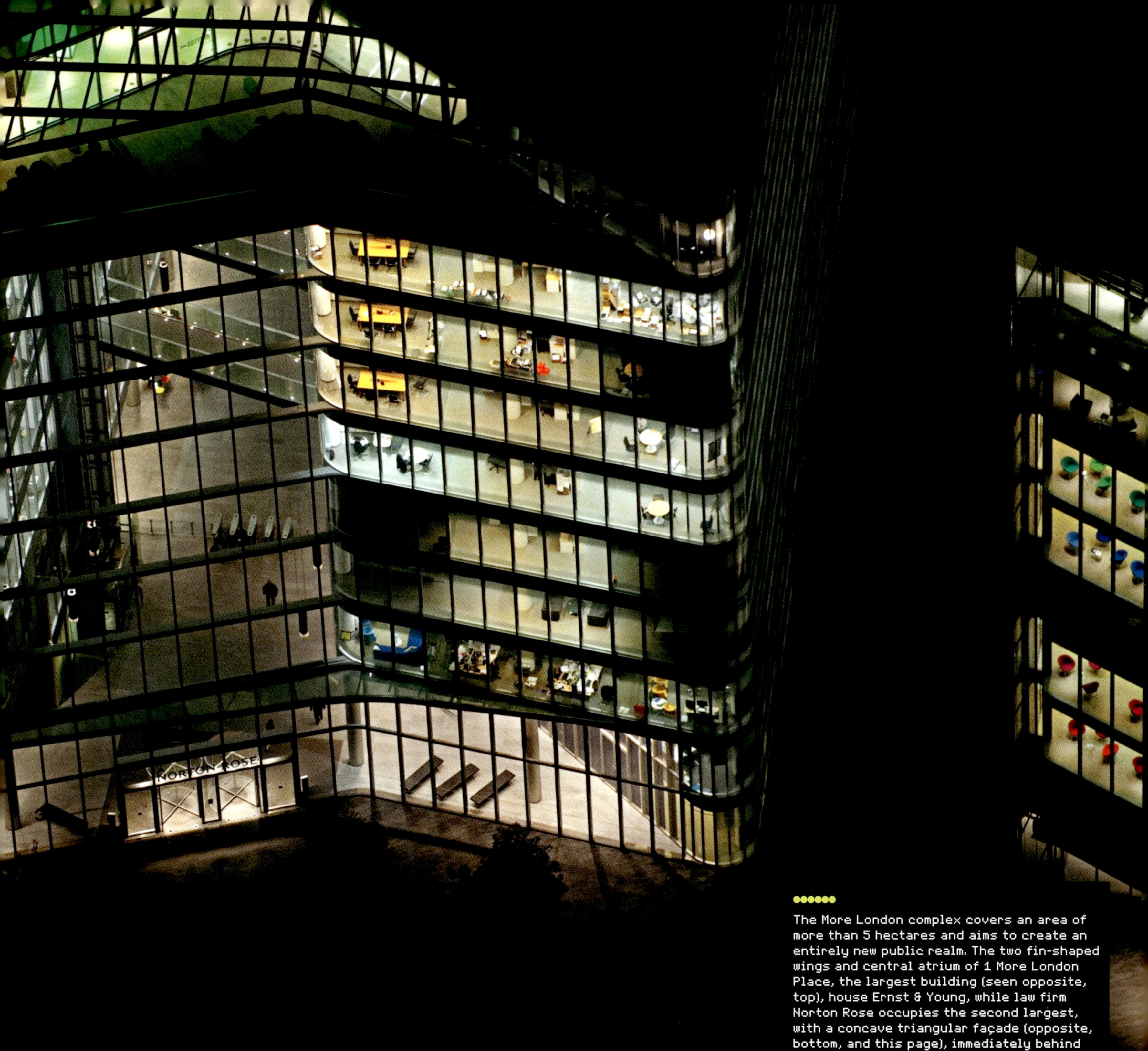

●●●●●●
The More London complex covers an area of
more than 5 hectares and aims to create an
entirely new public realm. The two fin-shaped
wings and central atrium of 1 More London
Place, the largest building (seen opposite,
top), house Ernst & Young, while law firm
Norton Rose occupies the second largest,
with a concave triangular façade (opposite,
bottom, and this page), immediately behind
City Hall. A sunken amphitheatre called the
Scoop plays host to free theatre, dance
and music events.

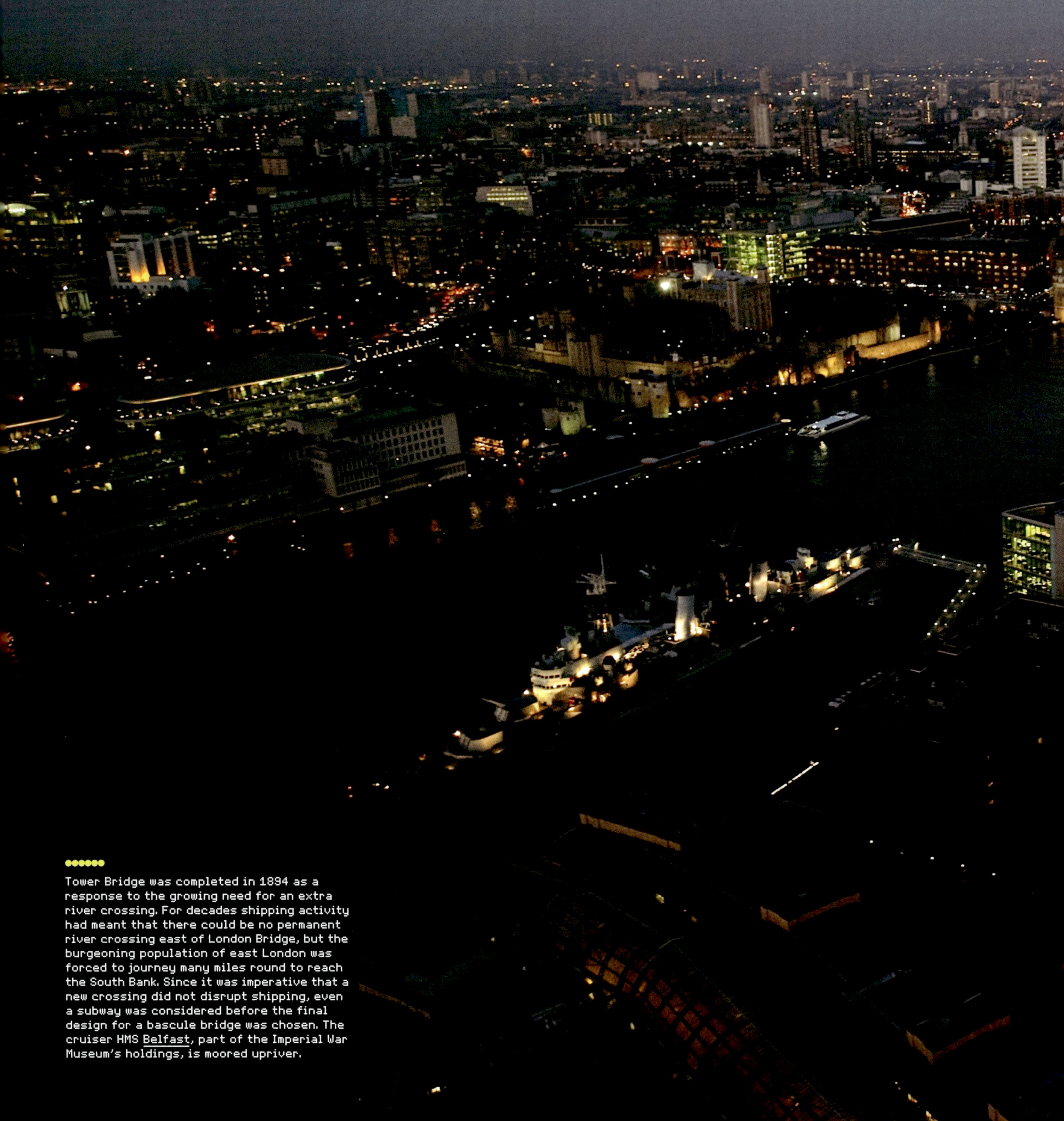

Tower Bridge was completed in 1894 as a
response to the growing need for an extra
river crossing. For decades shipping activity
had meant that there could be no permanent
river crossing east of London Bridge, but the
burgeoning population of east London was
forced to journey many miles round to reach
the South Bank. Since it was imperative that a
new crossing did not disrupt shipping, even
a subway was considered before the final
design for a bascule bridge was chosen. The
cruiser HMS Belfast, part of the Imperial War
Museum's holdings, is moored upriver.

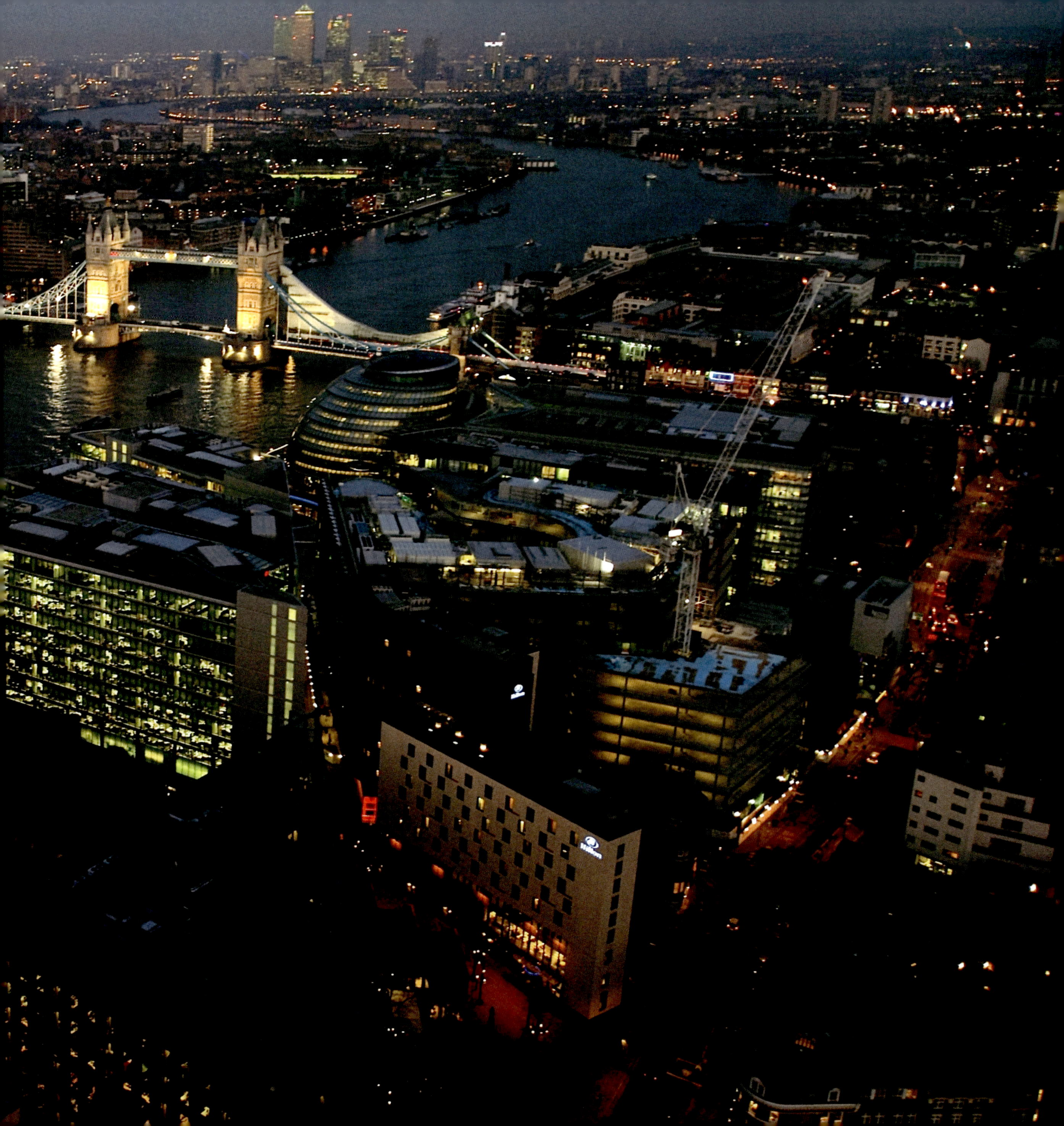

↓ From above, the dark skein of railway lines
is clearer than the brightly lit roads. This
triangular junction carries tracks over viaducts
to and from London Bridge, Cannon Street,
Blackfriars and Waterloo East stations.

→ A fire at Breams Buildings in Chancery
Lane on 18 March 2009 sends smoke into
the evening sky. New London Bridge House
(in the foreground), a rather short-sightedly
named office tower dating from the 1970s,
has now been demolished to make way for
Renzo Piano's 'Shard' (see overleaf).

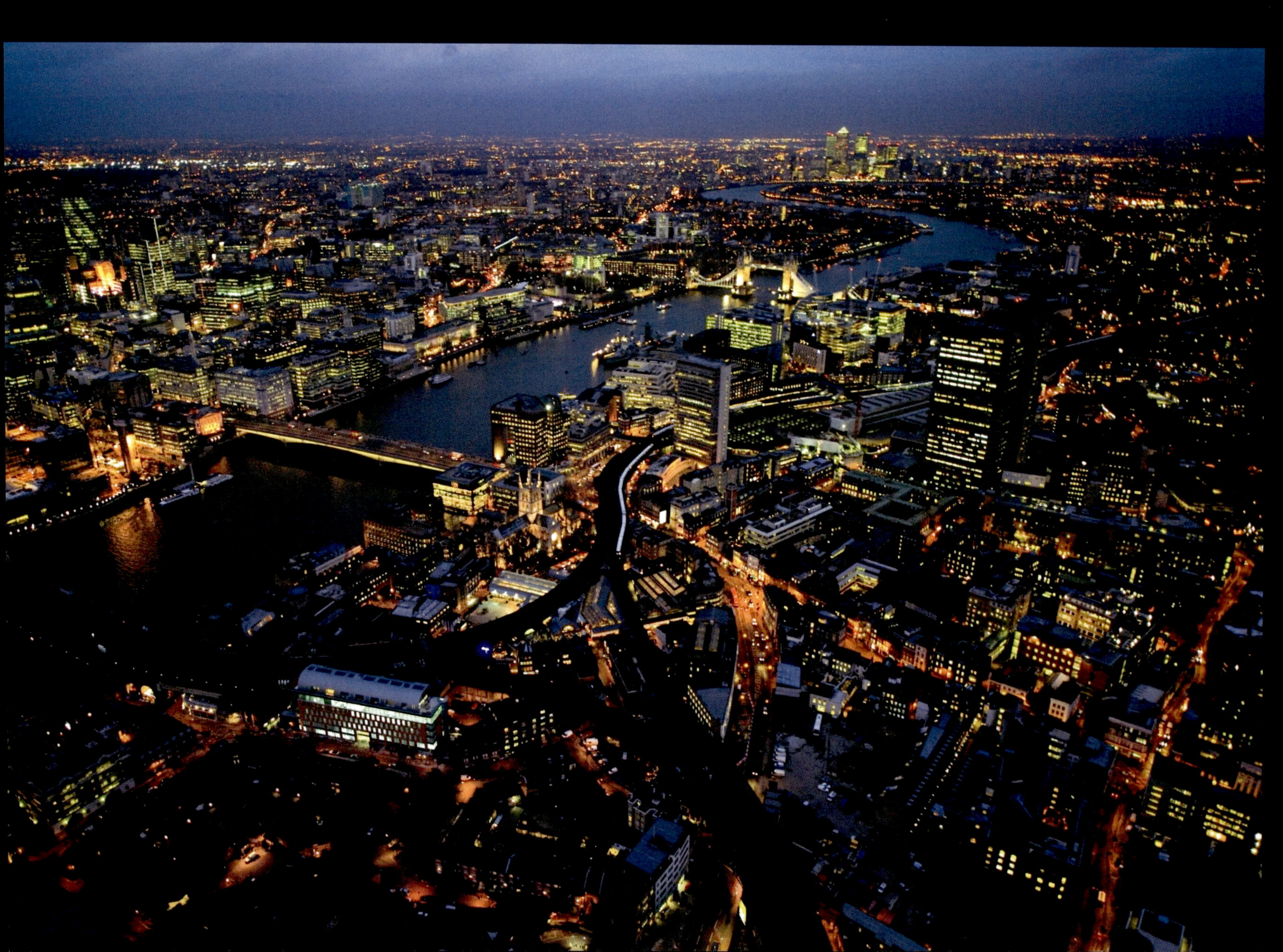

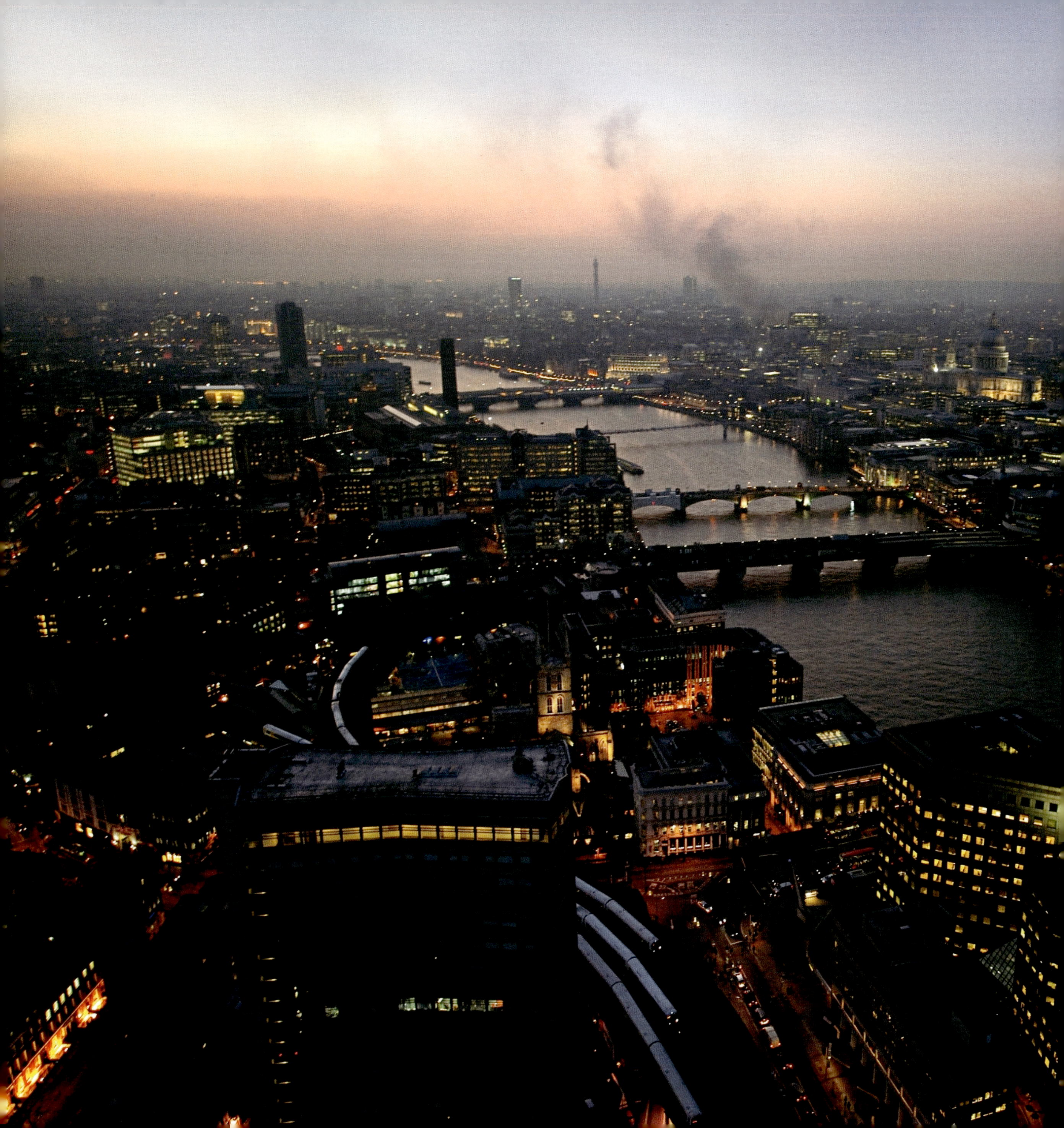

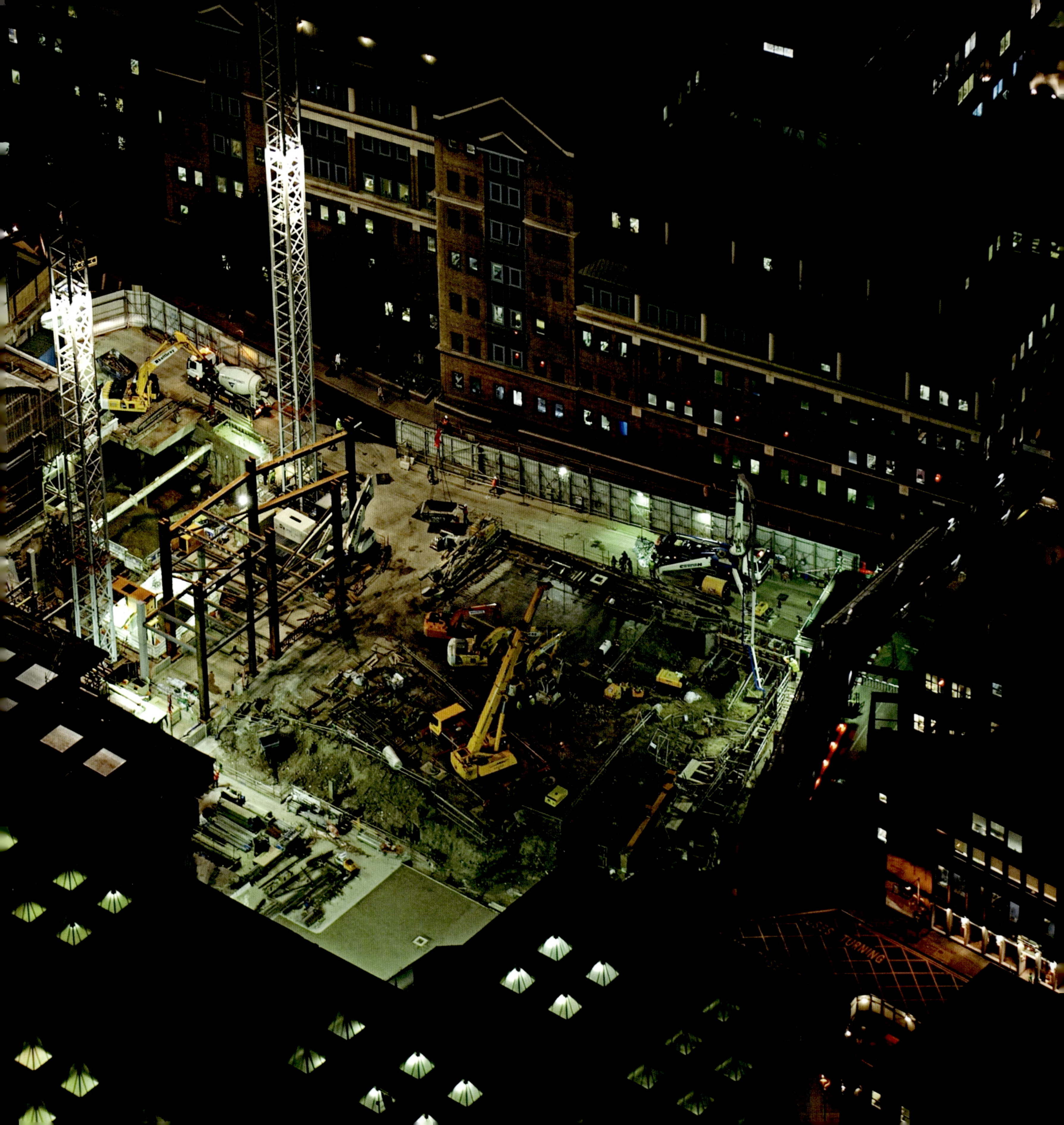

← From a site apparently no bigger than a postage stamp will rise London's tallest tower yet, and the highest in the UK. At 306 metres, London Bridge Tower (better known as the Shard), by Renzo Piano Building Workshop, will contain a 'vertical city' of offices, flats, shops and a hotel. Associated with its construction will be the refurbishment of London Bridge station, which serves around 42 million people a year.

→ Southwark Cathedral is marooned in a tangle of nineteenth-century railway viaducts. Once an Augustinian priory, it is the second most important medieval monument south of the river (the first being Lambeth Palace). It has been much rebuilt and extended and, as a result, contains parts dating from almost every century since its foundation in 1106.

→ The reconstructed Globe Theatre is a reminder of the former lively nature of Southwark, with its theatres, bear-baiting rings and prisons. The new theatre, opened in the 1990s, was founded by actor and director Sam Wanamaker. Although tall by the standards of sixteenth-century London, the structure's tiny scale by neighbouring office blocks is surprising. Riverside House (1966) by Southwark Bridge is a survival of an older era of building in the area; its refurbishment in 2002 led to the construction of two extra floors, the whole stabilized by a curious curved exoskeleton.

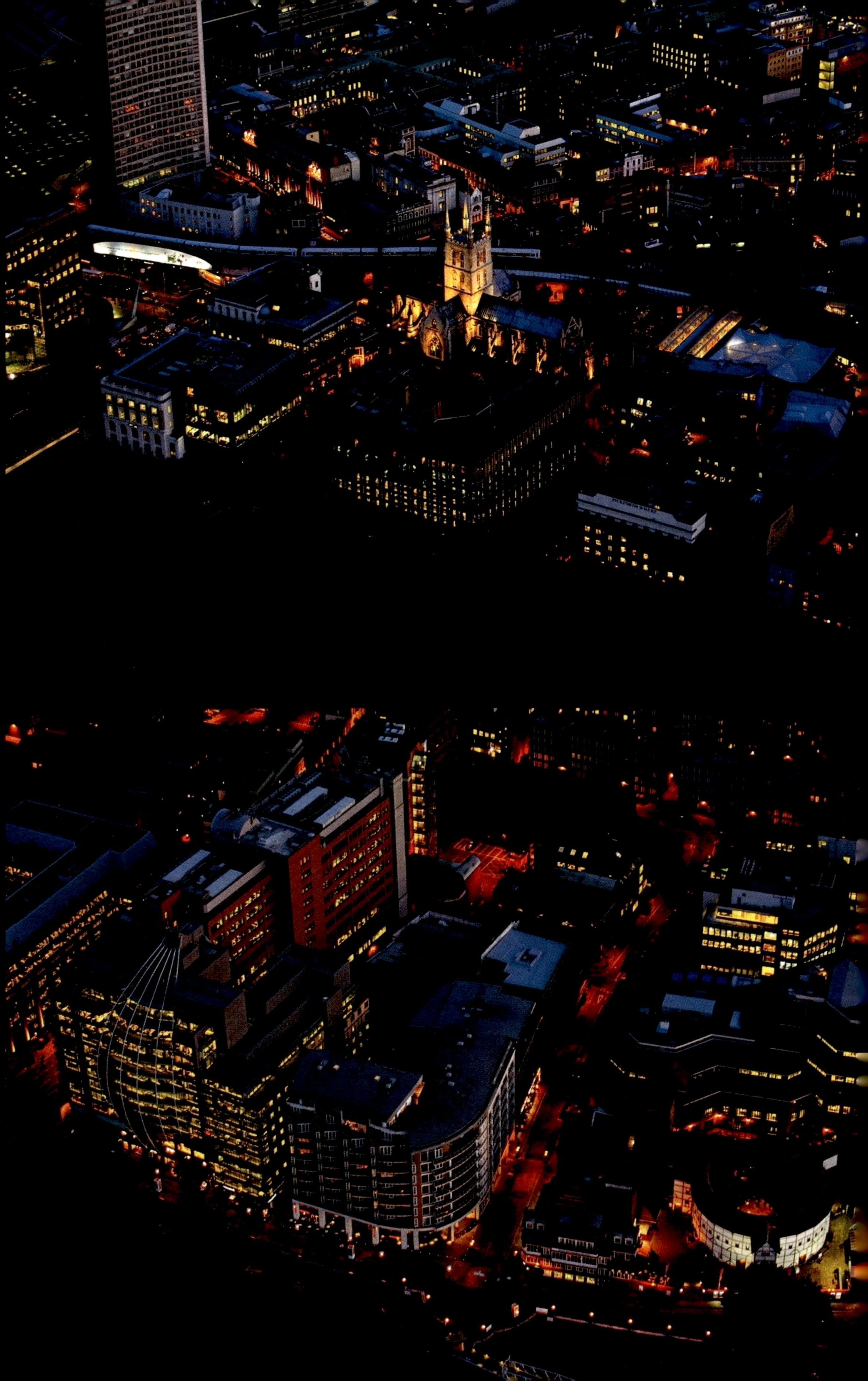

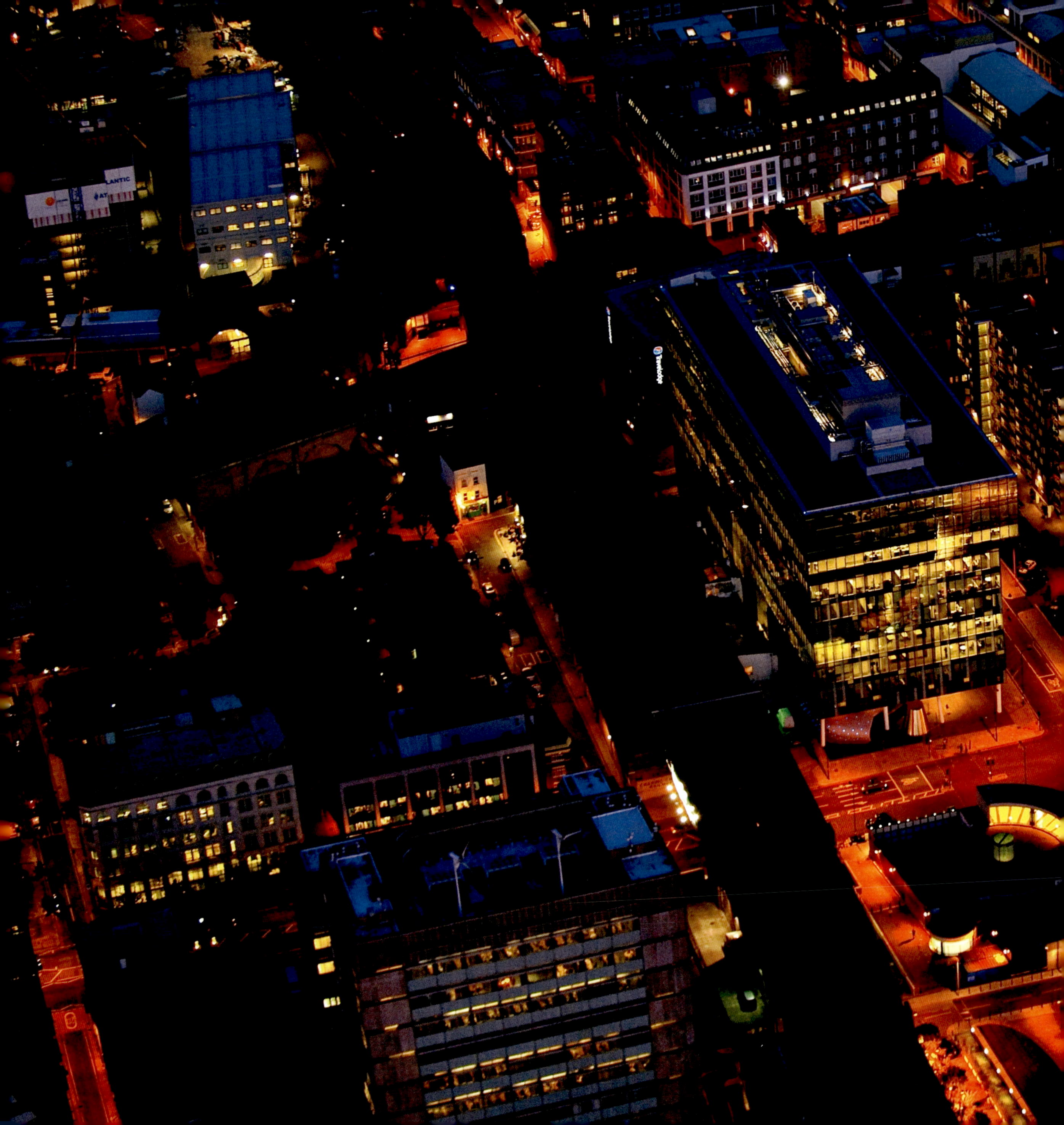

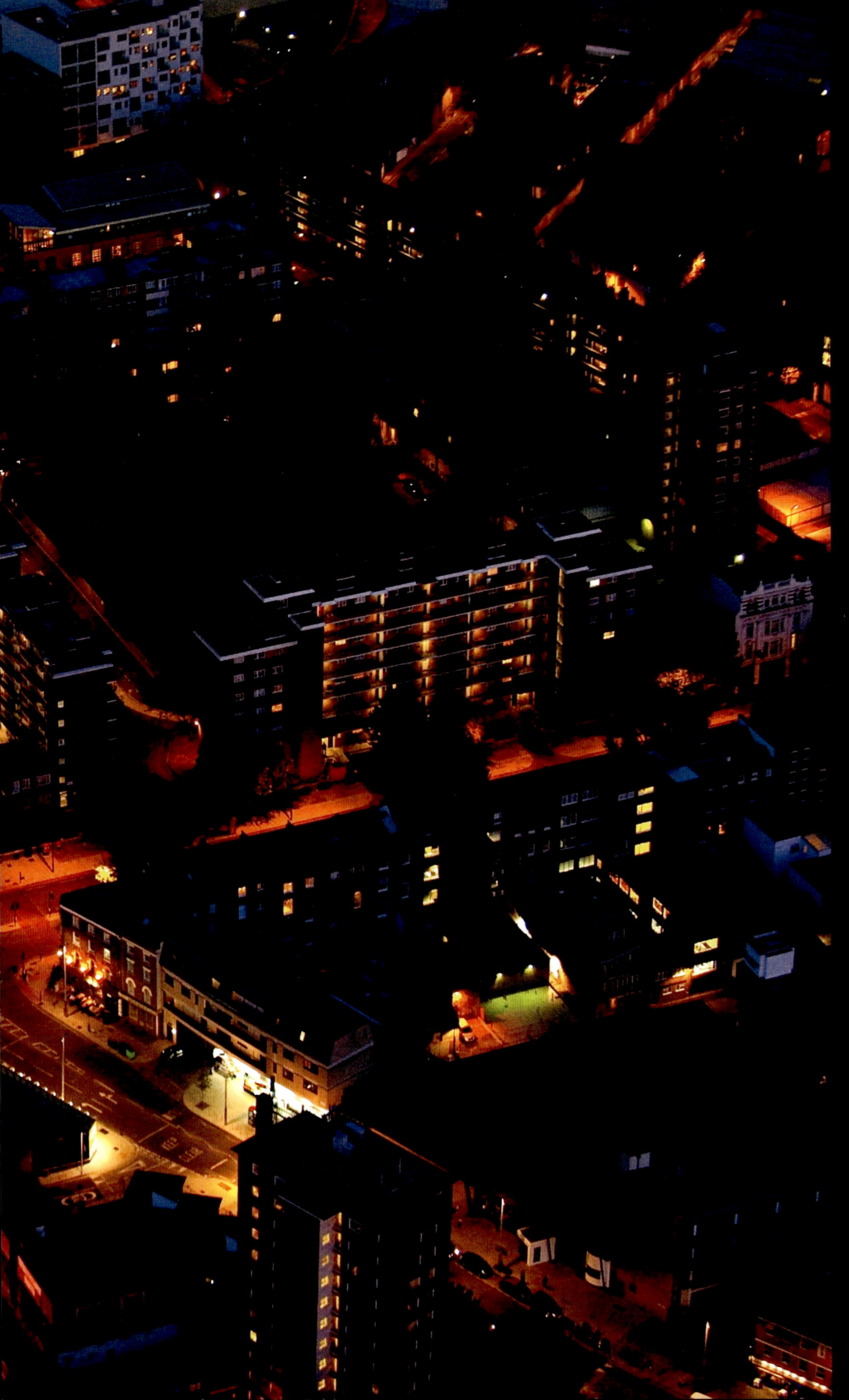

••••••
The area between Elephant and Castle and the
river was revitalized by the coming of the
Jubilee line in 1999. Palestra, an immense office
block by SMC Alsop, looms over the eastern end of
the Cut. Its top-heavy design makes it a powerful
addition to the streetscape, which – mid-
development – is still an uncomfortable mix of
council estates, non-descript office buildings,
new blocks of flats and isolated old pubs.

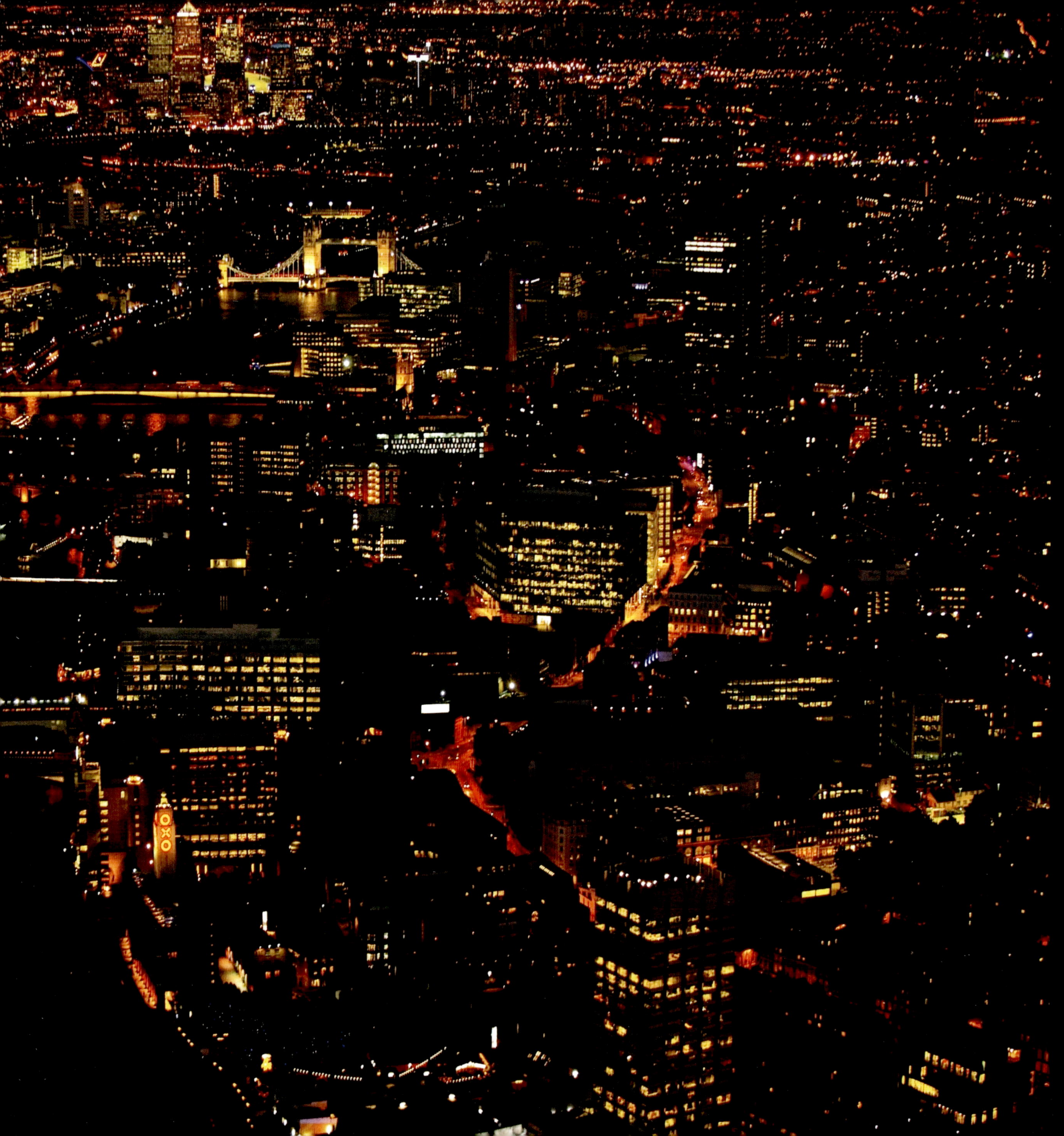

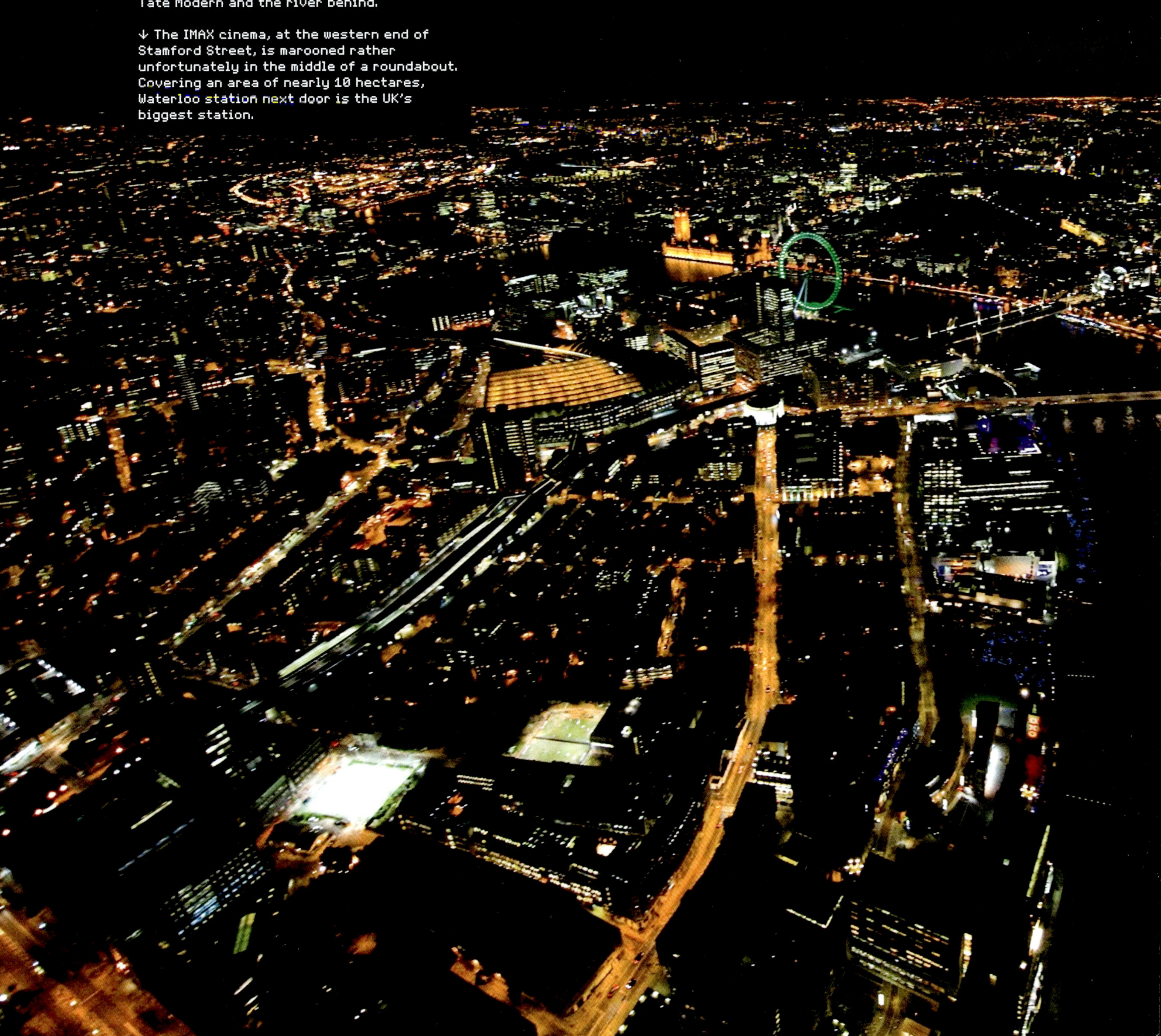
Tate Modern and the river behind.

↓ The IMAX cinema, at the western end of
Stamford Street, is marooned rather
unfortunately in the middle of a roundabout.
Covering an area of nearly 10 hectares,
Waterloo station next door is the UK's
biggest station.

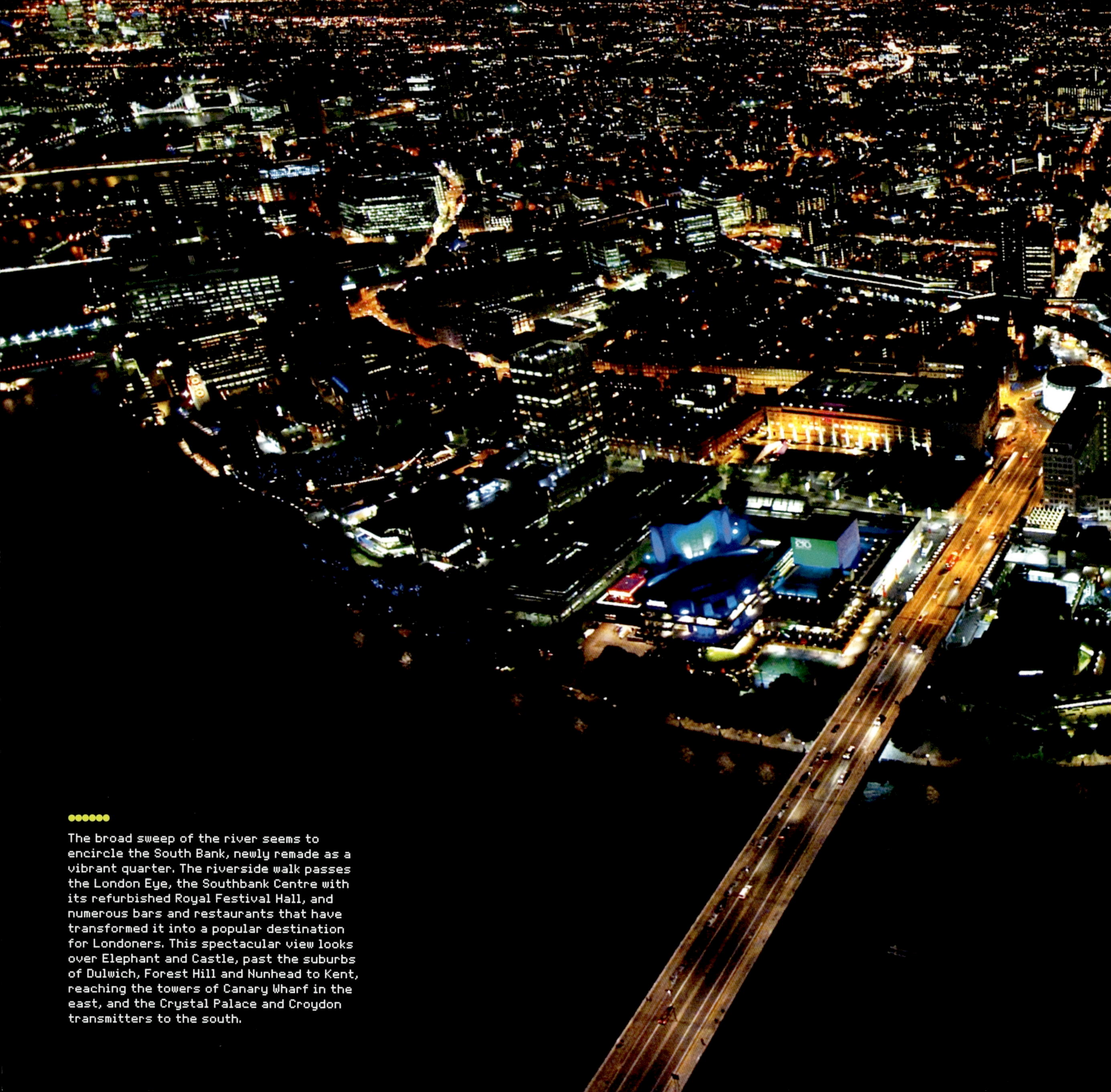

The broad sweep of the river seems to
encircle the South Bank, newly remade as a
vibrant quarter. The riverside walk passes
the London Eye, the Southbank Centre with
its refurbished Royal Festival Hall, and
numerous bars and restaurants that have
transformed it into a popular destination
for Londoners. This spectacular view looks
over Elephant and Castle, past the suburbs
of Dulwich, Forest Hill and Nunhead to Kent,
reaching the towers of Canary Wharf in the
east, and the Crystal Palace and Croydon
transmitters to the south.

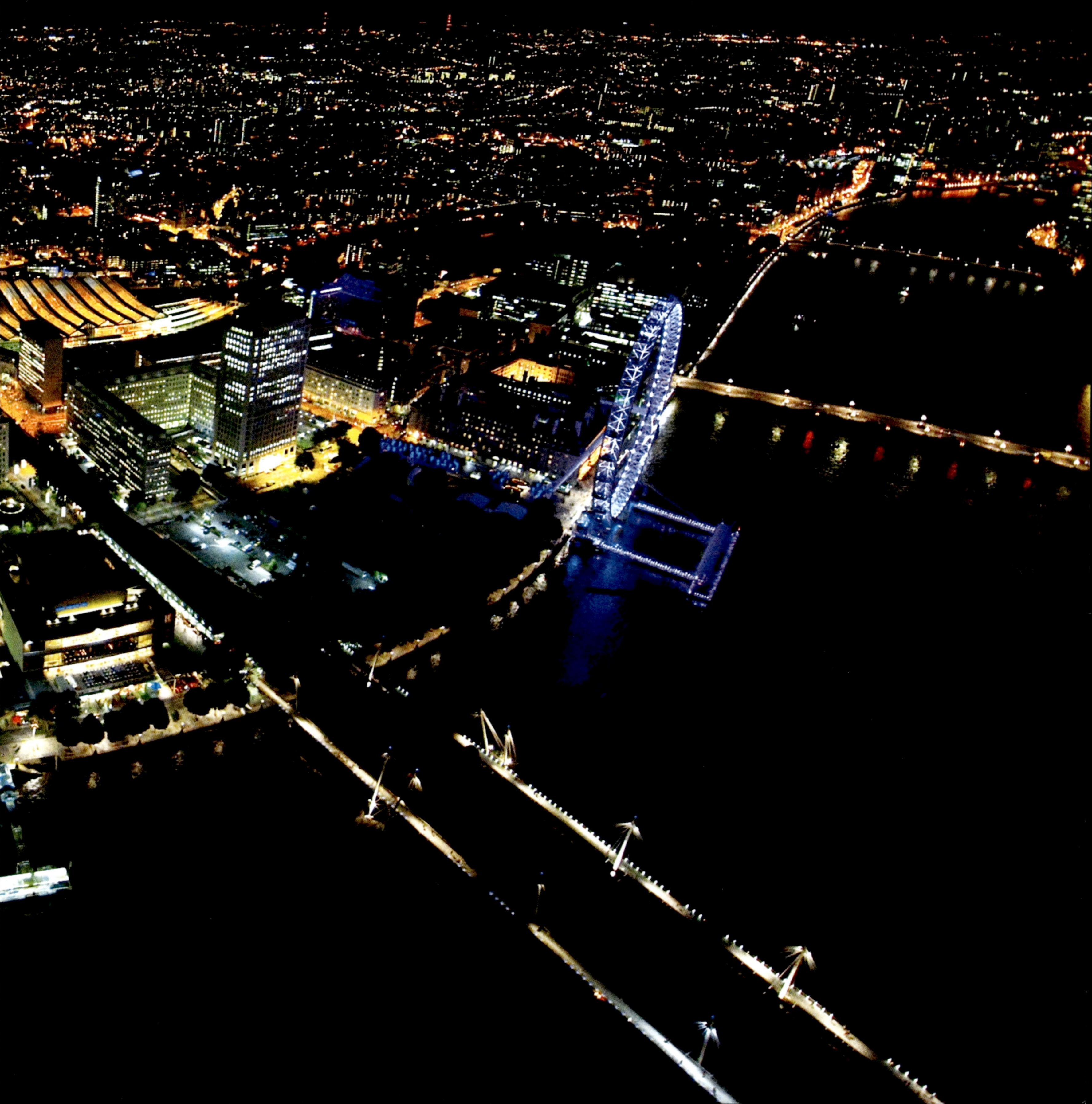

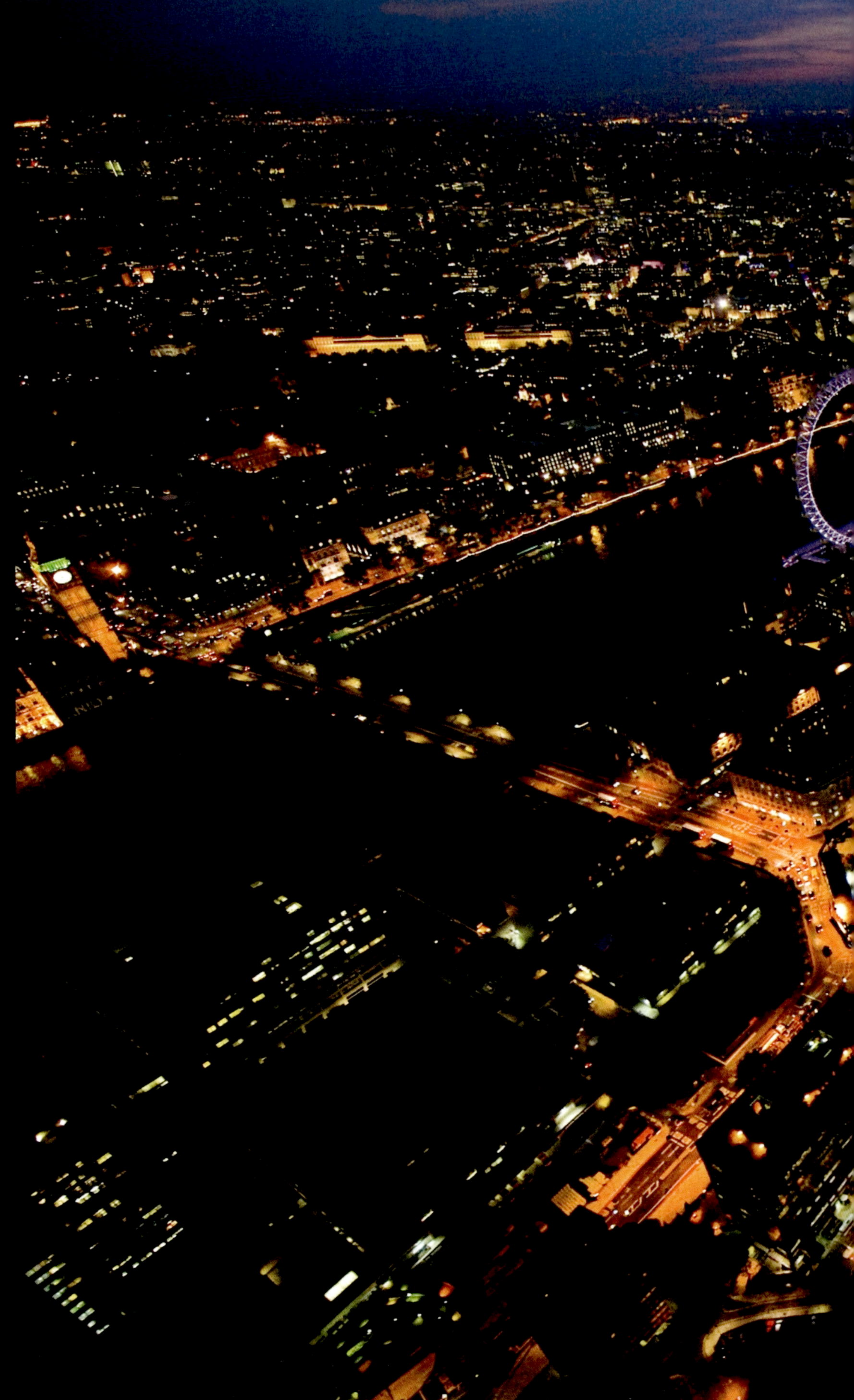

Waterloo station (also overleaf) first opened in 1848; the present structure was built in 1922. The area surrounding the station was once marsh crossed by causeways, and had to be drained before development could begin; this history now survives only in some street names, such as Lower Marsh, which runs alongside the station itself.

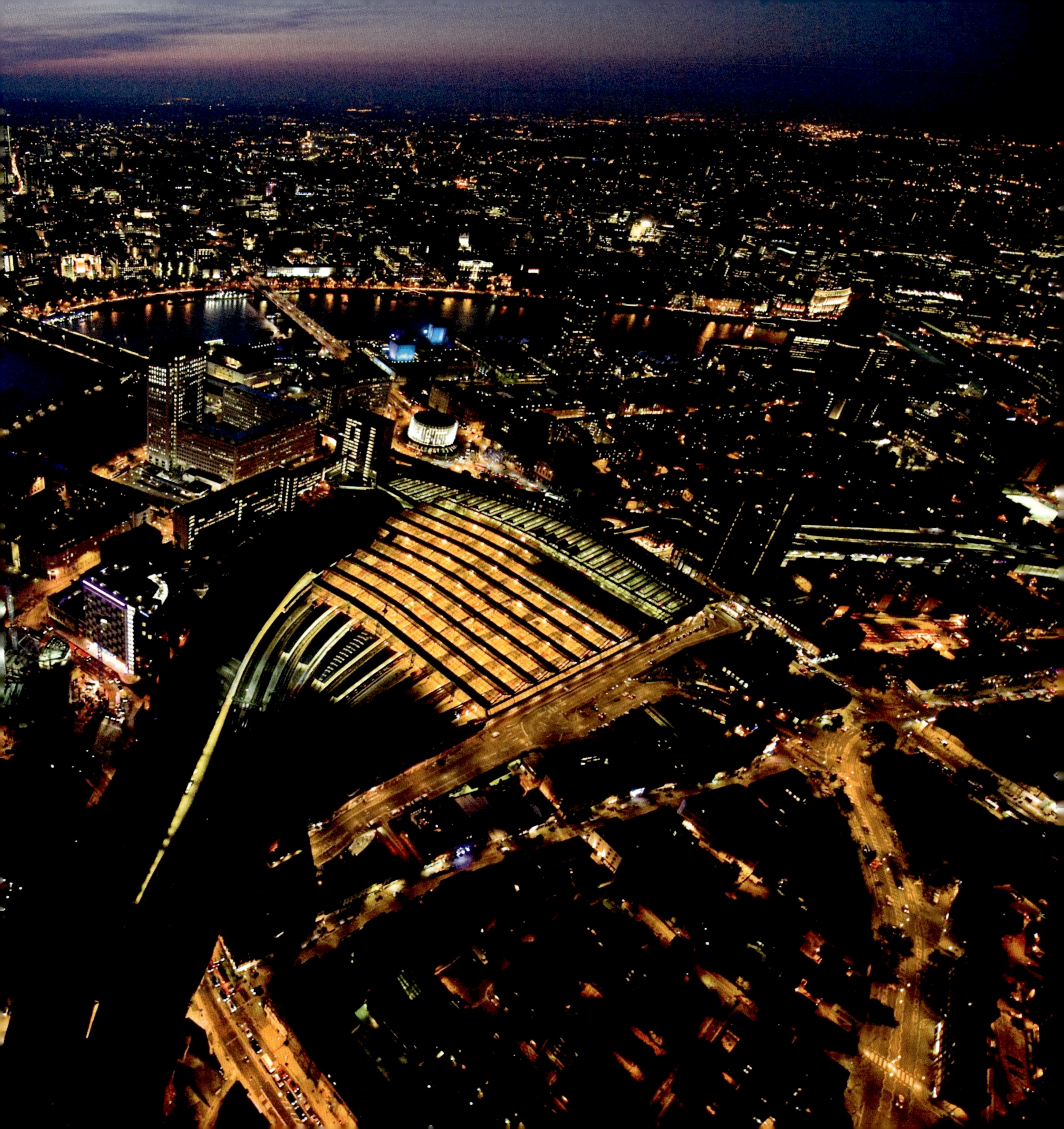

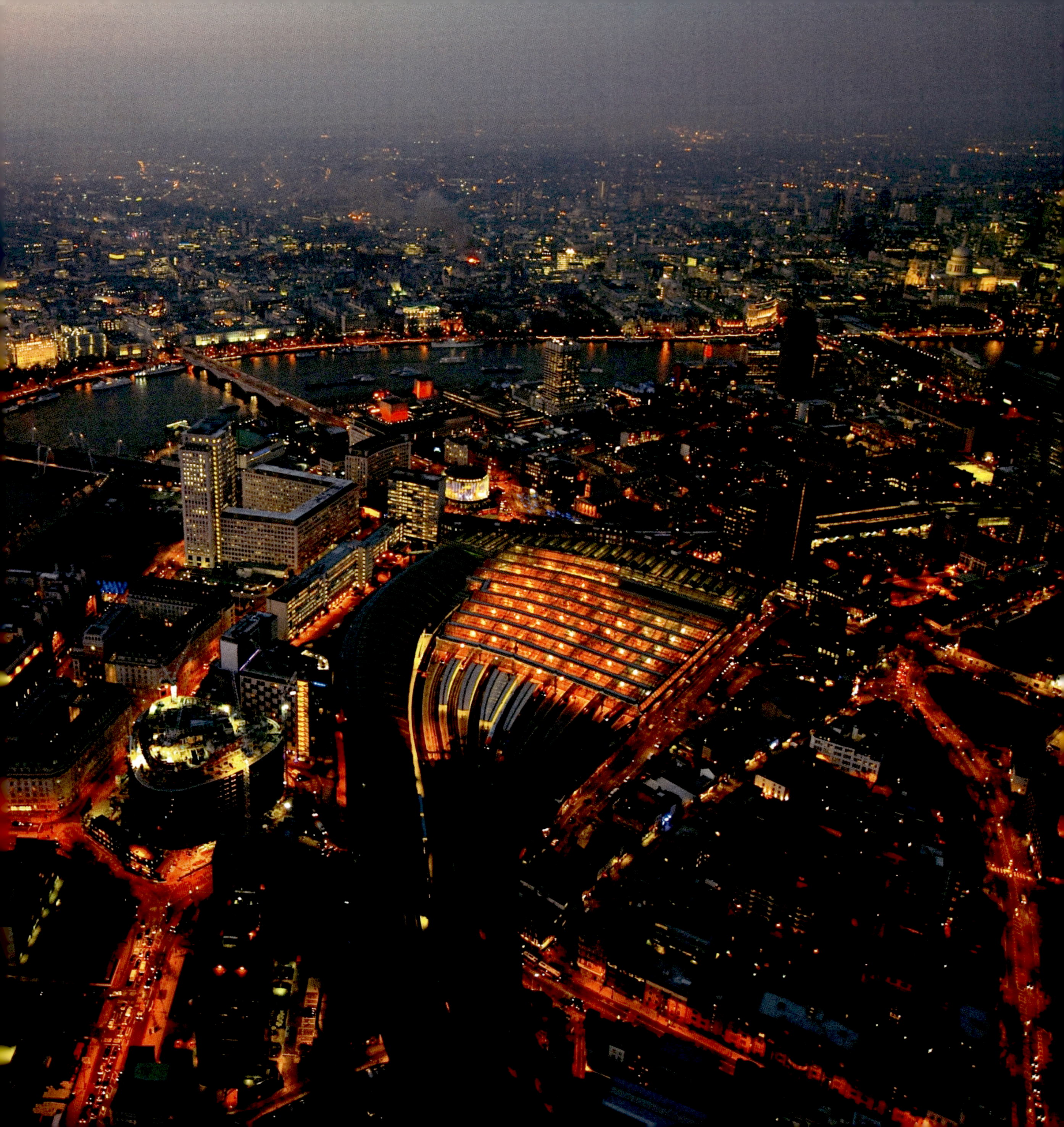

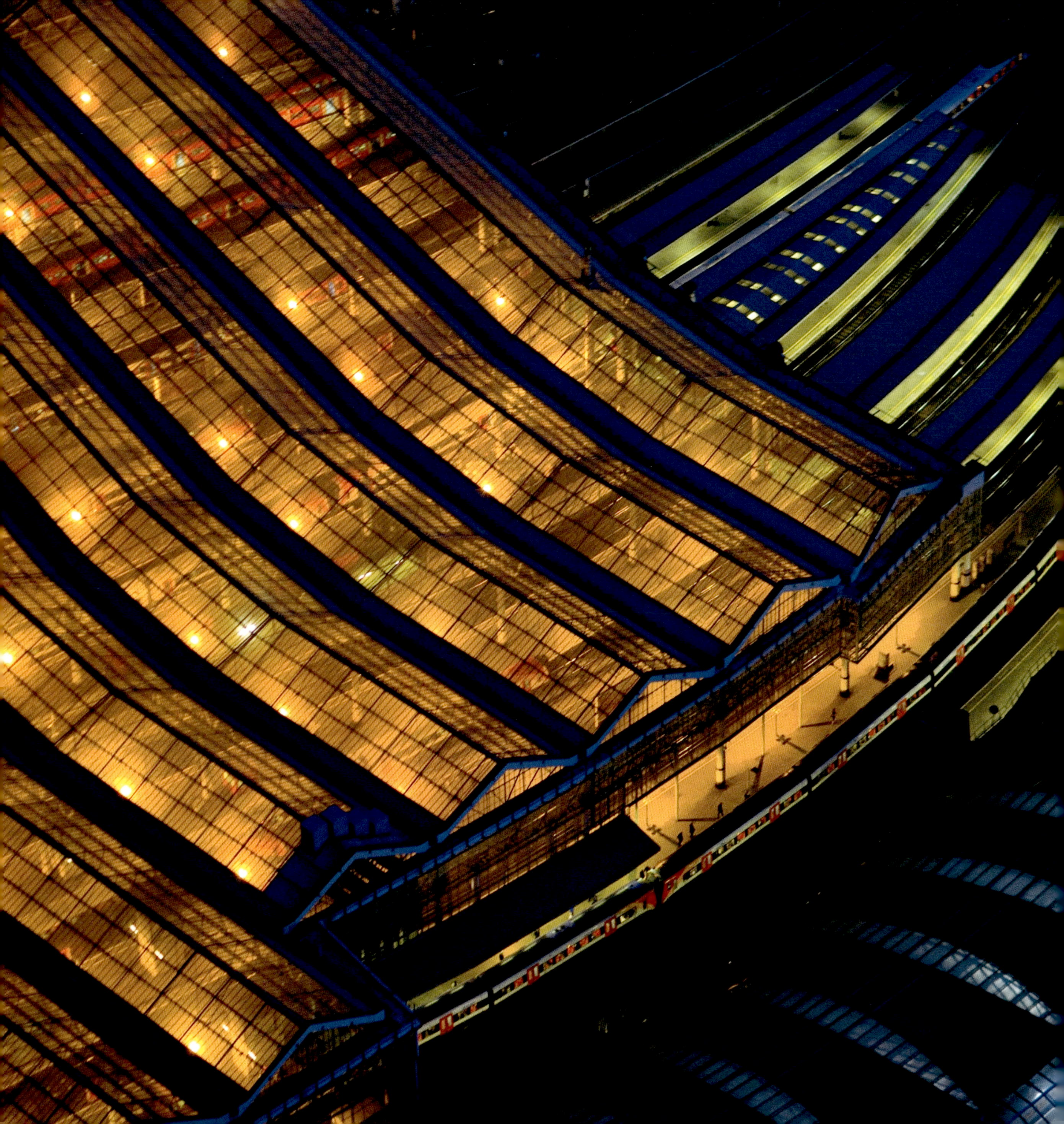

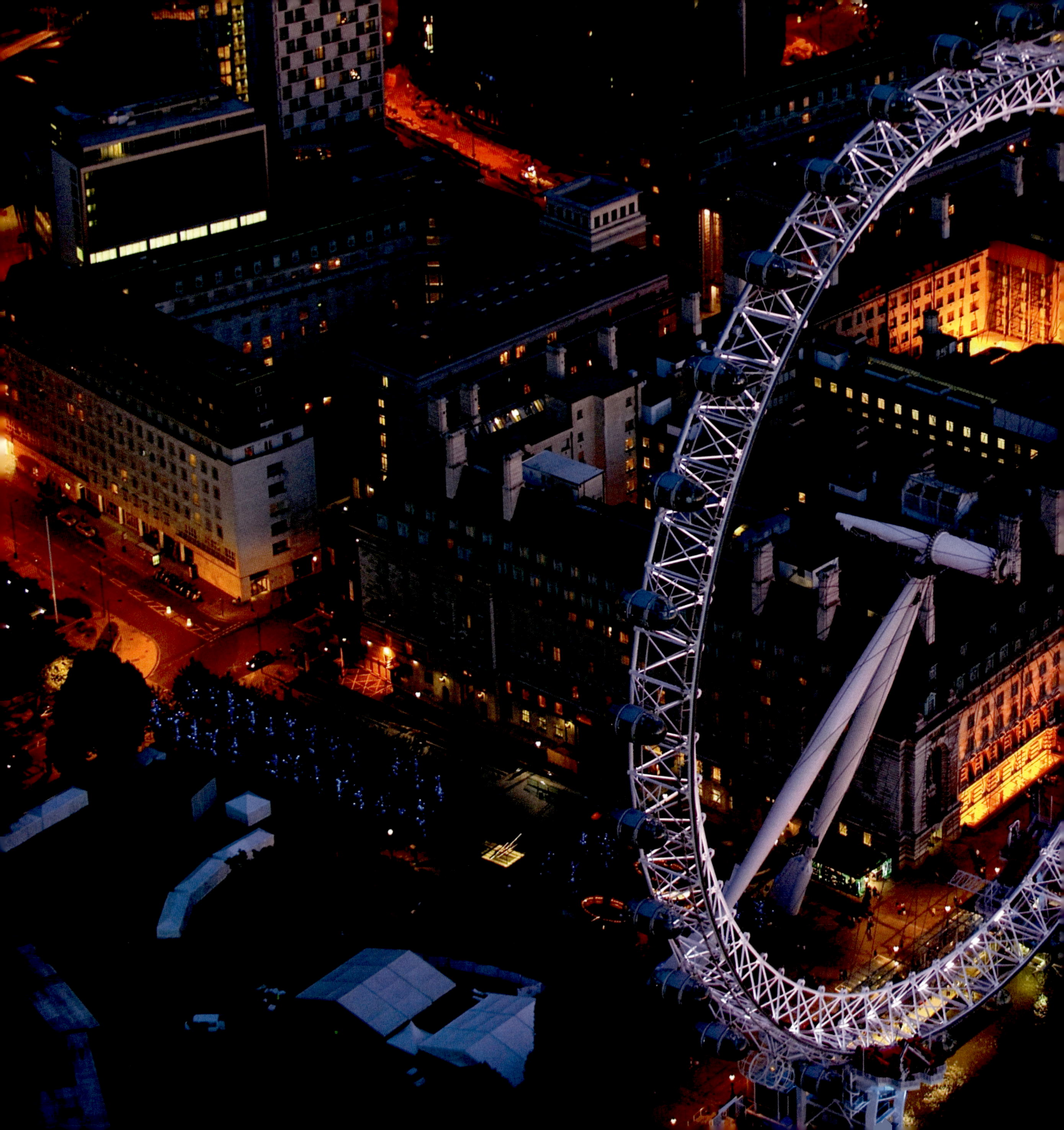

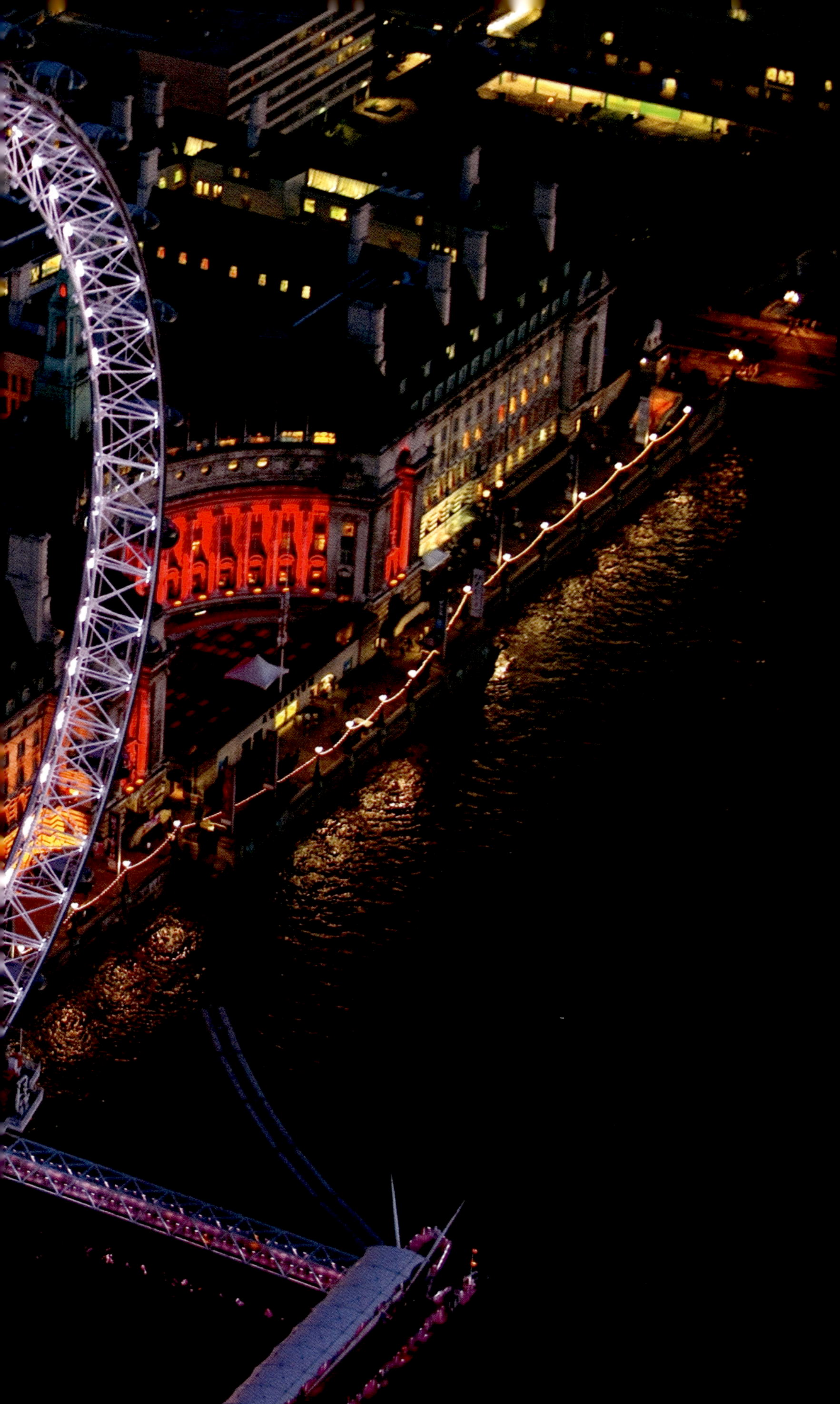

●●●●●●
The London Eye, an initiative of British
Airways, has always been set up as a rival to
the 'official' millennium monument, the Dome
at Greenwich. It has proved hugely popular.
Beyond is the old County Hall, now home to such
tourist attractions as the London Aquarium
and the Movieum, its chimneys perhaps
providing inspiration for those of Portcullis
House across the river (see pages 76–77).

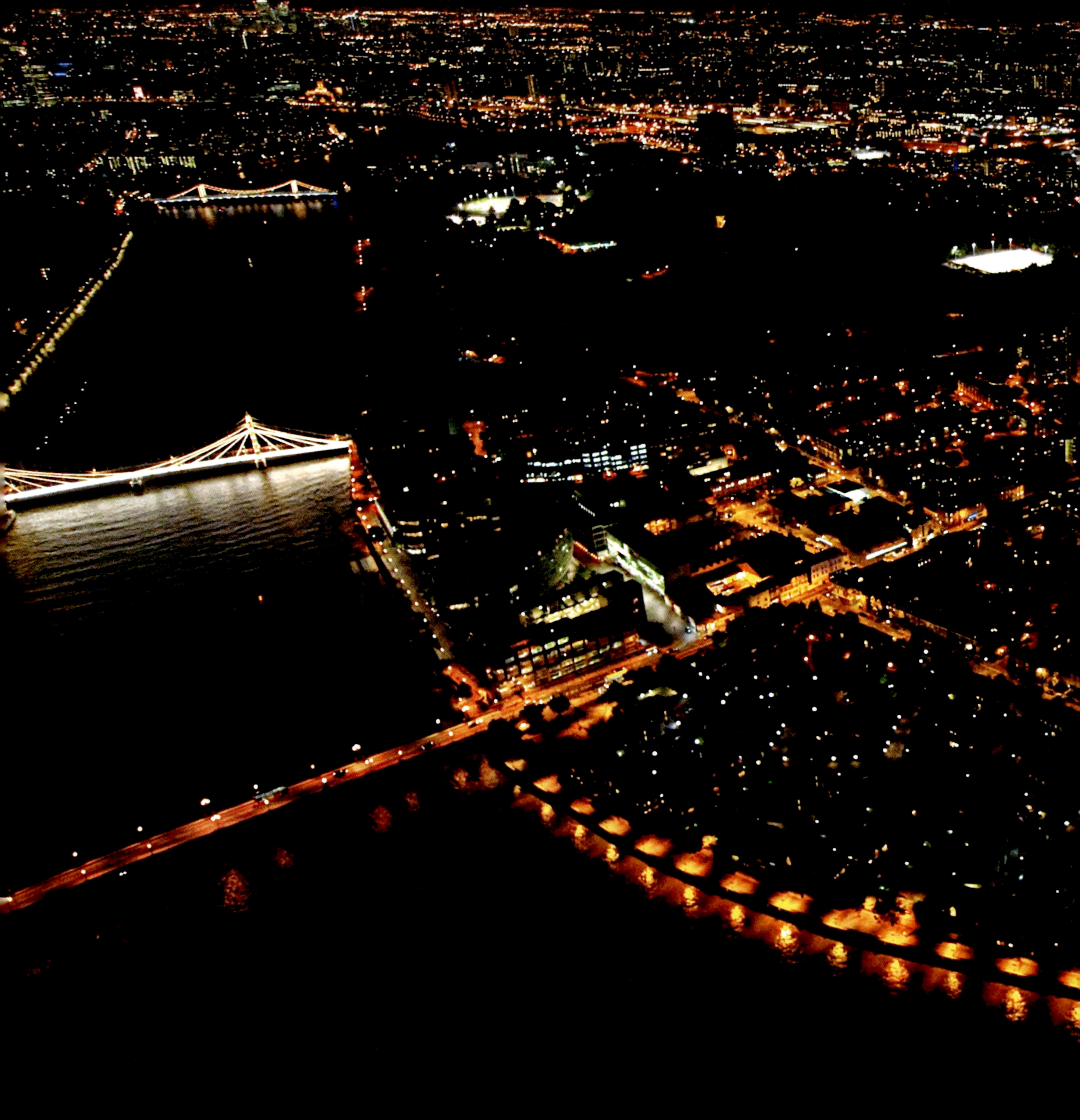

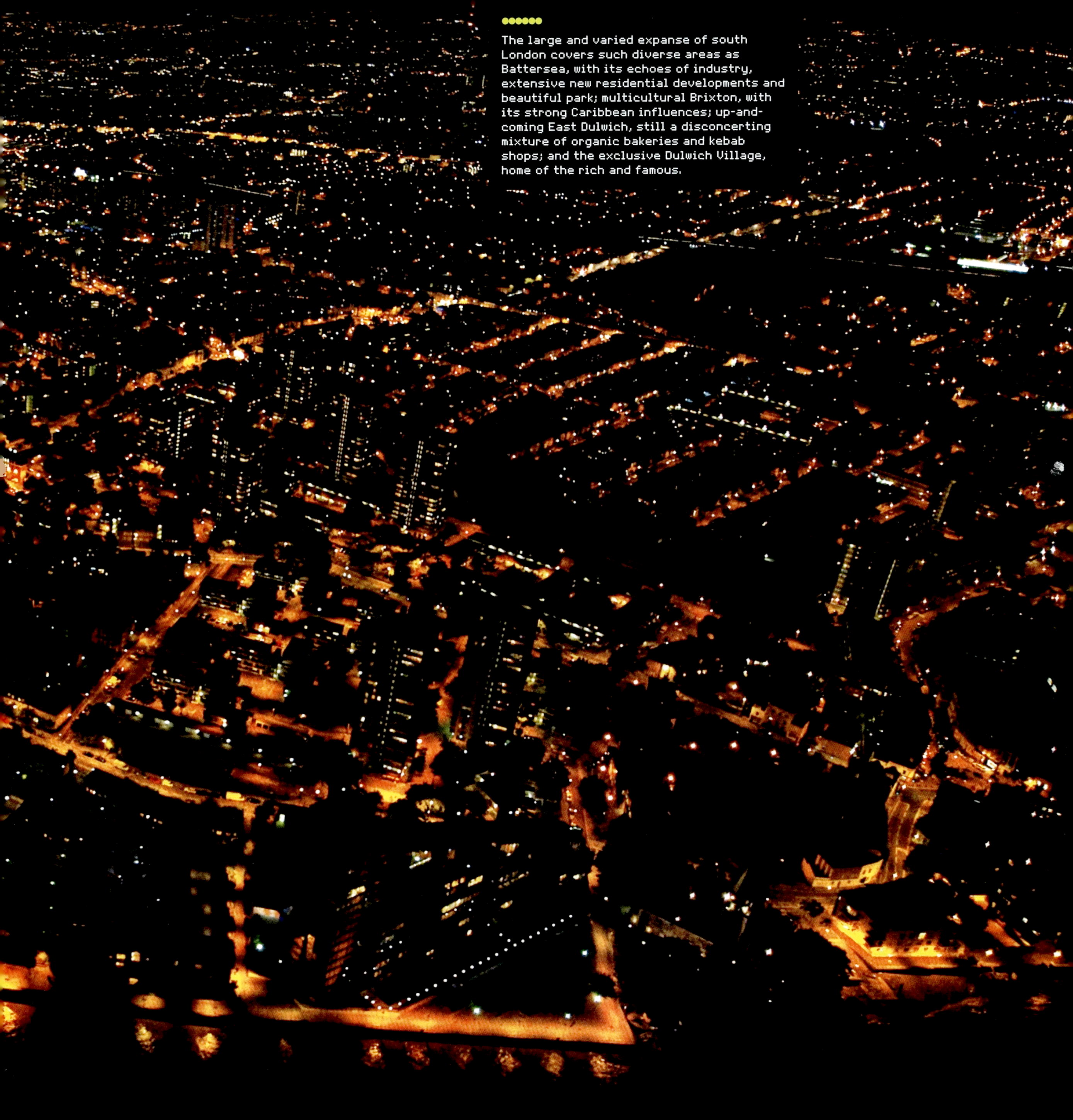

The large and varied expanse of south London covers such diverse areas as Battersea, with its echoes of industry, extensive new residential developments and beautiful park; multicultural Brixton, with its strong Caribbean influences; up-and-coming East Dulwich, still a disconcerting mixture of organic bakeries and kebab shops; and the exclusive Dulwich Village, home of the rich and famous.

WEST

West of Park Lane, the great expanse of Hyde Park and Kensington Gardens is central London's largest open space. South of it is Knightsbridge, anchored as a prime retail destination by Harrods, with the Peter Jones store marking the entry to King's Road beyond. This is fashionable, highly affluent territory, with Belgravia retaining its cachet as Britain's smartest address. The cultural quarter of South Kensington is familiar to millions of museum-goers, and to the crowds who annually pack the Albert Hall for the Proms. One of Britain's leading universities, Imperial College London, somehow packs 13,000 students into its expanding campus here. Notting Hill Gate is another destination for tourists, drawn by London's best-known outdoor market, along Portobello Road. And in one year alone 20 million people visited the vast Westfield shopping centre at Shepherd's Bush.

For many from outside Britain, west London is a place of arrival and a place to settle: it is on the road to and from Heathrow Airport (a city in its own right). Earls Court, with its famous exhibition centre, remains a popular destination for many new arrivals. Great expanses of Victorian housing in Hammersmith, Fulham and west Kensington have been colonized by the middle class, and developers have moved in on the riverside of Chelsea and Fulham, with brash new apartment blocks replacing industrial sheds and wharves. Lots Road Power Station once powered the Underground, but is now empty, awaiting conversion to shops and flats. Further west, the riverside retains a picturesque quality, with the remains of the ancient villages of Chiswick and Isleworth and the great houses of Osterley and Syon in their enclosed parks off the M4. It is a territory of contrasts – there is little picturesque about Acton – but London's drift to the west looks unstoppable.

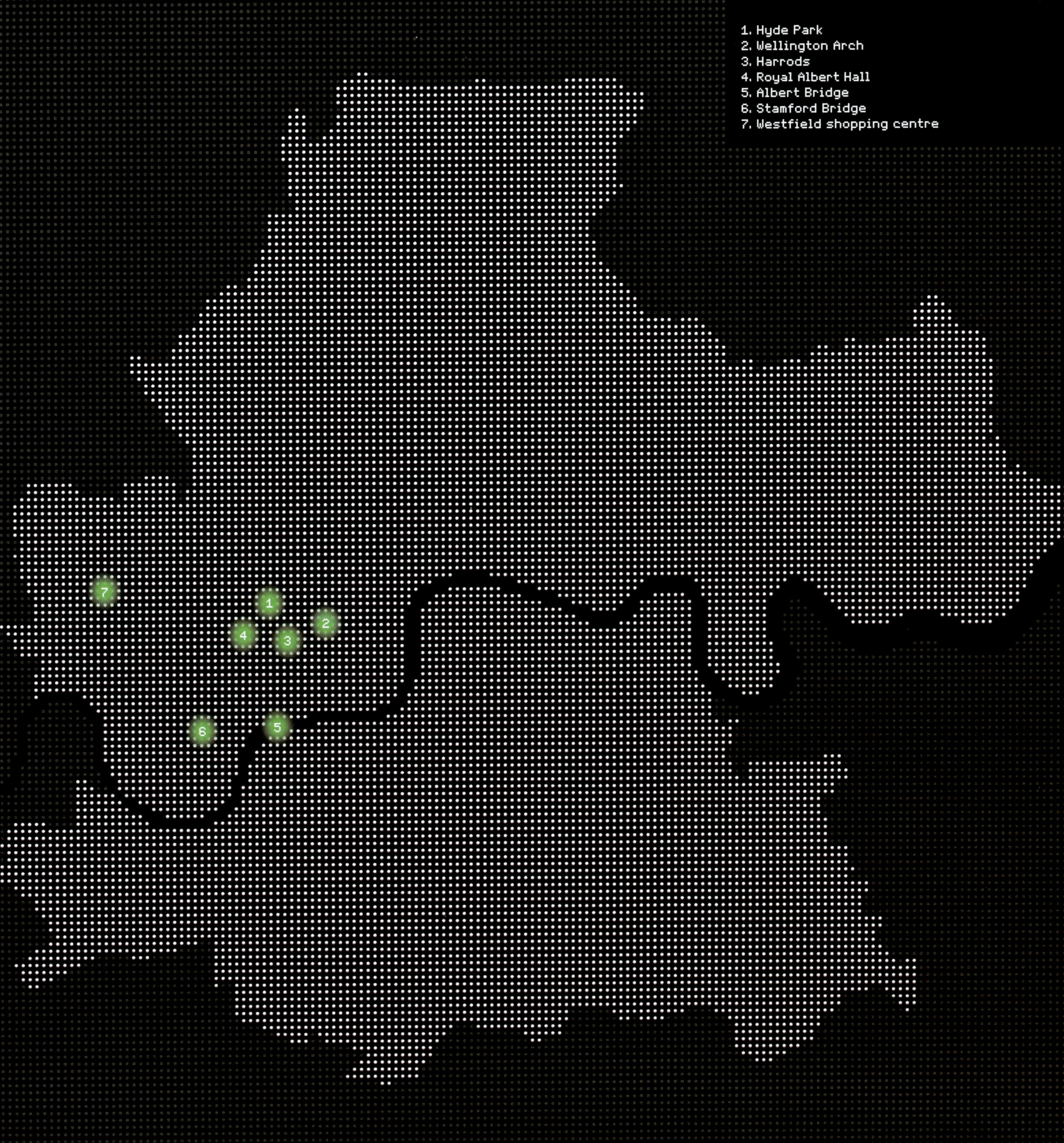

1. Hyde Park
2. Wellington Arch
3. Harrods
4. Royal Albert Hall
5. Albert Bridge
6. Stamford Bridge
7. Westfield shopping centre

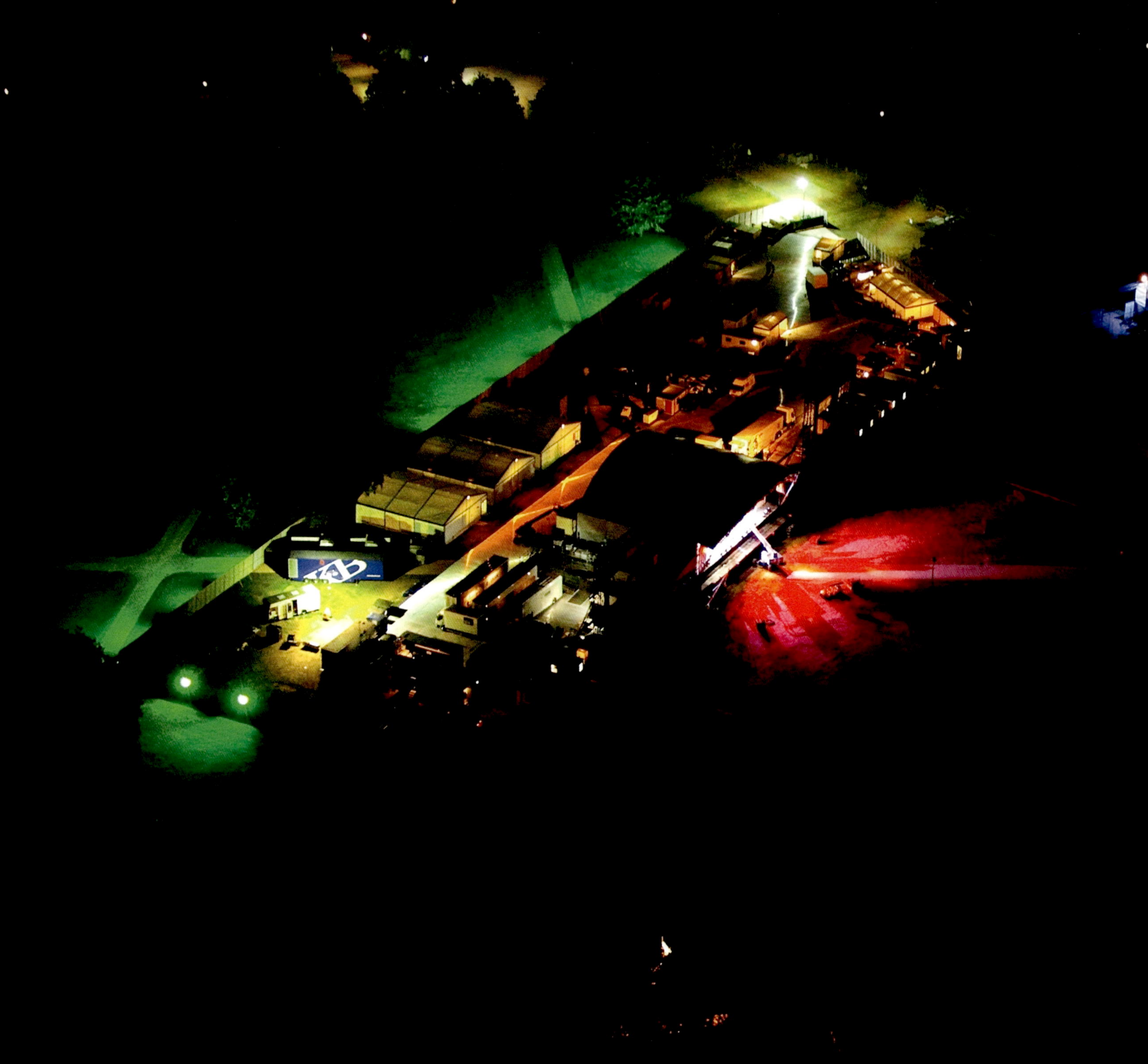

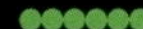

Hyde Park hosts the BBC Proms in the Park on
12 September 2009. Hosted by broadcaster
Terry Wogan, the event featured Barry Manilow,
Katherine Jenkins and the BBC Concert Orchestra,
and finished with spectacular fireworks.
Established in 1996, the Proms in the Park
concerts take place in various venues across
the country, to coincide with the last night of
the Proms in the nearby Royal Albert Hall.

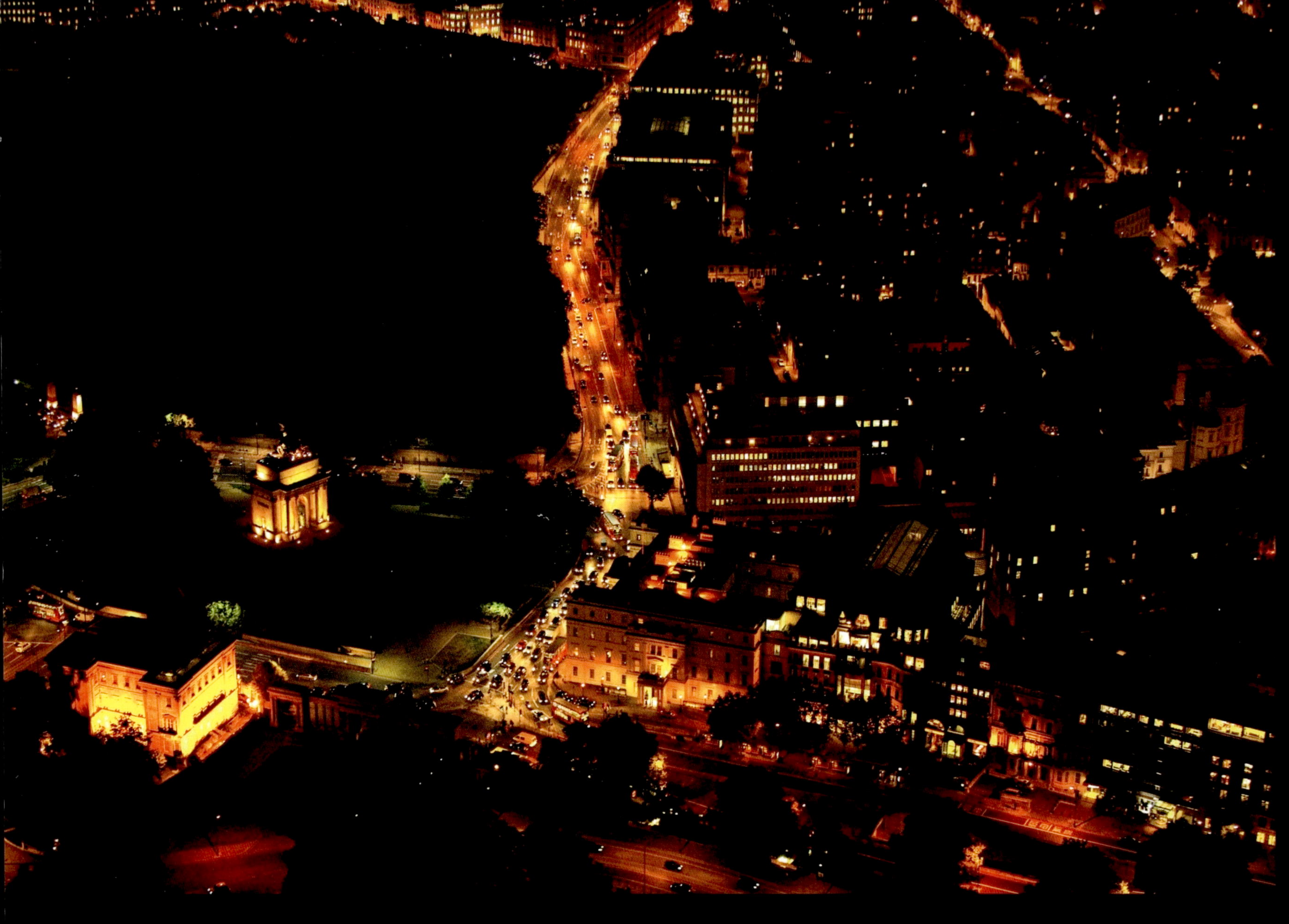

Hyde Park Corner was once the official
western boundary of London. Number One
London – Apsley House, the home of the Dukes
of Wellington – stands at the corner of the
park; although it is now open to the public,
an act of Parliament granted the family the
right to live there in perpetuity, and the 8th
Duke still has a flat in the building. Across
the road is Wellington Arch, a memorial to the
1st Duke, famous for his victory at the Battle

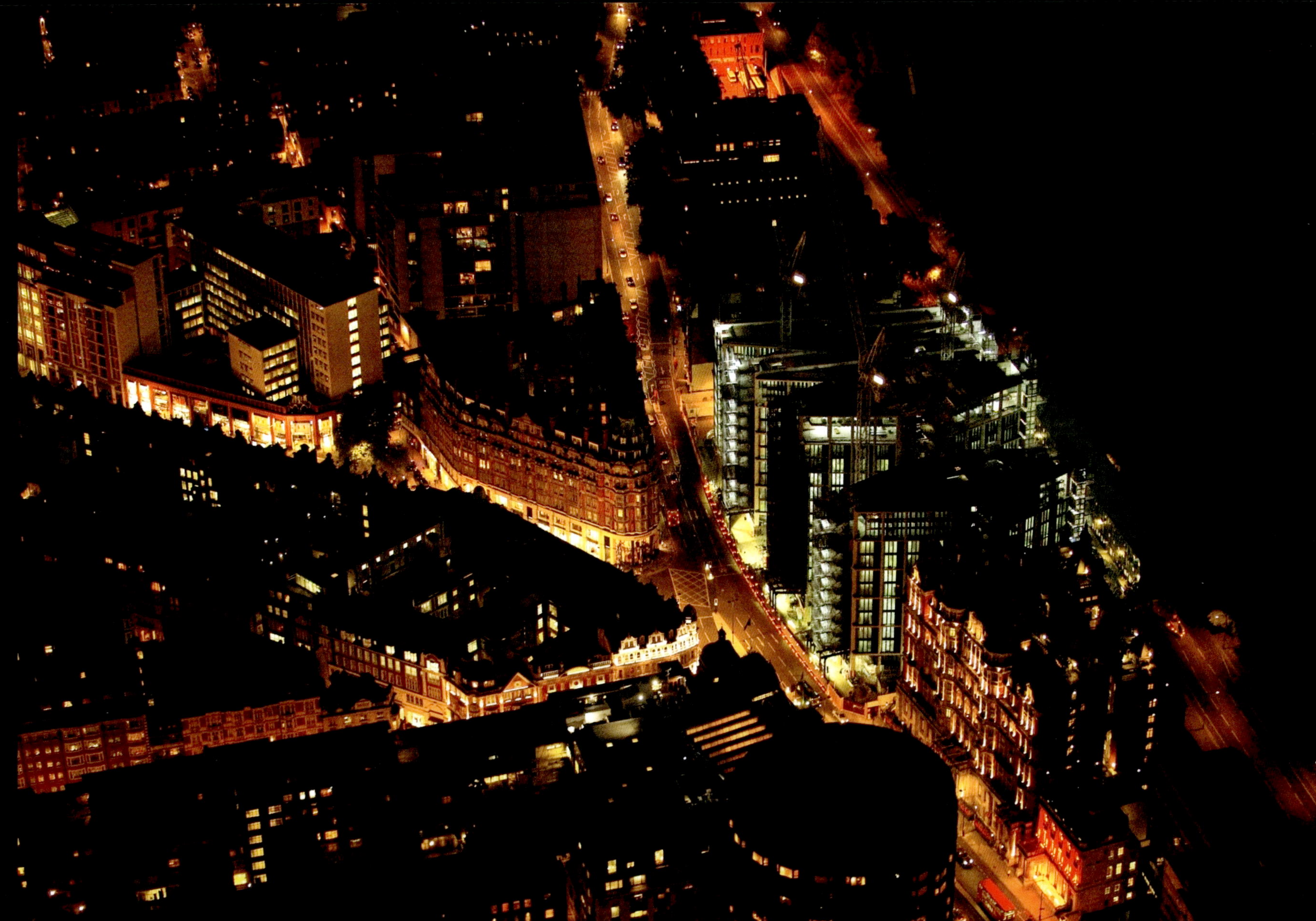

Knightsbridge runs westwards from Hyde
Park Corner towards Kensington. The wedge-
shaped buildings nearing completion on the
right-hand side make up Rogers Stirk Harbour
+ Partners' One Hyde Park, a development
of shops, a hotel and flats that seeks to
reconnect Knightsbridge with the park.

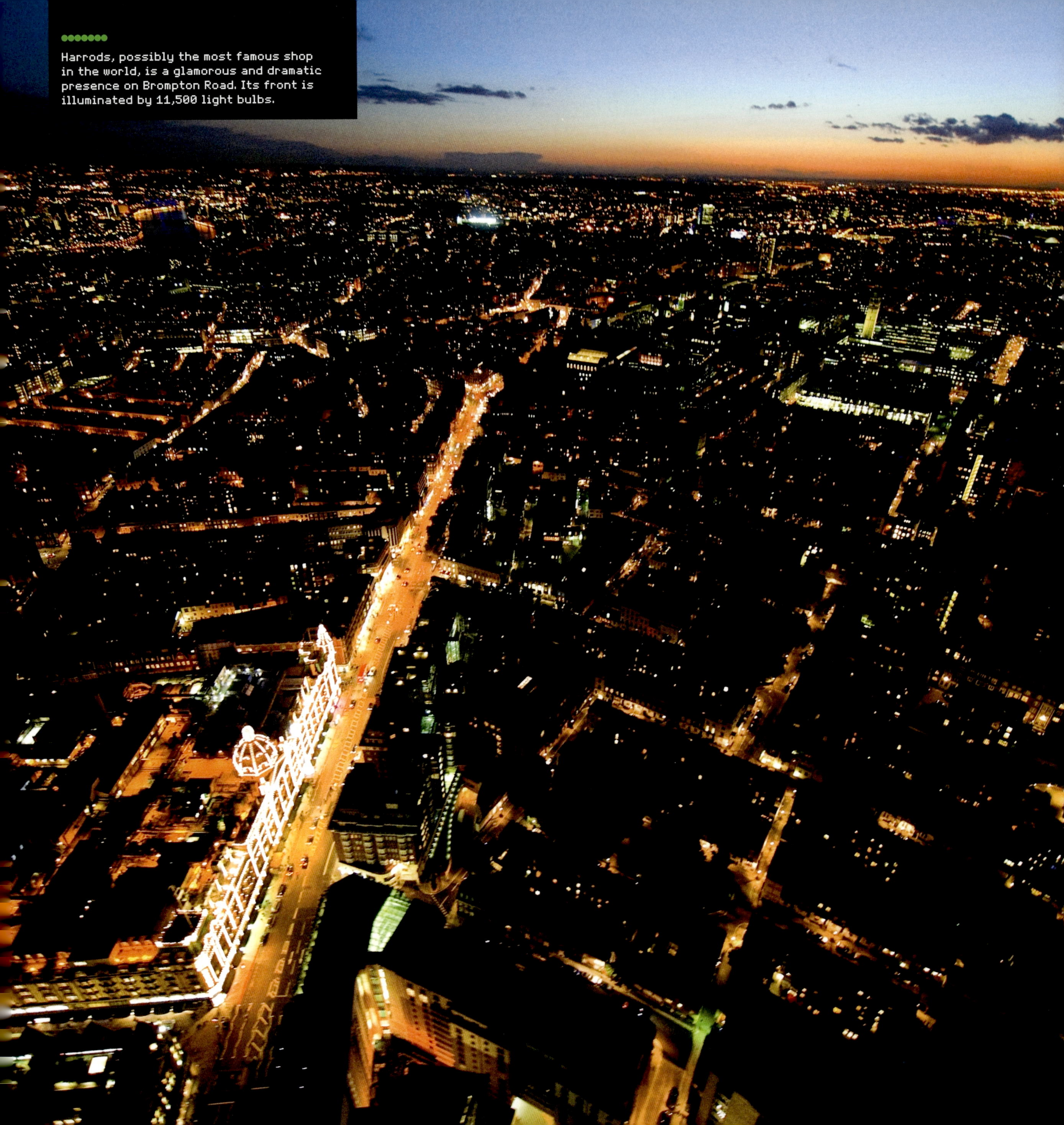

Harrods, possibly the most famous shop in the world, is a glamorous and dramatic presence on Brompton Road. Its front is illuminated by 11,500 light bulbs.

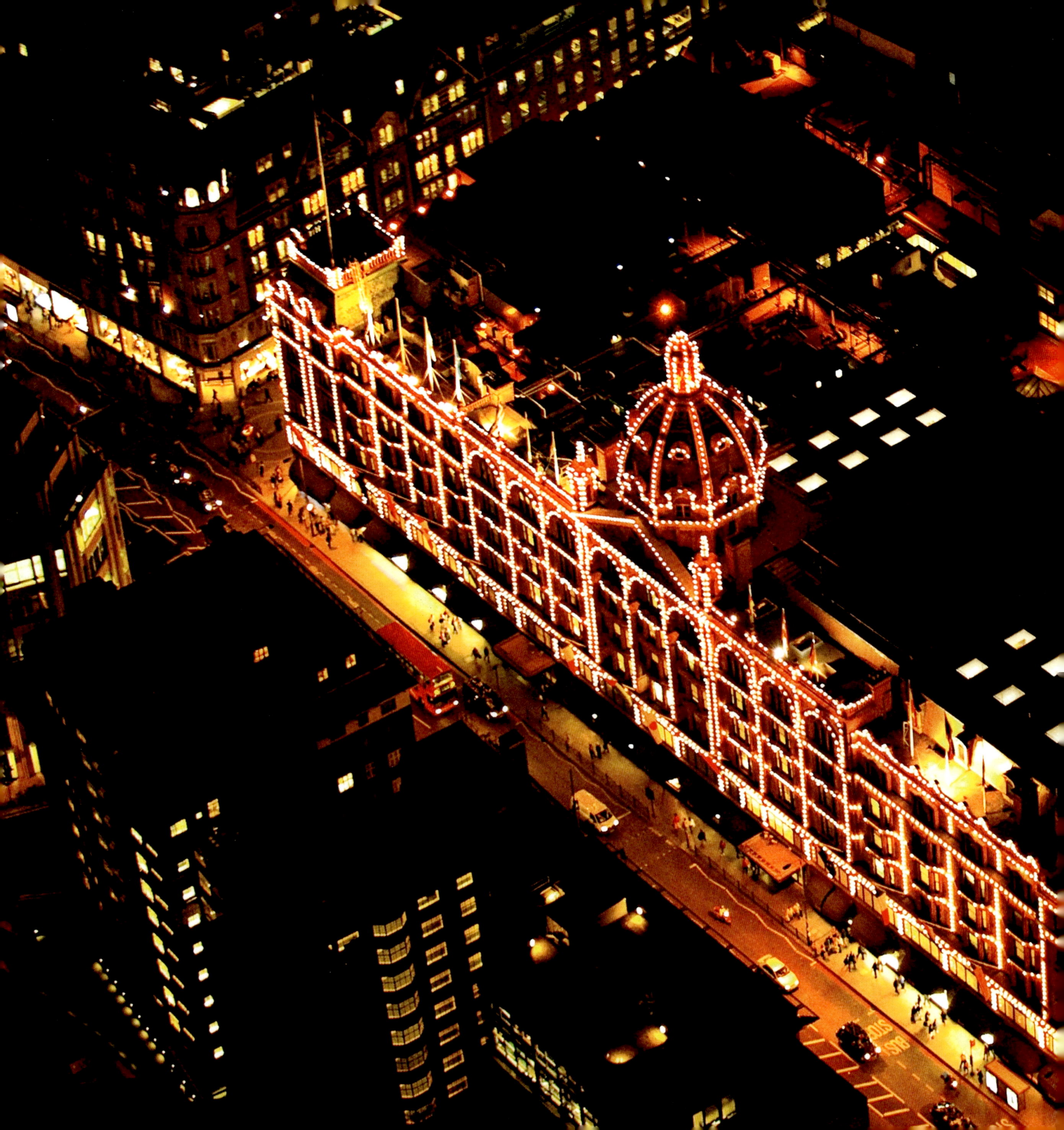

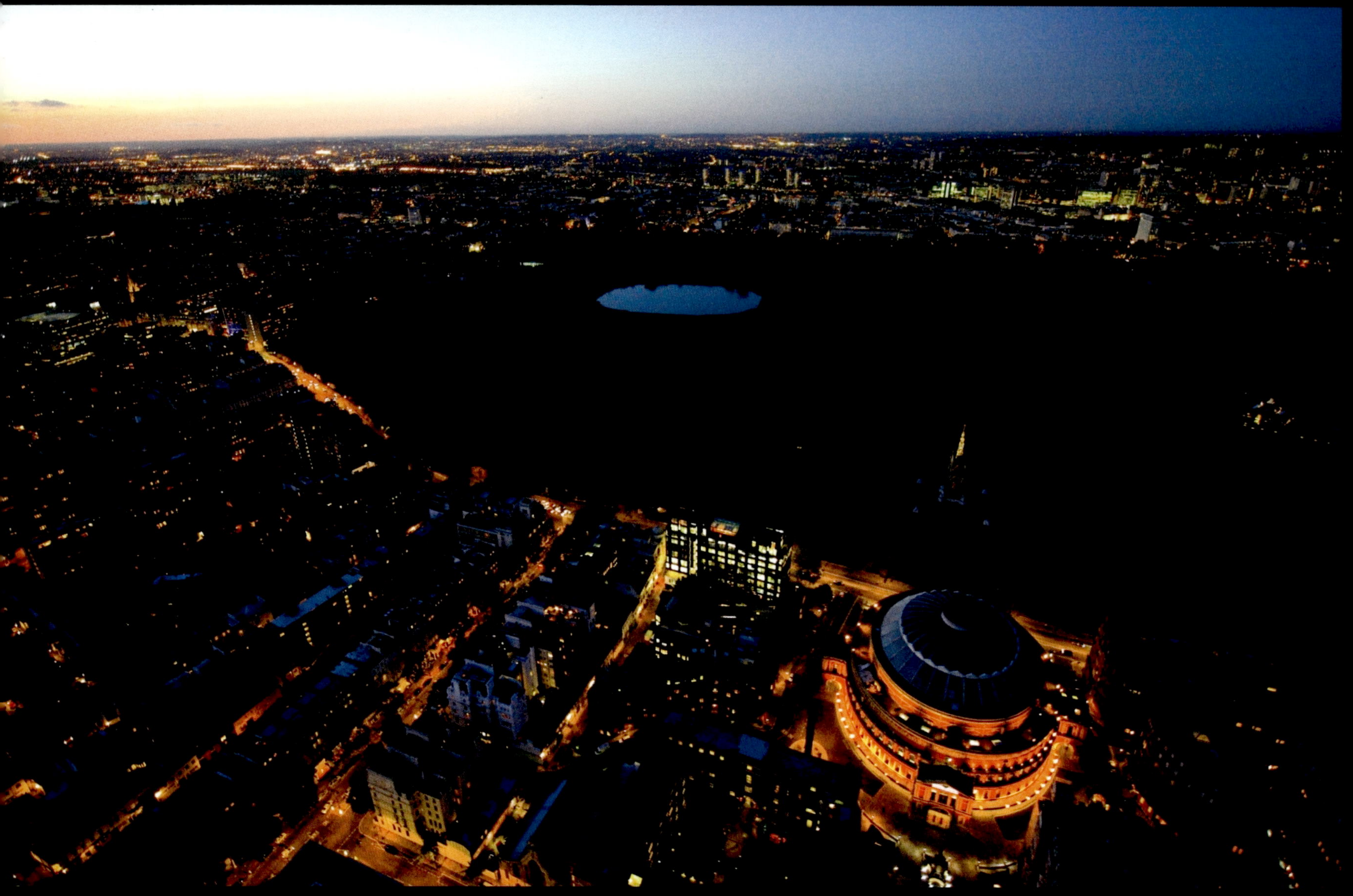

The dome of the Royal Albert Hall echoes
the round pond in Kensington Gardens,
which reflects the dusk sky. The impressive
streets and ordered squares of Knightsbridge,
Belgravia and Mayfair, which abut Hyde Park to
the south and east, are now home to both 'old'
and 'new' money, and include some of London's
most exclusive shops. The view south from over
Hyde Park (overleaf) stretches past the low-
lying districts on the south bank of the Thames,
as far as the television transmitters at Crystal
Palace and Croydon.

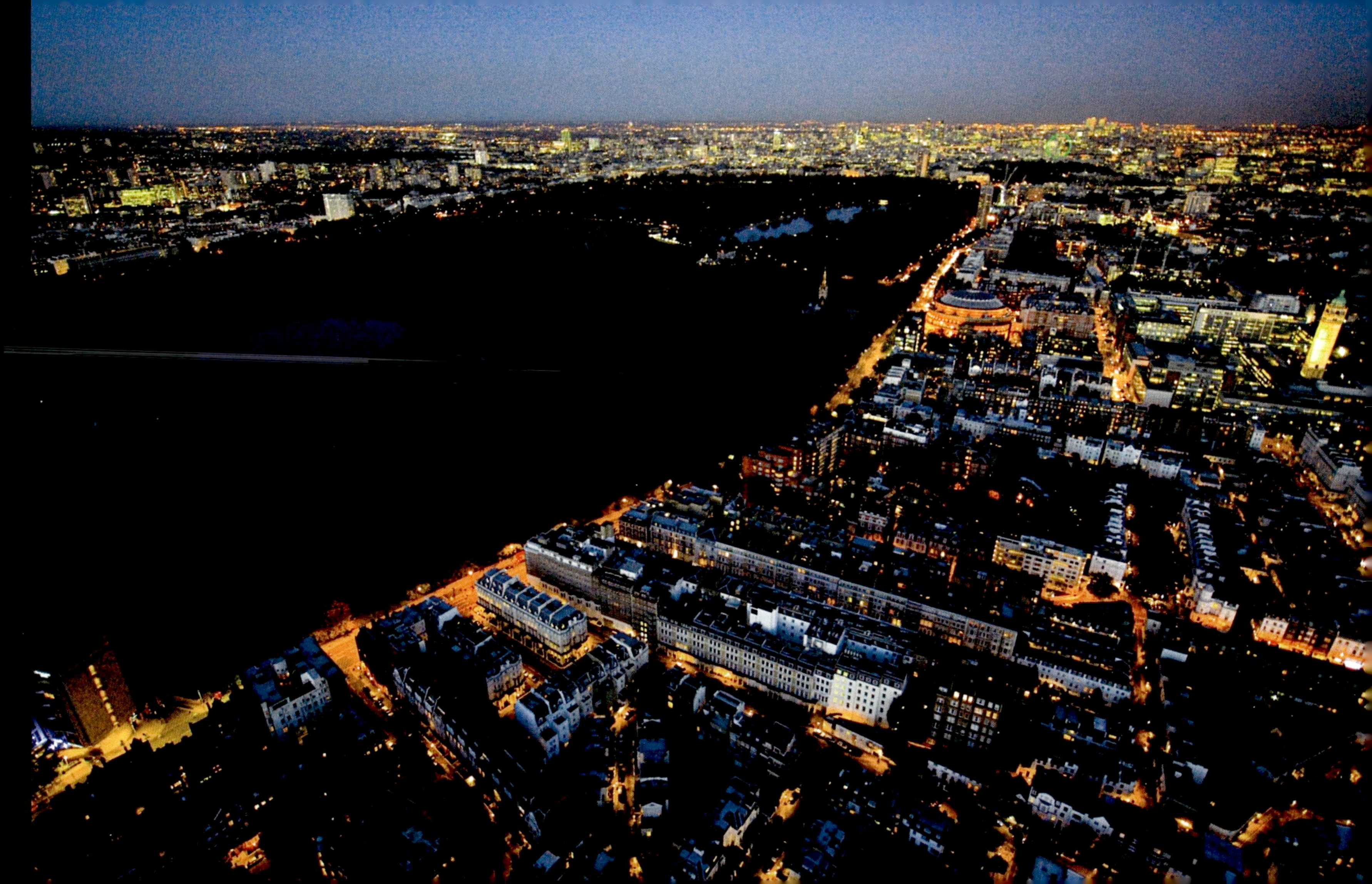

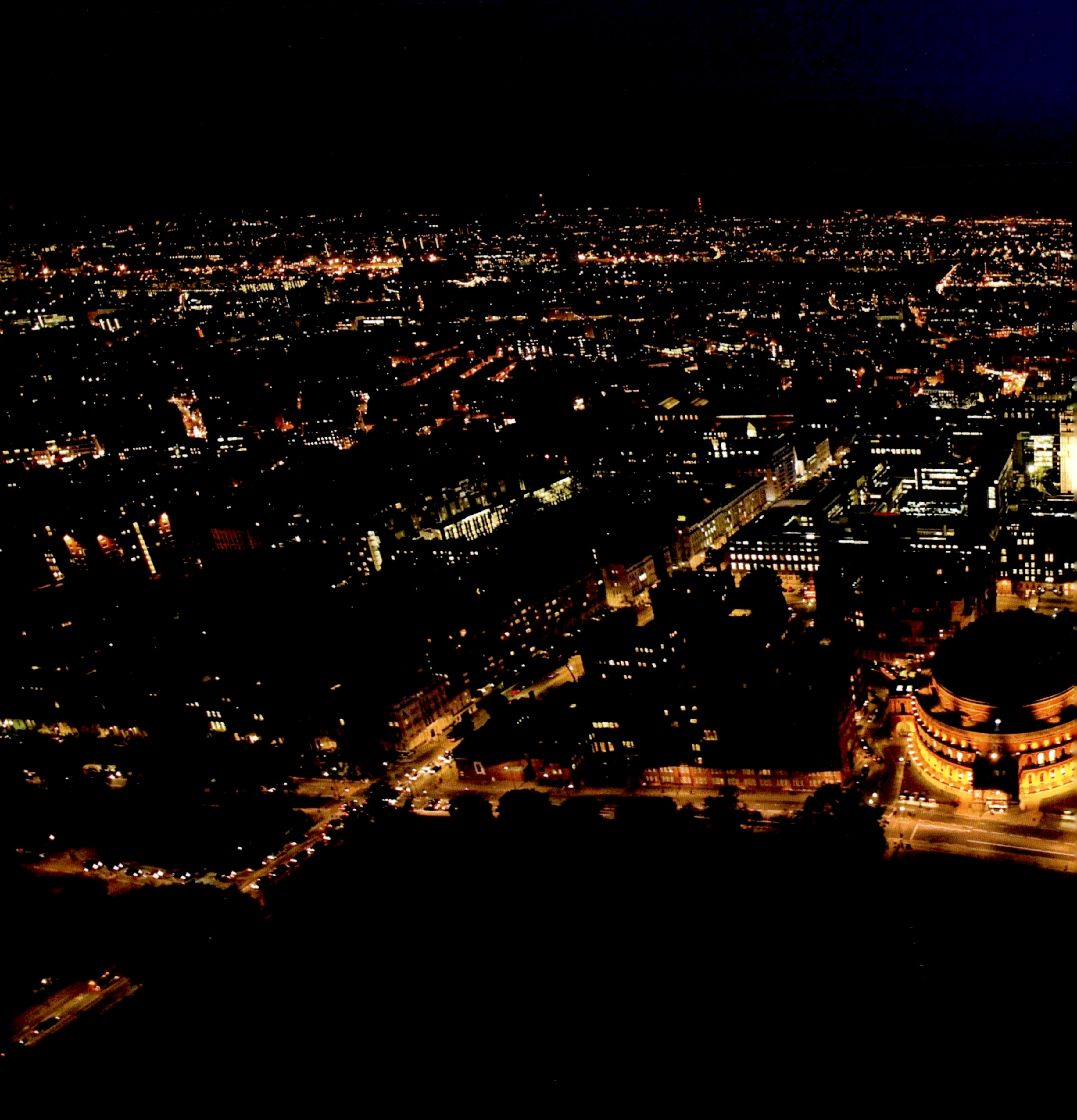

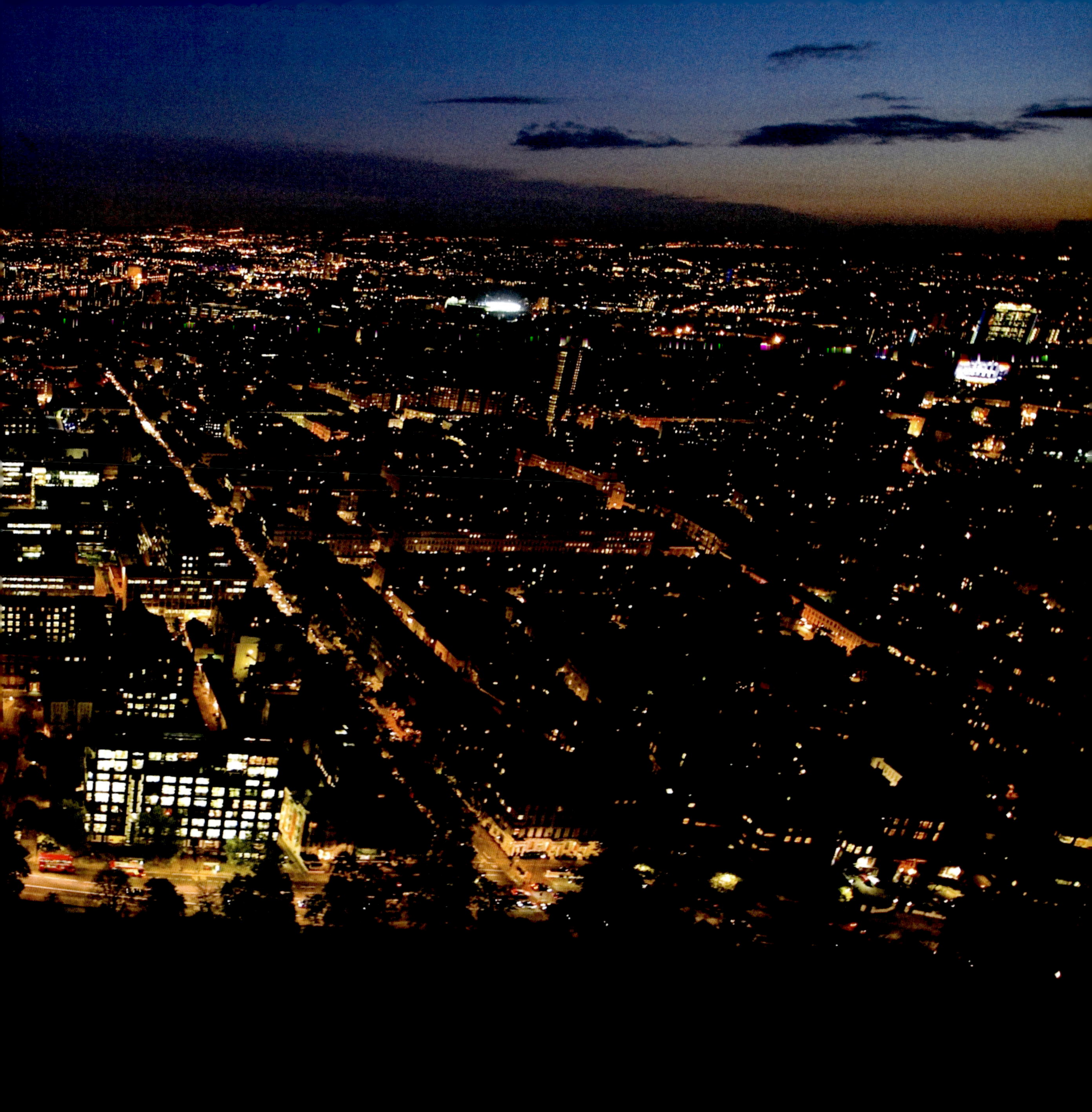

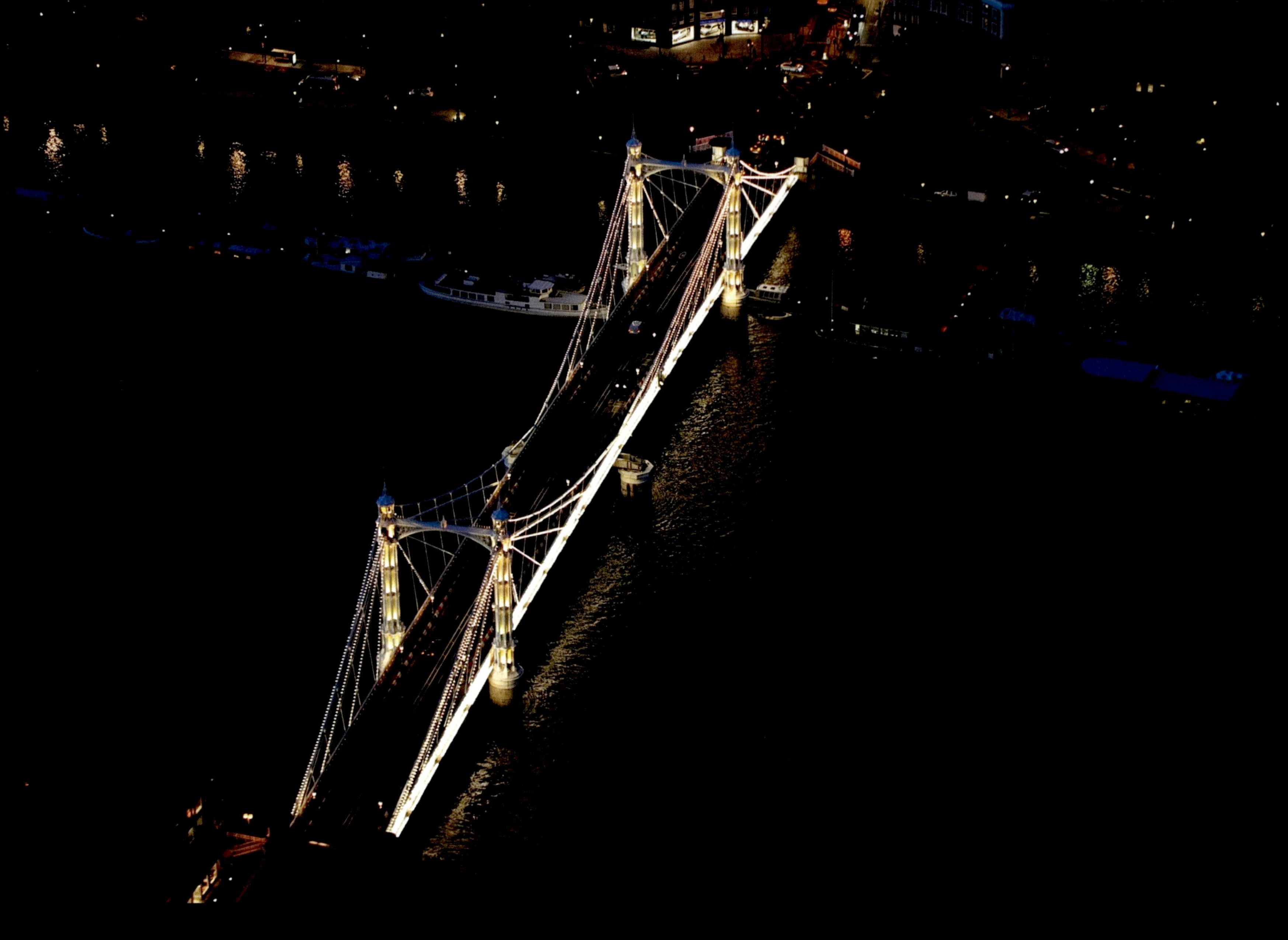

●●●●●●●

Until 1873, when Albert Bridge (by R.M. Ordish)
was built, there was no crossing from Chelsea
to Battersea. As a result, the two developed
very separately despite being so close.
Battersea, indeed, was comparatively remote
until the coming of the railways in the mid-
nineteenth century. The bridge's design is
simple and attractive, and enhanced after
dark by delicate white lighting. The only false
note – aesthetically, if not practically – is
the central support, which was added later.

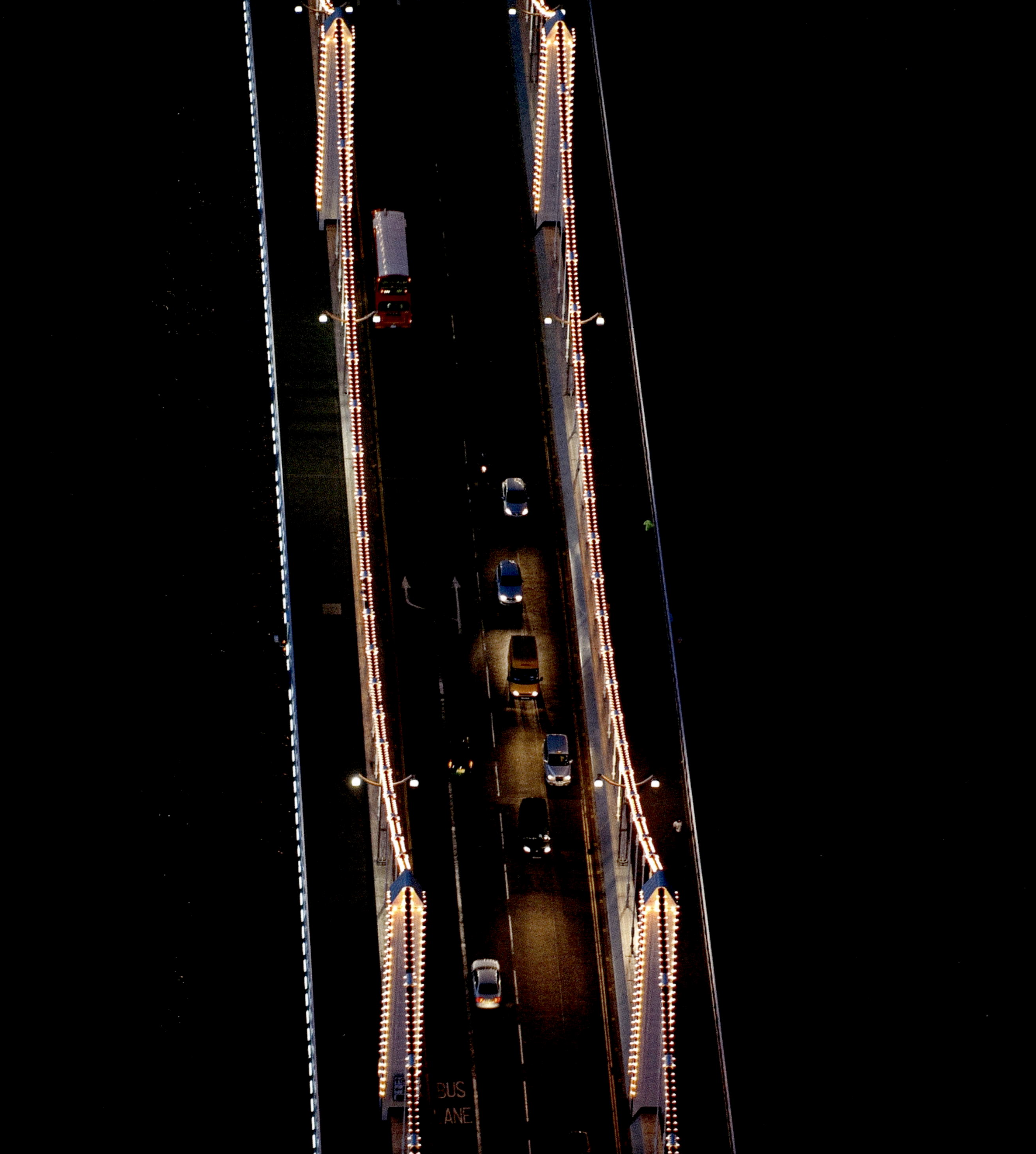
BUS
LANE

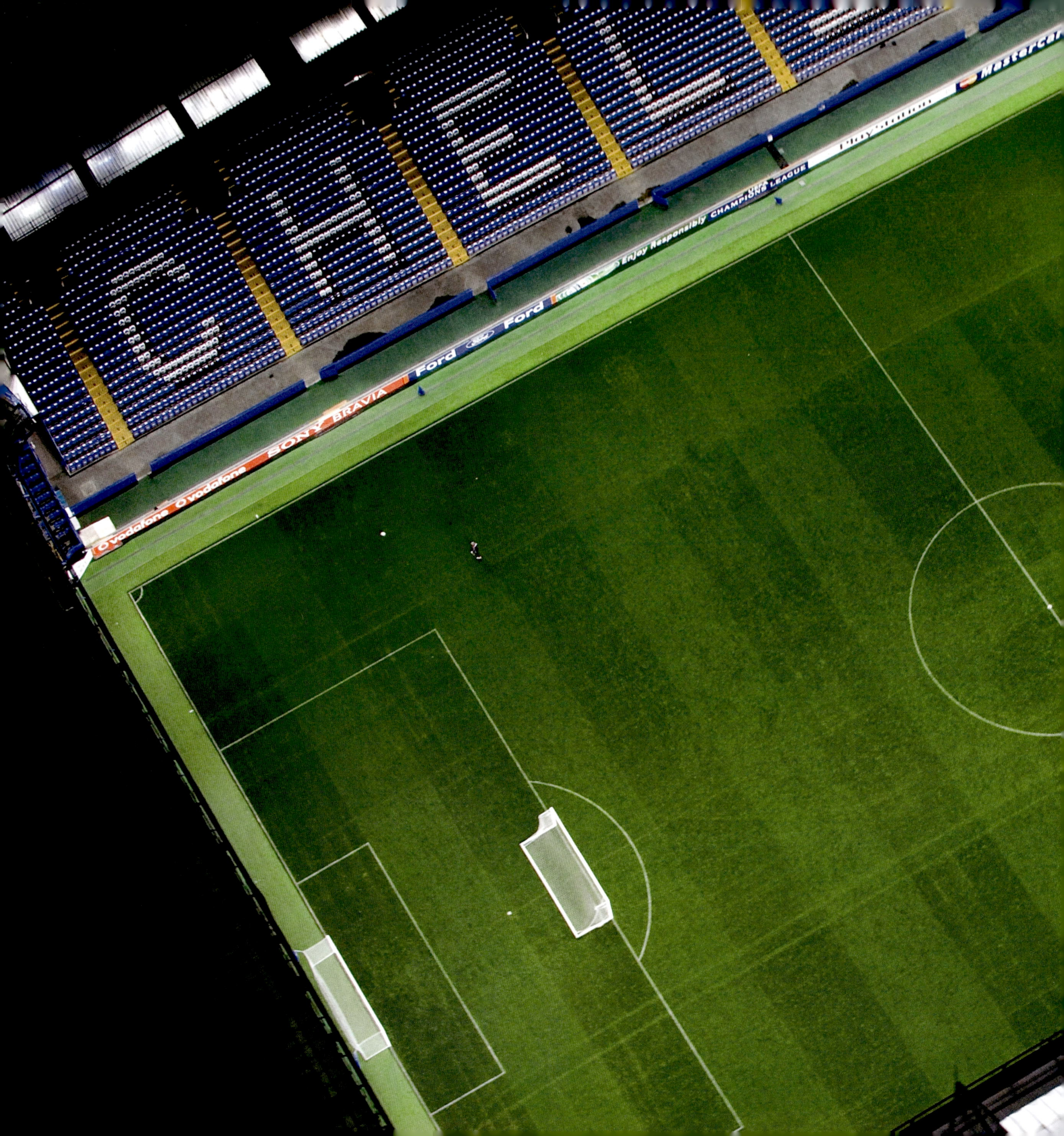

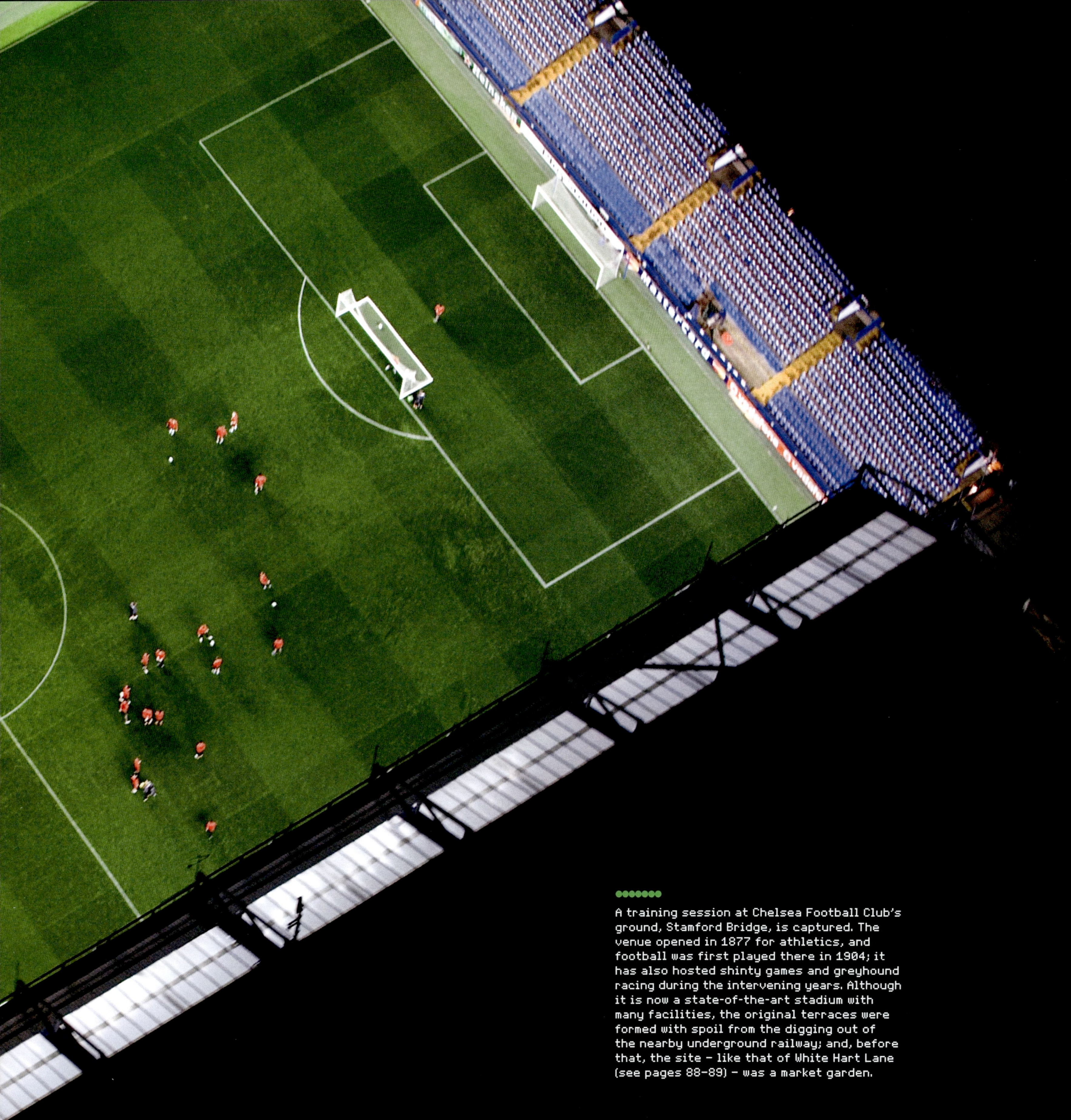

A training session at Chelsea Football Club's ground, Stamford Bridge, is captured. The venue opened in 1877 for athletics, and football was first played there in 1904; it has also hosted shinty games and greyhound racing during the intervening years. Although it is now a state-of-the-art stadium with many facilities, the original terraces were formed with spoil from the digging out of the nearby underground railway; and, before that, the site – like that of White Hart Lane (see pages 88-89) – was a market garden.

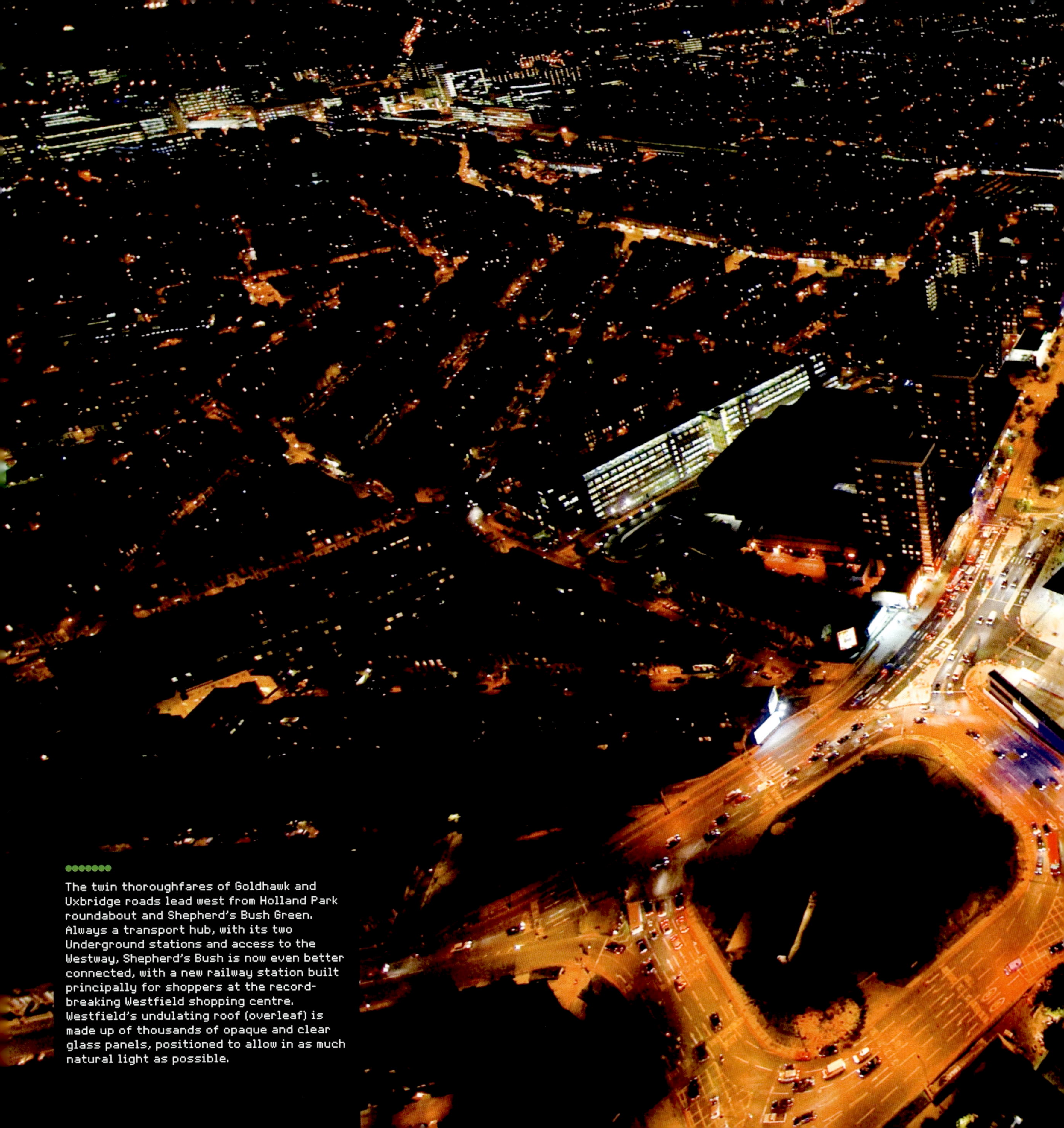

The twin thoroughfares of Goldhawk and
Uxbridge roads lead west from Holland Park
roundabout and Shepherd's Bush Green.
Always a transport hub, with its two
Underground stations and access to the
Westway, Shepherd's Bush is now even better
connected, with a new railway station built
principally for shoppers at the record-
breaking Westfield shopping centre.
Westfield's undulating roof (overleaf) is
made up of thousands of opaque and clear
glass panels, positioned to allow in as much
natural light as possible.

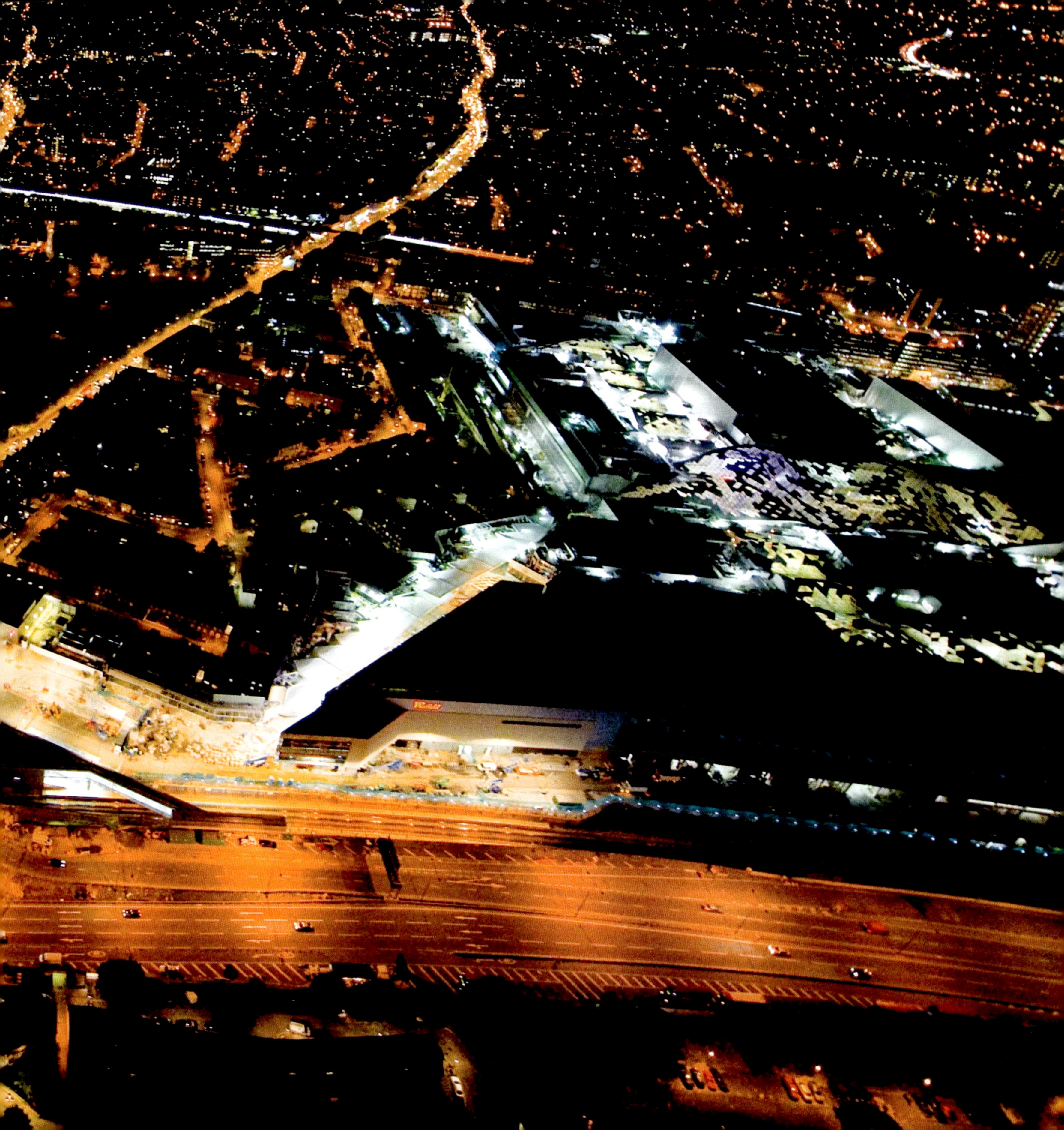

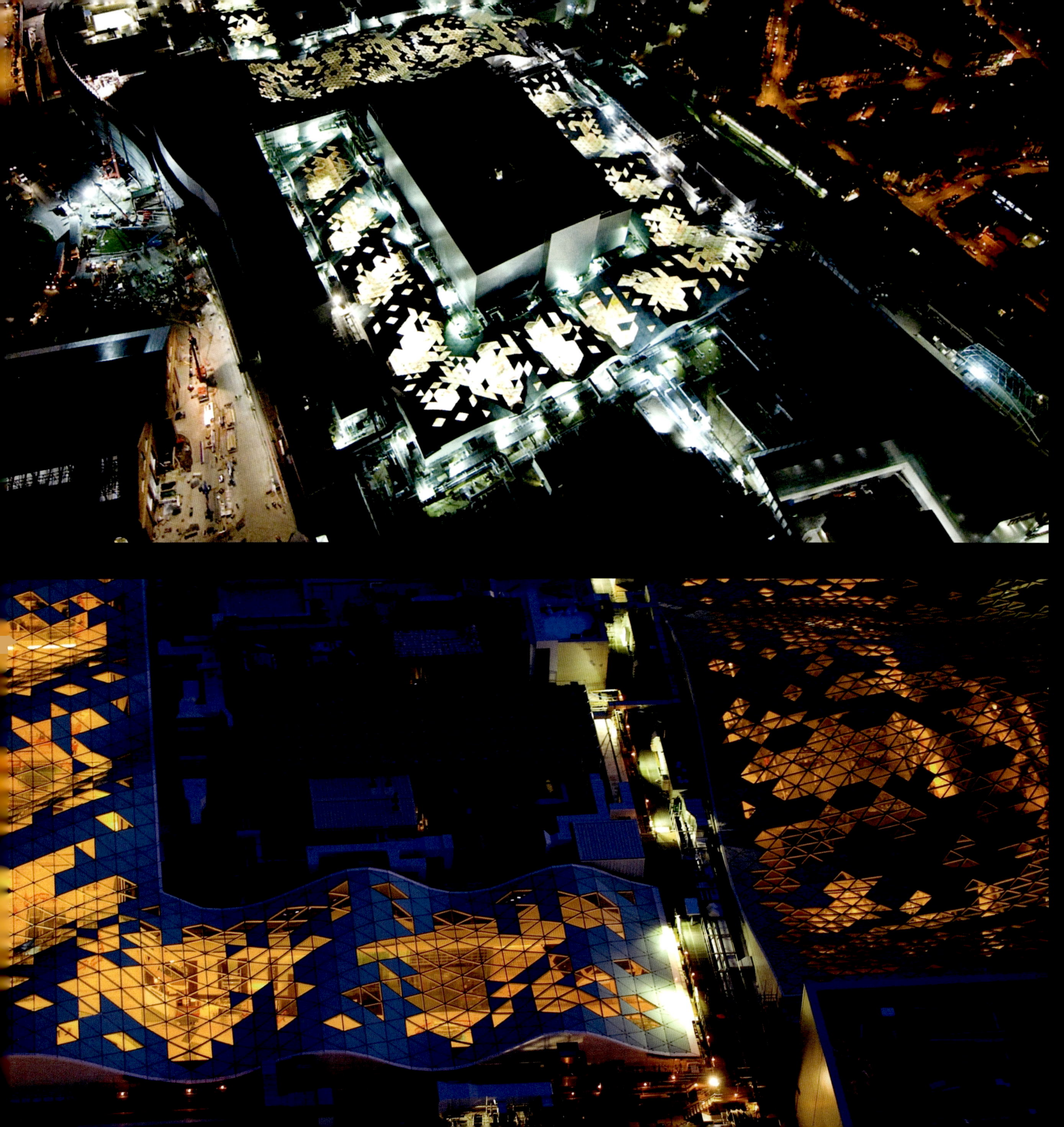

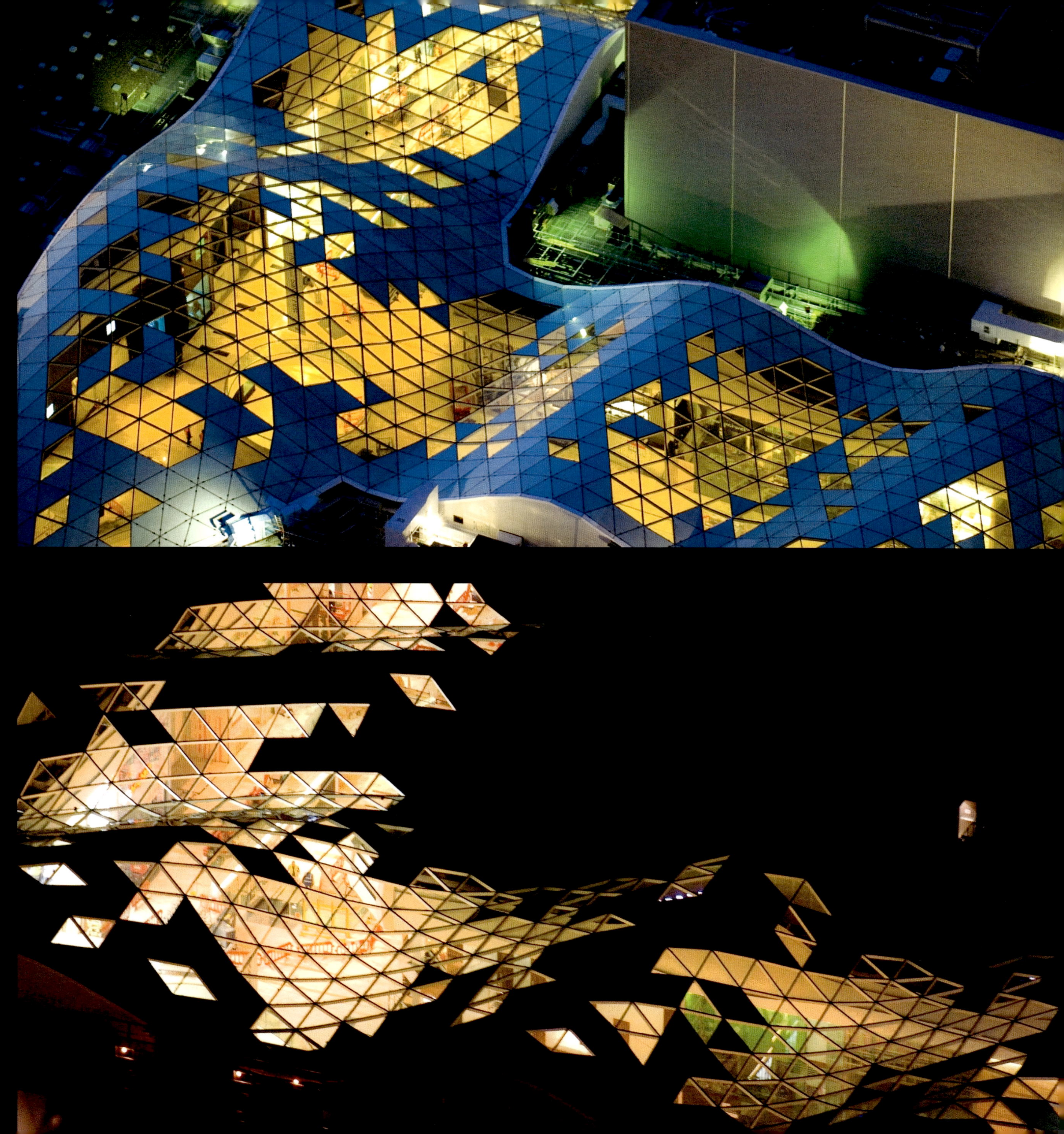

THE PHOTOGRAPHER'S VIEWPOINT

I have worked as an aerial photographer since 1991: almost straight out of college, apart from a brief stint assisting studio photographers in Covent Garden, London.

I tend to sit in (or occasionally hang from) the helicopter, having removed the door, which is roughly twice the size of an average car door. I am harnessed to a hard point in the helicopter, and wear a headset in order to talk to and direct the pilot. I sometimes also tether the camera to a MacBook laptop and a GPS. Given a decent pilot and an interesting location, it is not difficult to shoot some great images. The only real problem is the comparatively small time frame available. Flying in London, for instance, in a Eurocopter AS355 costs around £1200 an hour, and that includes the time required to get into position. Offshore it can be even more expensive: I remember one job in Norway where we burned through £13,000 of expenses in no time at all, flying Super Pumas (the Eurocopter AS332).

I have flown thousands of hours all over the world, and started shooting night images ten years ago on film. The results were adequate, but by no means great (see photographs opposite). To overcome the vibration of the helicopter I normally use a very high shutter speed, with the lowest ISO (sensitivity of film or digital sensor) I can get away with. At night this does not apply, and it took me many hours of testing different combinations of mounts, cameras (now, of course, digital) and processing software to achieve good results.

Various mounts are available: some sit on the floor of the helicopter and some need to be held. They stabilize the camera at night and allow sharp images even at very slow shutter speeds from a helicopter. They are very cumbersome and slow to work with, but can produce excellent pictures.

Over the years I have shot with pretty much every make of camera there is, but now I use only Nikon (D3 and D3X). They are beautifully made and a real pleasure to work with.

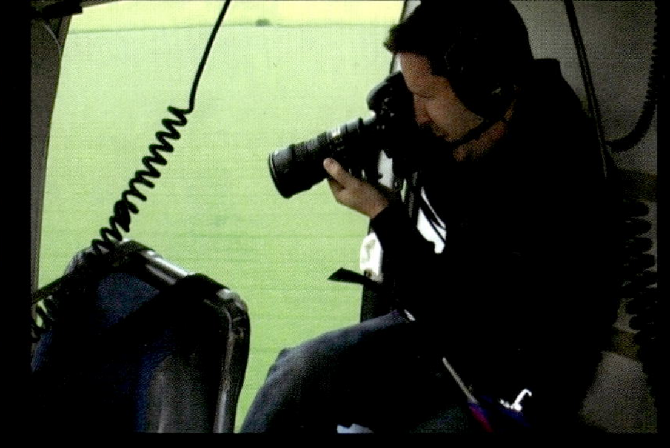 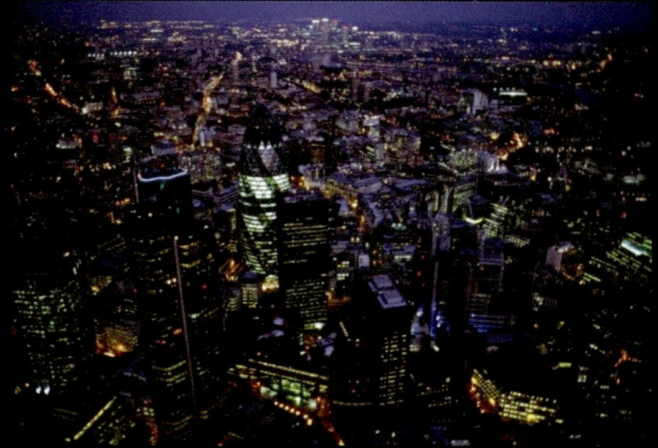 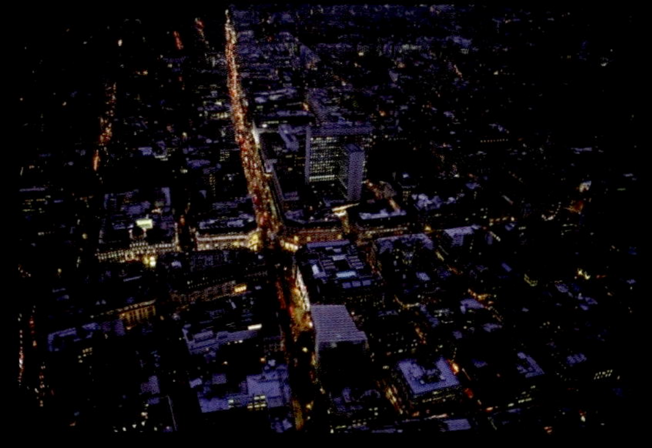

Digital cameras have a four-year product cycle, and halfway through that period manufacturers bring out a slightly updated version of the current professional model. While it is difficult to keep up with the constant stream of new camera bodies and software/firmware, it would be impossible to produce photographs like those in this book without them.

Working digitally has changed photographers' lives for ever. It takes a while to put together a good workflow, which will include captioning the photographs within the image's metadata, tweaking the white balance of the raw files and making sure everything is backed up at least three times. I use various RAID drives and then Archival Gold DVDs and Blu-ray disks. My one fear about digital files is that they may become unreadable in time. Recently, someone showed me amazing prints of his mother as a young girl, when she lived in our house. They were taken in 1933, but the quality was stunning, with great detail, and I was thrilled to see some of the history of our house. These days, there are various schools of thought about which file format to back up with – JPEG, raw, Adobe DNG – but who knows if any will be readable in another hundred years?

As I write, the new Nikon D3S has just been announced, and I'm looking forward to getting to grips with it. For the geeks among us (and I now count myself as one), its Hi3 extended sensitivity setting allows stills and movie capture at ISO 102,400. Now that was never available with film!

First published 2010 by

Merrell Publishers Limited
81 Southwark Street
London SE1 0HX

merrellpublishers.com

British Library Cataloguing-in-Publication data:
Hawkes, Jason.
London at night.
1. London (England) – Aerial views.
2. Night photography – England – London.
I. Title
914.2′1′00222-dc22

ISBN 978-1-8589-4517-0

Produced by Merrell Publishers Limited
Designed by Paul Arnot
Project-managed and captions written by Rosanna Lewis
Printed and bound in Singapore

Jason Hawkes has specialized in aerial photography
since 1991, and has received awards from D&AD and the
Association of Photographers. His previous publications
include Aerial: The Art of Photography from the Sky (2003)
and Britain from Above (2008). For more information, see
jasonhawkes.com

Kenneth Powell is an architecture critic, journalist and
writer who was made an Honorary Fellow of the Royal
Institute of British Architects in 2000. His many books
include New London Architecture and 30 St Mary Axe, both
published by Merrell.

Maps throughout indicate the position of key landmarks
featured in this book. The area shown in white represents
the inner boroughs of London.

Front cover: Tower Bridge and the River Thames,
    looking west.
Back cover, left to right, from top: British Telecom tower
    (pages 60–61); Great Court, British Museum (pages 58–59);
    Regent Street (pages 52–53); Harrods (pages 144–45);
    London Eye (pages 134–35); Lloyd's of London
    (pages 28–29); Westminster Abbey (pages 78–79);
    Piccadilly Circus (pages 46–49); Leicester Square
    (pages 44–45); Oxford Circus (pages 54–55); O2 arena
    (pages 102–103); Big Ben (page 75); Northway Circus
    (pages 86–87); Emirates Stadium (pages 90–91).
Frontispiece: 30 St Mary Axe (the 'Gherkin'; pages 32–33).
Pages 6–7: The junction of the M25 and the A1(M) at South
    Mimms, looking north.